A Guide to

THE WINES OF

ENGLAND
& WALES

Publisher	**David C Tennant**
Designer	**Liz Rowe**
Editor	**Blue Ryan**
Picture research	**Janey Gilbert**
Cartography	**Jamie Crocker, Artista-Design, UK**
Studio photography	**Tony Barrett**
Printing & binding	**Ashford Colour Press Ltd. England**

First published 2008
by BTL Publishing Limited
8 Jonathan Court
Windmill Road
London W4 1SA

info@winebehindthelabel.com
Copyright © 2008 BTL Publishing Limited
Text © 2008 Philip Williamson, David Moore, Neville Blech,
Professor Richard Selley, David C Tennant
Design © Liz Rowe

A CIP catalogue record for this book is available from the British Library.

ISBN-10: 0 9557657 1 4
ISBN-13: 978 0 9557657 11

Whilst every care has been taken in the preparation of this guide, the
publishers and authors cannot accept responsibility of any kind for
consequences arising from reliance upon information contained in it.

A Guide to
THE WINES OF
ENGLAND
& WALES

HISTORY • REGIONS • GRAPES • STYLES • WINERIES

BTL

Contents

FOREWORD
Julia Trustram Eve

The world of English and Welsh wines is changing rapidly.
The landscape looks very different now than it did even
10 years ago, in terms of acreage planted, the variety and
styles of wines produced and importantly the attitude to
these wines from the wine-buying public and the trade.

The industry now exudes confidence; boasting a level of
professionalism, training, expertise and commitment to
wine production that is second to none. This, of course,
ensures that many wines from the UK successfully
compete on the world stage against some of the giants of
the wine world.

This growing recognition has come not only in
international competitions held here in the UK, but also
increasingly in competitions abroad. The number of entries
from England and Wales, and the awards received,
multiplies year on year.

These successes make headlines; for once it is the good
news that is reported in the media. In fact, the breadth of
coverage by the press and frequent appraisal from notable
wine writers and personalities for English and Welsh wines
is proportionately higher than that of any other wine
producing country.

Another growing area within the UK is wine tourism. Along with many other wine regions of the world that have responded to the increasing thirst for knowledge from wine enthusiasts, England and Wales offer some fabulous experiences.

A renewed interest in local and seasonal food and drink has developed significantly through farmers' markets, speciality stores and even supermarket chains, and is now strongly supported across the country. English and Welsh wines are an active part of this growing sector and work alongside many producers and organisations involved in this promotion. The marriage of food and wine that the classic European regions have enjoyed over centuries is now alive and kicking over here.

The wine industry is also marketing itself more effectively. There are some major brands in the industry today who lead the way. Availability also is no longer a challenge, with many more high street names and independent retailers listing English and Welsh wines, responding to increasing demand from their customers. Our nation's wines are most certainly something to be proud of, and the dedication of the UK's many growers and winemakers is reflected in the pages of this book. There is so much to learn about this young industry and of course there is one thing that we can offer above all other countries — the opportunity to explore these many vineyards on your doorstep.

Julia Trustram Eve
DIRECTOR
English Wine Producers

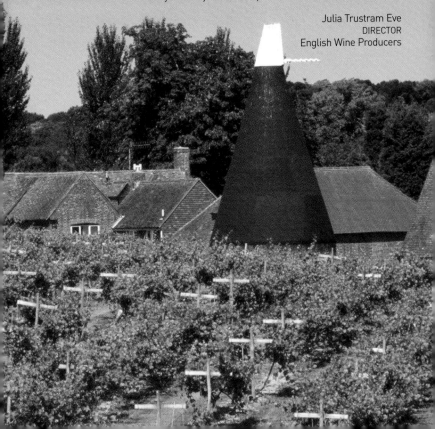

Introduction

The house at Nyetimber

You will find a great contrast between the many vineyards profiled on these pages. Some are set to become internationally renowned, others are by their own admission, little more than hobbyist operations. As well as a chance to get well-acquainted with wine production in England and Wales included are some surprising snippets of history along with some splendid locations to visit, be it in the Weald of Kent or the vineyard trail in Devon. For the leading wineries we have also included a short biography of the owner or the individual most important to the venture's success.

A new reality

When it comes to wine production there has emerged a new England to complement and sometimes remould the older order. A swing to larger scale sparkling wine away from often very small scale still wine production, while not universal, is having a major impact. One presents the possibility of an internationally renowned sparkling wine style, the other more of a local, hobbyist activity wedded to a more romantic view of struggle and perseverance against the climatic odds. But we've seen that the weather too is changing.

Yet despite evident climate change, at the time of writing in 2008 the stark reality is that the best combination of soil types and climate is largely restricted to southern England. At least until recently the quality of the grapes has been a major problem. In 2001 Stephen Skelton described growing grapes as 'our problem and in many vineyards the yield and quality of grapes is lamentable.' Sadly, in places this still holds true as there are still too many producers that are reliant on mediocre grape varieties planted in soils that are sometimes excessively fertile or are simply unsuited to the vine. But the industry really is coming of age and those who dedicate themselves to producing the best quality grapes will emerge with a growing reputation and survive. Of the recent spate of planting, the overwhelming majority of it to sparkling wine production, much of it is on the best sites available and even some of the visiting Champagne houses would attest to that. In most instances the new sparkling operators have also sought out the best clones and winemaking know-how and have the confidence to challenge the wines produced by that famous region in France. There is also an increased investment in people, equipment and a growing professionalism. A parallel might even be drawn with New Zealand where, from a standing start, the wine industry took a few Sauvignon vines planted in a virgin wine region to global recognition and economic returns in less than two decades. And it needn't be all about sparkling wine here — in addition to the Sauvignon success story, New Zealand now does handsomely with reds from Pinot Noir and fine whites from Chardonnay and other varieties.

Go visiting

The family at Fleurfields

Most vineyards can be visited, often without an appointment. We have provided details on location, how to get there and a summary of what's on offer. There are vineyards at leading tourist attractions and there are even some to be found at properties owned by the RHS and the National Trust. Sometimes vineyards have been put in where there has been little profitability in growing anything else. But then this is not uncommon with the vine, as can be seen in some of the world's leading wine regions. There are vineyards tucked away in beautiful valleys or lying close to the sea. Others command downland slopes or offer a quiet countryside oasis to retreat to on a Sunday afternoon.

Many of the smaller operations are also extremely welcoming and, for many visitors, provide them with their first taste of grape growing and wine production. Some also combine this with high quality products produced locally and so do their bit to support sustainable agriculture generally in the region. We have only profiled those vineyards that produce wines under their own label or will do so in the near future. Some do an admirable job of

The vines at Breaky Bottom

just growing grapes and these have been included in the Other Vineyards section near the end of the book. Many of the smallest operations do not have winemaking facilities of their own but use a winemaking 'centre' to process their grapes. Sometimes these are local but others use a winery that is further away. While not a guarantee of quality it usually means wines that are readily drinkable. The most important examples of these winemaking centres are wineries such as Chapel Down (Kent), Ridgeview (East Sussex), Stanlake Park (Thames Valley), Three Choirs (Gloucestershire) and Shawsgate (East Anglia).

For those vineyards that stand out for their wine quality we have also included profiles of the individual wines. These include the cream of current wine production in the UK and most are wines that stand up to international scrutiny. Where possible, taste the wines where they're made and return with some bottles in the knowledge that with wine too, good quality can now be sourced locally.

Bookers wine selection

A sparkling future

The English wine industry is already hugely blessed in having one of the best single marketplaces for sparkling wine in the world on its doorstep. There are outstanding restaurants, bars and numerous events that thirst for high quality 'fizz' and increasingly these opportunities extend well beyond London and the south-east. It is actually difficult at present to see how demand for top quality English fizz is ever likely to be satisfied. Where it can potentially go wrong is if the leading producers deviate from the pursuit of quality. There is always a danger that larger volume, more everyday examples are sold at inflated prices, something that is all too common in Champagne. Fortunately of those we've met in the course of writing this guide, there are plenty infected with a passion and dedication to making quality wine that goes well beyond any financial motivation.

We've been lucky enough during the course of compiling this guide to start to see the new shape of the map of English vineyards emerging. We have profiled many of the best new enterprises so you've time to keep tabs on them now and not miss the boat. While the picture is changing rapidly we've provided a foretaste of what's to come. 2012 and the London Olympics will offer an opportunity like no other for the wine producers to present this new reality to the world.

PHILIP WILLIAMSON & DAVID MOORE

A BRIEF HISTORY OF ENGLISH & WELSH WINE

There is evidence that grapes grew in the British Isles before the Romans arrived in Britain in 55BC but no absolute evidence that the Romans made wine during their 450 year occupation of these isles.

Certainly they drank wine during their occupation, there is evidence of wine cups and 'amphora' in several Roman cities, but it is possible that the wine they drank was imported from one of the nearby European countries that was also under the might of the Roman Empire. We do know that the Romans imported vines, probably in an effort to grow grapes and make wine or to eat the fruit. Indeed there is positive evidence of a Roman vineyard planted in the Neane valley in Northamptonshire. But the evidence to date does not conclusively prove that the Romans were the first winemakers in England.

Wine was drunk in Saxon times and England's Dark Age invaders would have increased the wine trade from Europe. The growth and spread of Christianity, after the arrival of St Augustine in 596, and the increase in monastic orders created a demand for wine for use in communion rituals. It was during these times that we see the religious orders planting vines and probably making wine. In 731, in his Ecclesiastical History, The Venerable Bede, wrote that, "wines are cultivated in several localities".

Undoubtedly it was the Norman Conquest of 1066 that had a major impact on wine consumption in England. William brought with him not only soldiers, but courtiers and their retinue and monks from French religious orders who founded more monasteries. Wine was their daily beverage and vineyards became more commonplace so that by 1086 the Domesday Book records vineyards in 42 locations of which only 12 belonged to monastic orders. Vineyards continued to grow in size and number to around three hundred. The 'Domesday Book' records a vineyard at Leeds Castle in Kent (see page 38) where vines for wine-making are still grown more than nine centuries later.

Two hundred years after the Norman invasion winemaking in England began a long decline. There was no single reason but rather a combination of factors. The marriage of King Henry II to Eleanor of Aquitaine in 1152 created a vast kingdom covering large parts of France where winemaking thrived. Wine imports increased because of an easy access to supply, reducing the need for home grown production. The mid 13th century saw a change in climate with cooler summers having a detrimental effect on the growing and ripening of grapes. The arrival of the Black Death in the mid 14th century had far-reaching consequences on the demographics of England, reducing both population and viticulture. The Dissolution of the Monasteries 1536-1539 under King Henry VIII increased the decline in English winemaking with an estimated closure of three- thousand religious houses.

Viticulture in the 17th century was confined to monarchs, nobles and a few of the landed gentry who

Wine making in the Middle Ages

were fascinated by the challenge of growing grapes and making wine. King James I (ruled 1603-1625) had a vineyard at Oatlands Park in Surrey and Robert Cecil, Earl of Salisbury, planted more than 2,000 vines at Hatfield House. John Rose, gardener to Charles II planted and tended vines at St. James's Palace, London and wrote a treatise on vine cultivation.

In 1738 The Hon. Charles Hamilton created a garden and vineyard at Painshill Place, Surrey, (see page 50) influenced by his travels in France and Italy. The vineyard fell into disuse at the end of the 17th century but has since been replanted on its original site, sloping down to the lake.

Wales was the site of the next experiment in viticulture when, in 1873 the Marquis of Bute instructed his gardener, Andrew Pettigrew, to plant a vineyard around his estate at Castell Coch outside of Cardiff. Pettigrew was sent to France to gain knowledge and to buy the vines that were planted on a south-facing slope opposite the Bristol Channel. The wines were made in a winery at Cardiff Castle. In 1900 the fourth Lord Bute succeeded his father and worked with Pettigrew's son who also took over from his father running the estate. The vineyard remained commercially productive until it was grubbed up after World War I.

After World War II, in the mid 1940s a new wave of pioneers showed great determination and belief in the possibility of wine production in Britain. They brought a more scientific approach to the problem by experimenting with different varietals and techniques that might be more suited to the vagaries of the climate. Ray Barrington Brock, who is considered one of the founding fathers of the English wine revival, at his Research Station in Oxted Surrey, trialled over 500 grape varieties over a period of 25 years. These were the revival years when Edward Hyams generated enormous publicity for British viticulture by his writing and broadcasting. George Odish was both a trained entomologist and economist who had worked in the Champagne region of France. When he returned to Kent he set up a small trial in his garden and published the results of his studies. His skill as a winemaker and his economist's mind led him to the commercial evaluation of grape yields and the viability of winemaking in Britain.

The year 1951 is considered to be seminal in the history of English wine with the planting of the Hambledon vineyard in Hampshire. This project undertaken by Sir Guy Salisbury-Jones was the first vineyard to be planted commercially for more than 75 years. Considerable interest was caused when the first wine was produced and the genie was finally out of the bottle.

The spread of vineyards was initially slow with only two other vineyards planted in the mid 50s, the Merrydown Wine Company at Horam, Sussex owned by Jack Ward and the vineyard planted on the Beaulieu Estate (see page 90) by Lieutenant Colonel Robert Gore-Browne and his wife Margaret, friends of Lord Montague. It was not until the late 60s and early 70s that expansion began in earnest.

Since the mid 70's England and Wales have seen an explosion in land given over to vine production. In 1975 an estimated 196 ha were under vine and 10 years later in 1985 this figure had more than doubled to 488 ha. The high point in grape production was 1993 with 479 vineyards cultivating 1,065 ha of vines. This figure in retrospect was artificially high and was caused by a rush to beat a possible EU vine-planting ban. Since that time both the number of vineyards and wineries has declined to 383 and 98 respectively.

The 70s saw the entry of some really serious players planting sizeable vineyards. These included Valley Vineyards (see page 86), Nyetimber (page 60), New Hall (page 182), Three Choirs (page 138) and Denbies (page 44) England's largest single vineyard with 94 ha currently under production.

English and Welsh winemaking is now serious business reflected by the change of styles from the Germanic tastes of the 60s and 70s to the drier styles of today and the increased production of sparkling wines (Méthod Champenoise) that reflect the vast improvement in quality and the dedication of the winemakers in Britain. The kings, nobles, landed gentry, and the pioneers of yesteryear would be proud that English, and Welsh wines, are now served by our Queen and her ministers on State occasions.

DAVID C TENNANT

THE IMPACT OF CLIMATE CHANGE ON BRITISH VITICULTURE

Professor Richard Selley, Senior Research Fellow, Imperial College

Vines under snow on Surrey's North Downs. Soon to be a sight of the past?

The impact of climate change on viticulture has been considered widely around the World in general and North America in particular. Viticulture occurs between the 10 and 20 degree C. average annual global isotherms. A poleward shift of winelands is taking place. Vineyards close to the former 20 degree C. isotherms are being abandoned, or replanted at higher altitudes. New vineyards are being planted further towards the poles in response to the polar drift of the 10 degree C. isotherm. In 2001 the UN's Inter-governmental Panel on Climate Change predicted a global temperature increase within a range of 1.4-5.8 degrees C. This was revised in 2007 to an increase of between 1.1-6.4 degrees C. The 2007 IPCC report concluded that global warming is anthropogenic, and largely caused by burning fossil fuels. The Kyoto and other international conferences have failed to agree to a World-wide dramatic decrease of green house gas emissions.

In the northern hemisphere the 10 degree C. isotherm traverses central Britain. In such marginal winelands the interplay of climate with geology is all important, controlling the landscape within which a vineyard shelters, and the soil in which it grows.

A recent study, summarised in the map shown, showed how the northern limit of British viticulture has migrated to and fro correlative with temperature over the last two millennia.

The Past

But to begin at the beginning: fossilized remains of vines have been found in the London Clay that was deposited across south eastern England some 50 million years ago when the climate was much warmer than today. Temperature has gradually cooled ever since, with the Earth entering an Ice Age some 2 million years ago. Temperature fluctuations during this

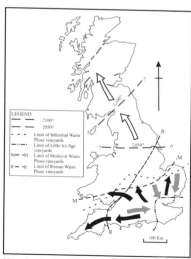

LEGEND

- ——— 2100?
- ——— 2050?
- – · – Limit of Industrial Warm Phase vineyards
- ········· Limit of Little Ice Age vineyards
- M——M Limit of Medieval Warm Phase vineyards
- R——R Limit of Roman Warm Phase vineyards

Map showing the to and fro migration of the northern limit of British viticulture since Roman times

Scientists predict that the south facing banks of Loch Ness will be suitable for viticulture by 2080

The north shore of Loch Ness may be one of the prime vineyards of the Côtes d'Ecosse in the 22nd century, with geology similar to the winelands of the Cape of Good Hope, a sunny south-east aspect and water at the foot of the slope to reflect the sun's rays up into the vines.

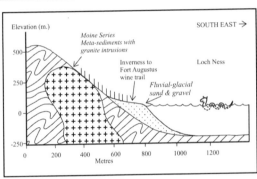

period have resulted in alternating glacial and interglacial episodes. Vines were absent from Britain during the glacial advances, but reoccupied Britain during each warm interglacial. Vine pips and pollen some 250,000 years old have been found in interglacial sediments in Suffolk. The first evidence of viticulture dates back to the Neolithic period in 2,700BC, though there is no evidence that viticulture led to vinification. The later Iron Age Celts, however, were described by contemporary Roman writers as heroic wine drinkers; a view amply corroborated by abandoned wine amphorae and drinking vessels in late Iron Age sites in general, and in high status graves in particular. There is no evidence of wine making in Britain before the Roman Conquest. A number of supposed Roman vineyards have been identified across southern England. Many of these are dubious. There is, however, sound evidence of viticulture as far north

as Thoresby in Lincolnshire. The best documented Roman vineyard is at Wollaston in the valley of the River Nene where over 27 acres (11 hectares) of vineyard have been excavated. This was viticulture on an industrial scale. The area has been described as the Roman Côtes de Northants. This was probably producing 'vin de pays' for the legionnaires stationed in York and elsewhere. It is generally held that the temperature in Britain during the period of Roman rule may have been warmer than today.

Temperature dropped as the Roman Empire collapsed, perhaps the two are linked. In the Dark Ages there is no evidence of viticulture in Britain until the end of the Saxon Period. Temperature began to rise with the Norman Conquest, and northern Europe entered the Medieval Warm Period. The Domesday Book (1086-7) gives a detailed account of early Norman vineyards planted as far north

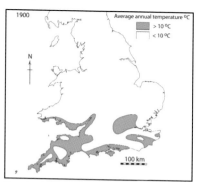

Map showing land with an annual average temperature above 10°C in 1900

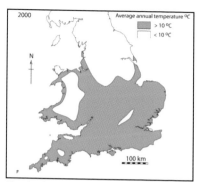

Map showing land with an annual average temperature above 10°C in 2000

as Yorkshire and into south Wales. English wine was of such quantity and quality that peace treaties at the conclusion of Anglo-French wars often included a clause forbidding the export of English wine to France. Temperature began to drop in the 14th Century. This, together with the general decline in agriculture caused by the Black Death, led to a collapse of viticulture in Britain. From the 15th to mid-19th centuries vineyards were restricted to the south east of England, though some of the vineyards of the period were large, long-lived, and produced quality wine — according to contemporary accounts.

The Present
Temperature began to rise again at the start of the Industrial Revolution in the middle of the 19th century. The renaissance of British viticulture commenced with the planting of 2000 vines over a 3 acre site outside Cardiff by the Marquis of Bute. This was later increased to 8 acres. White wines, 'still' champagne and red wines were sold as far afield as London. Alas it

was not to last. Wine making ceased at the outbreak of WWI. Little happened after this 'false dawn' until the establishment of the Oxted Viticultural Research Station in the mid-twentieth century. Subsequently vineyards have been established across most of England and parts of south Wales. These were originally planted with Germanic varietals that could survive in cool (13-15 degrees C. average summer) temperatures. Within the last two decades, however, varietals have been planted from northern France where summer temperatures average 15-17 degrees C. In southeast England the 'Holy Trinity' of Pinot Noir, Pinot Meunier and Chardonnay now produce medalliferous sparkling white wines. Some heroic vineyard owners have already planted Merlot, albeit in polytunnels.

The gradual increase in average annual temperature in Britain is shown by isotherm maps for average UK temperatures for 1900 and 2000. These maps delineate the 10 degree C. annual isotherm that roughly defines areas warm enough for viticulture. In 1900 only small

→ COOL ←	→ INTERMEDIATE ←	→ WARM ←	→ HOT ←
13 – 15°C	15 – 17°C	17 – 19°C	19 – 24°C
Muller-Thurgau	Pinot Noir	Merlot	Raisins
Reisling	Pinot Meunier	Viognier	Currants
Bacchus	Chardonnay	Syrah	Sultanas
Dornfelder	Sauvignon Blanc	Cabernet Sauvignon	Legbe
Rondo	Cabernet Franc	Grenache	
Regent	Semillon	Zinfandel	

Grape varieties for different average growing temperatures. In the last century English vineyards were largely planted with cool temperature Germanic varietals. They are now being planted with intermediate temperature varieties similar to those in northern France. A 5 degree centigrade increase predicted for southern England by 2080 will cause surviving growers to plant warm varieties

isolated areas of southern England were above the critical 10 degree C minimum average temperature necessary for successful wine making. By 2000, however, most of southern England and the Midlands were above the critical 10 degree C. threshold, except for the Chilterns, Bodmin moor, Dartmoor and Exmoor and the Welsh mountains.

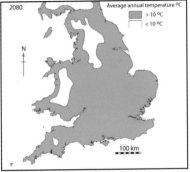

Map showing land with an annual average temperature above 10°C in 2080 based on IPCC and Hadley Centre predictions

The Future

Using the 2001 IPCC data the Hadley Centre (the Research Centre of the Meteorological Office) predicts that by 2080 there will be an increase of 5°C in average summer temperature in southern England. The increase will decline north-wards due to the ameliorating maritime influence of the Atlantic Ocean. The summer temperatures of 2003 will be normal in 2040 and considered cool by 2060. By 2080 most of England and Wales will have annual average temperatures above 10 degrees C.

It is possible to integrate these data with the temperature bands for cool, intermediate, warm and hot grape varieties shown in the accompanying table.

The results show that the Thames Valley, the Severn Valley, the Hampshire basin and the Cornubian Riviera will be too hot for conventional viticulture. These areas will only be suitable for producing dried fruit, such as raisins, and legbe, a wine made from the fermented sap of the date palm. Manchester Merlot and Sheffield Shiraz will be feasible. Sparking white wines may be produced over much of Wales and the Pennines. The presently typical British grape varieties, such as Müller-Thurgau and Reisling, will be restricted to the slopes of Snowdonia and the Derbyshire Peak District.

This research shows that the immediate future of the British wine industry is bright indeed. The long term future, however, is bleak. It is unlikely that there will be any vineyards left in Britain by 2080, let alone 2100. Climate change is going to cause, and is already causing, disruption to civilization across the Earth. By 2100 the surviving bands of hunter-gatherers searching for sustenance across the

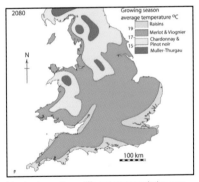

Map to show where different grape varieties may be grown in 2080 according to predicted isotherms

deserts of Europe will have more urgent matters on their minds than viticulture. We must use this narrow window of opportunity to plant our vines and drink our liquid assets while we may. Cheers!

References

Cowie, J. 2007. 'Climate Change'. Biological & Human Aspects. Cambridge Univ. Press. Cambridge. 487pp.

Houghton, J. 2004. 'Global Warming'. The Complete Briefing. 3rd Edn. Cambridge Univ. Press. Cambridge. 351pp

Lovelock, J. 2006. 'The Revenge of Gaia'. Allen Lane. London. 177p.

Selley, R.C. 2008. 'The Winelands of Britain: Past, present & prospective'. Second Edition. Petravin Press, Dorking. 119pp. ISBN 978-0-9547419-2-1. (Order from: www.winelandsofbritain.co.uk)

VITICULTURE IN ENGLAND

The British climate as illustrated by Professor Selley shows that climate change is indeed upon us. For the time being though English and Welsh winegrowers must work with a combination of early ripening Germanic style grapes and a few French varieties mainly for the production of sparkling wine and rosé. The reason for this is that grape varieties require differing levels of accumulated heat during their active growth cycle between the spring and harvesting in the early autumn. The average daily temperature during this period in southern England is still a little cooler than Reims in Champagne so it is clearly very important for growers to establish isolated, warmer mesoclimates. The best vineyards here all possess such sites.

All plant life requires photosynthesis for growth. This is clearly important in England with our many wet and particularly cloudy days. Although some light does get through in cloudy conditions it is a limiting factor. Ideal are those British summers with sunny and warm days like those enjoyed in 2003 and 2006. Most areas of southern England get around 1,200 to 1,300 hours of sunshine between April and October in comparison to Champagne which enjoys close to 1,350 proving once again that site selection is key here. All plants also need rain and vines

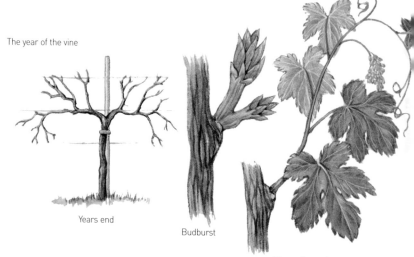

The year of the vine

Years end

Budburst

Flower formation

are no exception. English summers are marginally wetter than the more established of Europe's wine regions although not significantly so. Cool damp conditions do though encourage the development of rot.

Soil and aspect are both important in choosing where to plant. A south or south-east facing slope is ideal because the vines absorb a maximum of direct sunlight throughout the day. The nearby presence of bodies of water, lakes and rivers also assist in reflecting light back to the vines. You will not find English or Welsh vineyards planted much above sea level because an increase in altitude means a decrease in temperature, which will delay ripening in an already very marginal climate. Well-drained soil is ideal for balanced vine growth. It just needs to hold sufficient water and enable the vines roots to burrow deeply and absorb nutrition. Gravel, sand, loam and chalk soils are all good for grape growing and the limestone character of chalk helps to promote good acidity and is prized for growing grapes for sparkling wines. Heavy and fertile soils, particularly clay are far from ideal because they will encourage vigorous growth in the vines and reduce the build up of natural sugar.

The perennial early season problem for British grape growers is the risk of spring frosts. If this happens after budbreak the

Budburst

year's growth can be killed off. In most cases a second bud will grow back but the yield will be reduced and quality will often be negatively affected. A number of vineyards employ frost busters, pots which increase the air temperature in frost pockets where cold air forms and sits. Vineyards with slopes are again beneficial because the cold air can drift away and windbreaks, natural or planted, will help to ward off cold winds.

Having established which vine varieties to plant and having isolated their site, growers need to consider a few other factors. Almost all wine grape vine varieties need to be grafted onto American vine rootsocks. The reason for this is a root feeding aphid, phylloxera which devast-ated most of Europe's vineyards in the 19th century. It feeds off the root system of the vine and eventually kills it. There are other considerations as well. Certain rootstocks will work better in certain soils and the marriage between rootstock and vine is a complicated one. Certain types of other vine maladies can be minimised and the growth and vigour of a vine can also be better controlled. The training and trellising methods employed in the vineyard are also important in ensuring maximum light exposure and consequently greater sugar in the grapes. Geneva Double Curtain is widely adopted while others use various

Bloom

Fruit buds

Veraison

Maturity

forms of vertical shoot positioning and vines are both spur and cane pruned. Spur pruning is done from a fixed cordon with the spurs pruned back to a few buds each winter. Cane pruning involves retaining one and sometimes two shoots each year with a greater number of fruiting buds on each cane. The archetypal training system that uses this method of pruning is the Single or Double Guyot.

A year in the vineyard

November to March – this is the dormant period for the vine where the average temperature is below 10 degrees Celsius and the vine ceases to grow. During this time the vines will be pruned to set the potential crop for the following season. Other tasks can also be carried during out this period such as ploughing and repairing damaged trellising.

April to May – the sap in the vine rises as the temperature warms and budbreak will generally take place in April and in May the vines begin to sprout inflorescences. Frost during the period is a constant concern. The vines are moving into their most vigorous growth period and new canes retained after pruning are tied to wire trellises.

June to July – vigorous growth during June which begins to slow in July and canopy management is all important and vegetative growth is cut back where necessary. In June the grapes bloom and then the fruit sets. In July the grape bunches begin to develop.

August to October – during August sugar reserves are built up in the roots and wood of the vine and véraison takes place and can be noticed on red varieties where the colour of the grapes changes from green to a red/blue colour depending on the grape variety. Further work must continue on the vine canopy, opening it up and maximising light exposure. After véraison at the beginning of September the sugar in the wood is transferred to the grapes, this is known as the sugar flux. Throughout September and into October the fruit will ripen and warm dry days are what all growers will be praying for. Harvesting takes place and the winemaking cycle begins.

The interior of a modern English winery

In the winery

Many of the winemaking processes are similar when vinifying white or red grapes. Most wine produced in England is white and we will run through the processes involved and then highlight the differences in making red, rosé and sparkling wines. The one component shared in vinifying all the fruit is the process of adding yeast to the juice which reacts with the natural sugars and transfers this must into roughly equal proportions of alcohol and carbon dioxide. The presence of CO_2 can make winemaking facilities potentially dangerous places. In order to ease the process and maximise the final quality of the fruit they have harvested, many vineyard owners have invested heavily in their winemaking equipment with crusher de-stemmers, bladder presses and the provision of stainless steel tanks, many with temperature control. In trying years the winemaker has the option to chaptalise, in the form of grape must addition to increase the potential strength of the wine. Up to 2% potential alcohol is possible with this process. In the larger wineries they have also put in cool rooms and separate warm rooms. This enables fruit and must to be kept in perfect condition and red wines can be hastened through their malolactic fermentation.

White winemaking

1. After the fruit has been picked it may be sorted to eliminate any rotten grapes.
2. The grapes may be taken straight to the press without crushing them or they may be crushed and then passed to the press. Going direct to press avoids picking up any tannins from the grape skins or bitter flavours from the pips
3. A pectic enzyme may be added. This helps to release juice from the pulp and can also speed up the settling of the juice. At this juice handling stage some sulphur dioxide (the all purpose wine antiseptic) can be added to avoid juice oxidation. It also has the benefit of inhibiting wild yeasts.
4. The juice is then racked to a settling tank, where it will stay for up to 24 hours. Carbon dioxide can be added to the tank and guards against oxidation because it is heavier than air.

A sample being taken using a pipette

5. The clear juice is then racked to tank to commence fermentation. In most cases a yeast culture will be prepared and added. Fermentation tends to be long and cool running for up to 6 weeks.

6. After fermentation the wine will be left to settle for a period which helps to naturally filter the wine from any impurities.

7. The wine is then cold stabilised by chilling down to – 4 degrees Celsius which precipitates out any unstable tartaric acid. This is quite harmless but looks like little shards of glass and may be off-putting to consumers. The wine is then held in cold store prior to bottling.

8. Almost all English white is filtered. Only a limited number of wines are aged in oak, which will afford a natural period of stabilisation. The wine tends not to kept on fine lees, certainly not for any length of time because of a need to preserve as much of the delicate aroma and flavour as possible and lees would tend to add a rich creamy component, particularly if regularly stirred. A number of wineries will though keep wines on lees for a limited period to add weight. A rich lees character may be desirable in a Chablis but not necessarily an English white. Wines can be either filtered through diatomaceous earth or through a sheet effectively ensuring the wine is sterile.

9. Blending for consistency will be done just before bottling.

10. The final filtration will be done at bottling. The wines may also have an addition of Süssreserve (back-blending) if necessary. All equipment is steamed beforehand because of the risk of stray yeasts. Otherwise it would always be possible then to get a refermentation in bottle.

Red winemaking

1. Grapes will go though a crusher/de-stemmer. Some whole bunches may be retained for the fermentation, which is popular in vinifying Pinot Noir.

2. Must may be held at low temperature for up to 5 days before commencing fermentation to extract colour and fruit flavour.

3. Fermentation is at a warmer temperature than for whites but still relatively cool. The objective with most UK made reds is to provide wines with good fruit and a well-rounded, supple structure for short ageing.

4. After fermentation the wine may be racked to tank or to small oak barrels.

5. Malolactic fermentation will then take place. All reds should go through the malolactic fermentation for stability. The process converts harsher malic acid into softer lactic acid. It is stimulated by the addition of bacteria not yeast. Most aromatic white wine will not be put through the process.

6. Wine may then be aged in oak barrels. Avoiding too much new oak and having some wine in one or two year old barrels is advisable, the fruit is unlikely

to stand up to 100% new wood. Some wineries use oak staves in stainless steel tanks to pick up a little oak character.

7. After ageing there will be the option of filtering. Many UK reds may have a light filtration.

Rosé winemaking

1. The grapes will be crushed and then given a limited period of skin contact to pick up colour and some of the fruity flavour of the red varieties but very little tannin. How much depends whether the winemaker wishes to produce a more food-friendly wine.

2. The winemaking process then follows a similar path to white vinification. Some rosé is also a blend and may be for example 50/50 red and white fruit. This tends to produce paler wines.

3. Like whites the wines will be bottled young.

Sparkling winemaking

1. With top quality sparkling wines, particularly those that growers wish to make here, the press juice must be of the highest quality. The juice must have excellent levels of acidity and sparkling base wine is generally higher in acidity than other wine. This first press will release better juice and higher overall acidity.

2. Yeast will be added for fermentation that works well at lower potential alcohol levels. After primary fermentation some wine may go through malolactic fermentation to reduce the overall acidity of the wine.

3. The finished wine will then be blended for the desired house style and bottled under crown cap after a little sugar is added. The secondary fermentation then takes place in bottle. The longer the wine is left on its yeast lees the more bready, toasty complexity that you find in top Champagnes, is possible. Wine generally aged for less than 18 months on lees will be more fruit driven in style.

4. For 6 to 8 weeks before bottling the wine will be riddled, the yeast cells moved gradually towards the neck of the bottle. Wineries here tend to use giropallets, which are electronically driven and controlled on a computer cycle.

5. The wine is then disgorged by freezing the necks of the bottles in a freezing brine solution and removing the crown cap with a disgorging machine.

6. The final style of the wine is determined by the dosage, which is a topping up mix of wine, sugar syrup and brandy. Most sparkling wines are produced in a "Brut" style and will generally have between 6 and 15 grams of residual sugar.

A note on vintages

The majority of English wine should generally be drunk within at least four to five years of the vintage and much of it a good deal sooner than this in the case of many whites and rosés. A lengthy vintage report in this context is not really relevant to what readers will have the opportunity to

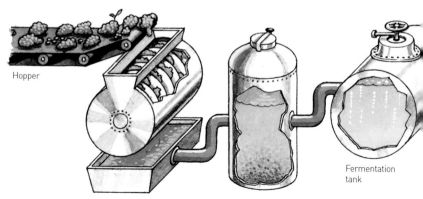

Hopper

Destemmer & Wine press

Settling tank

Fermentation tank

sample and buy. The conditions of the vintage year though can have a very significant effect on crop levels. Also of crucial importance are the weeks immediately prior to the harvest, from late September to late October for most. There is also some regional variation during this period giving rise to different outcomes.

2007 was very trying for many growers with wet weather in the early summer and many vineyards suffering significant yield losses with a poor flowering. At Three Choirs they processed just 80 tons of grapes in comparison to 250 tons in 2006. However in the south-east a warm finish to the harvest in 2007 provided better than expected quality in the grapes for sparkling wines. There is always likely to be a potential scarcity of supply depending on the year. This is one of the reasons why Waitrose, who have been tremendous supporters of English wine, have decided to plant their own vineyard for sparkling wine.

What does appear to be clear is that the very warm summers enjoyed in 2006 and 2003 produced wines of much greater weight and ripe fruit flavour than has normally been the case. The global trends would tend to suggest years like these will be more frequent. However, once again, a damp finish and the rapid spread of rot took the edge off quality in 2006, for some growers at least. A tasting of Nyetimber base wine from the 2003 vintage showed the tremendous potential for top quality sparkling wines in such years. Perhaps the only downside for growers in these vintages and with very early ripening varieties being that the wines will be a little fat and with

Grapes conveyed by a hopper to the wine press

less balanced acidity. 2005 has turned out to be a fine vintage, the best wines show the health and fruit quality enjoyed by many regions in France and Germany that year. While not of quite the same level, 2004 produced well-ripened grapes and reasonable yields.

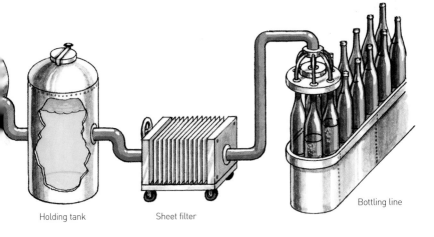

Holding tank   Sheet filter   Bottling line

SOUTH EAST

South East

Philip Williamson

Kent
1 Barnsole
2 Biddenden Vineyard
3 Chapel Down
4 Elham Valley
5 Gusbourne Estate
6 Harbourne
7 Herbert Hall
8 Hush Heath Estate
9 Leeds Castle
10 Meopham Valley
11 Sandhurst
12 Surrenden
13 Throwley

East & West Sussex
14 Bookers Vineyard
15 Breaky Bottom
16 Carr Taylor
17 Davenport
18 Henners
19 Nutbourne
20 Nyetimber
21 Plumpton Estate
22 Ridgeview
23 Sedlescombe Organic
24 Storrington Priory
25 Stopham Vineyard
26 Wiston Estate
27 English Wine Centre

Surrey
28 Denbies Wine Estate
29 Iron Railway
30 Painshill Park
31 RHS Garden Wisley

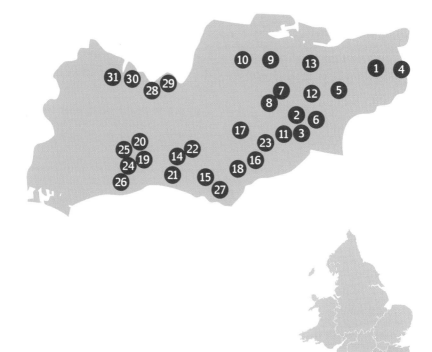

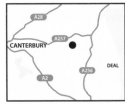

BARNSOLE
Staple, Kent

A small vineyard located between the iconic Kent towns of Canterbury and Sandwich. Devoted to a traditional English wine production from Germanic varieties, there is red as well as white, the opportunity to taste, and to tour the vineyards.

VINEYARD FACTS

- The 3 acres (1.2 ha) of vineyard are dominated by Huxelrebe and Reichensteiner but also includes Rondo, Regent and Pinot Noir Précoce (Frühburgunder).
- The vines are trained on a Double Guyot system on a south facing site.
- Particular attention is paid to canopy management to ensure ripe, healthy grapes.

The Barnsole vineyard was planted in 1993 but only after 16 years of research and experimentation with regard to both the trellising system and which varieties to plant. There are just 3 acres (1.2 ha) of vineyard but these are carefully tended by the owners, the Danilewicz brothers. Canopy management plays a key role in getting ripe, healthy grapes. This means both a large well aerated leaf area and maxi-mising the grapes' exposure to light.

Barnsole's Red Reserve

Wine production

All the Barnsole production appears under the Canterbury Choice label. There are just three wines to ensure a consistent style in each. All are vintage dated. The Dry Reserve is made to emphasise fruit and freshness while Pilgrim's Harvest is a med-ium-dry style that seeks to balance sweetness with fruit and acidity. Red Reserve sets out to provide all the colour, body and tannin that might be expected from a red based largely on the Rondo variety.

Visiting

Barnsole lies just south of Ash and not far from Sandwich or the coast at Deal. Visitors are welcome to taste or purchase the wines. In fact visiting the winery is the best and cheapest way of buying these wines. There is only a small charge for a full guided tour of the vineyards which must be booked in advance. The winery is open daily from 10:30 until 5pm between April and October. In the winter months telephone to check opening hours.

Effective if slightly comic-looking fermentation vessels at Barnsole

HOW TO FIND US

- Fleming Road, Staple, Canterbury, Kent CT3 1LG
- From Canterbury take the A257 towards Sandwich but leaving the bypass road for Ash itself before turning right almost immediately towards Staple along Durlock Road. Turn left at a T-junction in Staple and continue on for about half a mile. From the east, leave the A256 at Sandwich following the A257 for Ash.

Tel: 01304 812530
Email: vineyard@barnsole.co.uk
Web: www.barnsole.co.uk

BIDDENDEN VINEYARD
Biddenden, Kent

Biddenden is a model of commitment, perseverance and the willingness to adapt in order to maximise the potential of vineyard site and location. Embracing diversification whilst maintaining quality in every facet has proved a formula for survival (and more).

VINEYARD FACTS

- 22 acres (9 ha) out of the estate's 65 acres (26 ha) are planted to vines.
- Some newer vineyards on adapted Lyre trellising to help combat mildew.
- Ortega, Huxelrebe, Bacchus and Reichensteiner are the most important white grapes.
- Dornfelder is the leading red but Gamay and Pinot Noir are also significant.

Today Biddenden Vineyards is owned and run by Julian Barnes. His father Richard Barnes came from a Rochdale 'mill family' that processed waste cotton. As that business became less economic in the late 1950s he turned his sights southwards, purchasing a farm in Kent. In the beginning it was an estate based on arable crops, orchards and pigs and the catalyst for change was to come from an unlikely source: Julian's mother heard about a new vineyard being established in Hampshire on the BBC's 'Woman's Hour'. A subsequent decision to plant some vines of their own (in 1969) made these the first to be planted in Kent, or anywhere in the south-east, in the modern era.

The vineyard
The first vines were a small plot of Müller-Thurgau which have subsequently disappeared but the vineyard has expanded to 22 acres (9 ha). The relatively sheltered site has sandy loam soils over clay. All the rows, mostly trained on the GDC or Geneva Double Curtain system, are south or south-east facing. A stroll through the vineyards reveals a succession of different planting dates. There has been an almost continuous evolution in the mix of varieties as an understanding of the local soils and mesoclimate has grown. This process continues, as do adaptations to the type of trellising used in order to produce a healthier, more consistent crop. Some of the new vineyards are trellised on an adapted version of Lyre with a higher and straighter curtain than usual. The improved air flow both under the vines and within the canopy helps in combatting mildew that often affects parts of the vineyard from July onwards. One consequence of the recent warmer vintages are earlier harvest dates, now starting 2-3 weeks earlier, typically in the last week of September.

Wine production
Biddenden do everything themselves from picking, pressing, vinification and bottling, and this includes the sparkling wine production (the disgorging alone is carried out at Chapel Down). Technical expertise comes from Geoff Taylor of Corkwise. This ensures the very best expression of the fruit that Julian works so hard to provide.

The wines are characterised by a clean, fruity, well-balanced style and deserve to have wide appeal, not just to visitors but also to wine lovers anywhere. As well as the fine regular Gribble Bridge Traditional Method sparkling wine profiled here there is a rosé version, based on Gamay, Pinot Noir and Reichensteiner in the 2005 version. A complex red fruits pastille quality precedes a soft, supple and slightly off-dry palate. It is very drinkable, if missing the structure or finesse of the best English sparkling rosés. In addition to the Gribble Bridge Ortega

BIOGRAPHY — Julian Barnes

Julian Barnes is no superstar winemaker but a seasoned wine grower and hugely experienced winery manager who learnt much of his craft from his father, Richard. As a boy, Julian grew up on the then new farm in Kent and has seen the vineyard expand, working with his father as many of the changes took shape. He left school at an early age but now employs up to 37 people. Julian considers Biddenden his life rather than just a job and speaks of his passion for grapes and getting them right. This means getting out into the vineyard whenever it is necessary to safeguard the health of the fruit, whatever the sacrifice. Julian's three sons have all gone off to agricultural college but none have yet committed themselves to viticulture.

Wine tasting area of the shop

VISITING

Guided tours can be booked for groups of 15 to 45 people while a new addition is holiday accommodation for two in The Vineyard Loft. As 80 per cent of Biddenden's wines are sold at the winery a visit to this pretty part of Kent, with Sissinghurst gardens close by, seems difficult to resist.

Dry there is a regular Ortega made in a slightly off-dry style which is soft and deliciously fruity. While a lot of the black grapes, other than Dornfelder, go into the blends for the 'fizz', the Gamay was produced varietally in the hot 2003 vintage.

Cider and apple juice from bought-in fruit are also an important part of Biddenden production. They also make cider and apple juice for others, including the Hush Heath (see page 36) pure apple juice. The production of Kentish cider, around 300,000 litres dwarfs that of wine (40,000 bottles) and plays a key part in the profitability of the family's operations. Around 80 per cent of the wines are sold through the winery so the easiest way to buy them is to pay a visit in person or go online.

HOW TO FIND US

- Gribble Bridge Lane, Biddenden, Kent TN27 8DF
- From the A21 take the A262 eastbound through Goudhurst and Sissinghurst as far as Biddenden. At a sharp turning in the road less than a mile south of Biddenden turn right (effectively straight ahead) into Benenden Road.
- Open throughout the year. Closed only from noon Christmas Eve until New Year's day and on Sundays in January and February. Monday to Saturday from 10am until 5pm. On Sundays and bank holidays the opening is an hour later.

Tel: 01580 291726
Fax: 01580 291933
Email: info@biddendenvineyards.co.uk
Web: www.biddendenvineyards.com

The Wines

2007 Gribble Bridge Ortega Dry

A fine example of this slightly perplexing variety that provides a mix of hedgerow, citrus and melon aromas as well as attractive spicy, appley flavours. Essentially dry, there is good intensity and enough structure that it doesn't need to be drunk straightaway.

2001 Gribble Bridge sparkling

Good quality Traditional Method sparkling wine based on the unlikely combination of Ortega, Pinot Noir, Reichensteiner and Scheurebe. Reveals a fine herbal, citrus and Champagne-like yeastiness. Balanced with an inviting apple and citrus fruit intensity.

2007 Gribble Bridge Rosé

From 100 per cent Dornfelder. A very pale cherry pink with refined floral aromas. Fresh, supple and expressive, it is everything a good English rosé should be but needs to be drunk in the summer or autumn following the vintage.

2006 Gribble Bridge Dornfelder

Pale in colour but with lightly spicy cherry, berry and herbal scents. This is a light, supple clear-fruited red with soft tannins and good length of flavour.

CHAPEL DOWN
Tenterden, Kent

The expanding facilities at Tenterden Vineyard Park, fuelled by a network of grape supplies from the surrounding countryside, constitute the single most important cog powering the English wine industry into the next decade.

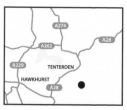

Chapel Down is the leading brand of the English Wines Group which has been headed up since 2001 by its highly regarded CEO, Frazer Thompson, chairman of the Kent Institute of Directors. It started out in 1992 as a purely winemaking operation, both buying in grapes and making wines for others but with the express intent of processing larger quantities of grapes. It has subsequently grown into the UK's biggest wine producer. David Cowderoy made the first wines from grapes grown on Chapel Farm on the Isle of Wight, which gave rise to the company's name. In 1995 they bought Tenterden Vineyard which had been established by Stephen Skelton in 1977. The winery facility, the third to be utilised by Chapel Down, has been adapted and expanded ever since, with a further phase of development in 08/09. In purchasing the 62 acre (25 ha) farm it also secured its first vineyard of 21 acres (8.5 ha).

Also important as a component of English Wines plc since 2000 is Lamberhurst Vineyards. The vineyard itself

The bottling line

VINEYARD FACTS

- Grapes, all hand-picked, are sourced from different sites with a wide range of soils and growing conditions.
- Much of the new planting is of Chardonnay and Pinot Noir for sparkling wine production.
- Only healthy grapes are purchased on a payment scale based on sugar and acidity levels.

was first planted back in 1972 but its subsequent expansion and the winery operation made a huge contribution to the commercialisation of English wines, especially in the 1970s and 80s. Remarkably this 20-acre (8.1-ha) vineyard is a north-facing site, and although more elevated than Tenterden, it is well-protected. The best Bacchus grapes, like those from Tenterden Vineyard are bottled separately as Chapel Down estate wines. The two vineyards have been significantly augmented with the recent explosion of plantings.

The vineyard
The composition of the Tenterden vineyard has evolved from one dominated by Germanic varieties to one with a strong bias towards Chardonnay and Pinot Noir (used for still wines as well as 'fizz'). Original plantings of Seyval Blanc,

Owen Elias has become arguably the best known winemaker in the UK. Given that Chapel Down also produces by far the biggest percentage of the country's wines he is, at least in one sense, also the most important. Born in Liverpool, Owen came to wine via art school (Chelsea School of Art) and music label management in London. The latter included co-founding DiscAfrique, one of the first World Music labels. After marrying and moving to the Lake District the idea of becoming involved with wine took seed. A part-time course at Plumpton College and a start as an assistant wine-maker, to David Cowderoy at Rock Lodge, followed. Owen soon joined Cowderoy who helped found Chapel Down in 1992. He had intended to head off for New Zealand but instead steadily acquired his expertise through handling all the different grapes that were funneled through Chapel Down, culminating in being made the head winemaker in 1999.

Reichensteiner and Müller-Thurgau have all gone. Yet Bacchus has done well here and plantings have been expanded since its introduction whilst the relatively recent additions of black grapes, Regent and Rondo are likely to be retained. The changing vineyard composition reflects the general evolution taking place in the group. Away from the Tenterden headquarters, there is a simply incredible amount of new planting going on, supplemented by many new sources for bought-in grapes coming on stream. It is envisaged that there could be as much as 1000

Part of the Tenterden winery complex

acres (400 ha) either owned or under contract by 2010. It is clear that Chapel Down intend to remain England's largest wine producer.

The 2008 plantings include a very significant chunk of chalk downland near Aylesford, called Bluebell Hill which was identified and overseen by the company's viticulturalist,

The Wines

2006 Bacchus Reserve

A notch or two up from Chapel Down's regular Bacchus, this has riper fruit as well as much better con-centration and intensity. There is both citrus and stone fruit as well as more exotic hints but not the individuality of the Tenterden or Lamberhurst bottlings.

2007 Bacchus Reserve Lamberhurst Estate

From a cooler and more elevated site this is a very distinctive example of Bacchus. With a Sauvignon-like pungency there is intense nettle and mineral fruit on the nose. The palate is structured, dense and very stylish for this variety. This and the Tenterden version rival the best Bacchus made in England.

2002 Pinot Reserve Brut

A blend of Pinot Noir and Pinot Blanc this sparkler is scented with citrus, herb and wild strawberry. Soft and flavoursome, there is plenty of fruit, balanced acidity and good length

2001 Pinot Prestige

A classic Pinot Noir/Chardonnay cuvée, this is currently Chapel Down's most expensive wine and it shows. Aromas of redcurrant, strawberry and a light yeastiness precede white currant and citrus fruit on the palate. There is impressive length of flavour, precision and an added intensity and fruit purity not found in the other sparkling wines.

Harvesting at Tenterden Vineyard

CEO Frazer Thompson

New Zealander Craig Daly. These 72 acres (29 ha) will be complemented by grapes produced by Squeyrres at Westerham — further west beyond Sevenoaks but also part of the Kent Downs. Squeyrres is just one example of a new vineyard estate that Chapel Down is working with. In 06/07 they planted almost 29 acres (11.5 ha) here entirely for sparkling wines. Part of the crop will find its way into Chapel Down wines but the balance will be made for Squeyrres to sell under its own label. Half of the vines are Chardonnay while the balance includes some Pinot Meunier as well as Pinot Noir. The Pinot Meunier portion is unusual for Chapel Down who have mostly shunned this, the third of the big three Champagne varieties. In general, much of Chapel Down's new planting is on chalk. This makes for an interesting contrast this with rivals Ridgeview and Nyetimber who have mostly greensand soils and significant plantings of Pinot Meunier. However in terms of the approach to planting, Chapel Down is not dissimilar, either in terms of planting densities or the training being employed (Single Guyot with Vertical Shoot Positioning), to that seen in other new vineyards dedicated to sparkling wine production.

Wine production

Chapel Down production is now heading towards a ratio of 70 per cent sparkling wine to 30 per cent still wine, almost the reverse of what it was five years ago. The change reflects a big increase in the sparkling wine output rather than any change in the volume of still wines. The winery operations are many but grape processing tends to fall into one of four categories. First there are the wines made from the group's own vineyards, then there are the contract bought-in grapes from growers or farmers. Thirdly, there are arrangements with other wineries where part of the crop goes into Chapel Down production and part is retained for the owner's own label (see Squeyrres above). These three components show

Inside Chapel Down's winery shop

Chapel Down moving closer to the model employed by many Champagne houses. That is, a grape supply derived in part from owned vineyards, a part from that bought under contract, with a further component coming from 'spot' buying. Lastly, there is dedicated contract winemaking for smaller operations without their own facilities. Others just require help with a single operation such as disgorging of their

sparkling wines.

With Owen Elias now overseeing all wine operations Chapel Down have taken on a new head winemaker, Lucy Clements. She comes armed with experience from Grant Burge, where they make a very creditable Pinot Noir/Chardonnay sparkling wine, and Champagne Taittinger. At present all the grapes are whole-bunch pressed and the temperature controlled fermentation is yeast inoculated. In fact, there is much experimentation with yeasts, which can be a very useful tool at the winemaker's disposal. None of the Chapel Down sparkling wines undergo a malolactic fermentation, nor are they de-acidified. The time spent sur lattes ranges from 18 months for the regular cuvées up to five years for the Pinot Reserve. The use of a series of gyro-palettes, each of which can be loaded with 500 bottles, means riddling times are reduced to just four days which together with state of the art disgorging and bottling facilities make for a large throughput of sparkling wine bottles. This is essential given the number of wines being processed for others as well as the Chapel Down wines.

Netting provides protection for the ripening grapes

Visiting

In the Tenterden Vineyard Park facility Chapel Down has a first rate visitor facility that wouldn't look out of place next to some of the more commercially astute new world wineries. There is a 'Fine Food' shop as well as the full range of Chapel Down wines. There is also a restaurant and wine bar and dedicated tasting facilities. The vineyards, grounds and herb gardens may be visited unaccompanied but access to the winery is by guided tour only for which there is a charge. Group tours are also possible by prior arrangement and can even be included as part of a joint itinerary to other local attractions such as Smallhythe Place (run by the National Trust) and the Kent and East Sussex Railway. Chapel Down also offers a vine lease scheme that includes personalised wine labels, a lunch and tutored tasting at the vineyard and the opportunity to harvest your own grapes. Lamberhurst Vineyard with a shop, bistro and function room popular for wedding receptions and conferences can also be visited.

HOW TO FIND US

- Chapel Down Winery, Tenterden Vineyard, Small Hythe, Tenterden, Kent TN30 7NG
- Tenterden lies within the Weald of Kent. Make for the town whether coming from Maidstone (A274, A262, A28), Ashford (A28), Hastings (A21, A28) or Royal Tunbridge Wells (A21, A262, A28). At the southern entrance to Tenterden exit left (if travelling south) on to Smallhythe road (B2082). Continue for 2.5 miles until a sign for Small Hythe. A further 300 yards on the right is the entrance to Chapel Down. If coming from Rye join the B2082 from the southern end.
- Lamberhurst Vineyard can reached directly off the B2169 (exit the A21), soon after it crosses the B2100 if travelling west.
- Tenterden Vineyard Park is open 7 days a week including bank holidays from 10am until 5pm. Lamberhurst is also open daily from 9:30 until 5pm.

Tel: 01580 763033

Tel: (shop and group tours): 01580 766111

Email: (sales and mail order): sales@englishwinesgroup.com

Email: (group tours): retail@englishwinesgroup.com

Web: (Chapel Down): www.englishwinesgroup.com

Web: (Lamberhurst): www.lamberhurstvineyard.net

The Wines

Chapel Down Brut Rosé (Non-Vintage)

Made from 100 per cent Pinot Noir, this pale copper-salmon pink rosé exudes floral, strawberry and cherry aromas. There is more refinement than in the regular Chapel Down sparklers (that are based instead on Reichensteiner and Müller-Thurgau) as well as a prosecco-like lift and freshness. A touch off-dry but well-balanced.

English Rose (still wine)

Usually based on Schönburger, Rondo, Dornfelder or Regent, and Pinot Noir. This is perfect, undemanding summer drinking in the year following the vintage. Perfumed with herbal and cool red fruit aromas, this is light, fresh and supple. It is also clean and not in the least confected unlike some of the bigger brand imports.

Flint Dry

A more basic blend that includes Reichensteiner, Müller-Thurgau, Schönburger and Bacchus yet it is consist-ently light, clean and round with a vaguely grapefruity and herbal character. It is drink-able and soundly made — in contrast to many English wines of a similar composition and price.

ELHAM VALLEY
Breach, Kent

This is a very small vineyard but one of special interest. Here adults with special needs get the opportunity both to work in the vineyard and later to assist in selling the product of their labours in the teashop.

Elham Valley Vineyard is owned by Family Investment Homes as the Vale of Elham Trust, a registered charity. The organisation provides homes for adults with learning difficulties. The site was originally planted in 1980 and not purchased by the Trust until 1995. It lies within the Kent Downs Area of Outstanding Natural Beauty.

Wine production
While only Müller-Thurgau, Reichensteiner and Seyval Blanc are currently planted, there are plans to replant much of the vineyard in order to enhance quality and give the vineyard a sustainable future. Climate change and advances in clonal selection now present new opportunities however decent wines are currently possible with ripe grapes and professional winemaking. At present this is in good hands as the grapes are sent to Chapel Down for

Elham Valley

vinification and bottling. Both dry whites and sparkling wines are made.

Visiting
A fine oak beamed teashop is set amongst the vines and offers light lunches and well as the opportunity to taste and buy the wines. Also on display and available to purchase are pottery and other arts and crafts that have been made by the students. Larger groups such as coach parties are requested to make an

The current range of wines

appointment before visiting. Elham Valley also includes two residences of the great Polish-born writer Joseph Conrad. Oswalds, at Bishopsbourne, where he spent his last years, can be passed on a walk up the valley.

GUSBOURNE ESTATE
Appledore, Kent

It is early days yet for Gusbourne Estate but this enterprising project looks set to becoming a significant player in the new wave of Traditional Method sparkling wine production over the next four to five years.

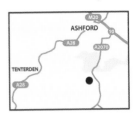

Andrew Weeber, an orthopedic surgeon of South African origin was living in Yorkshire when he chanced upon 500 acres (200 ha) of land when visiting his daughter near Appledore in Kent. An ambitious planting programme ensued taking place over four successive vintages from 2004 to 2007. Each year a large single plot was added. The task of maximising the quality of the grapes has fallen to Jon Pollard who has been entrusted with the management of the vineyards. Jon followed up a BSc in Agriculture with an HND in Wine Studies at Plumpton College (see page 64). The balance of the land is mostly given over to arable farming.

Wine production
The vineyards sit on low slopes and face south or south-west just above the medieval shoreline of southern Kent above the Romney Marsh. The Marsh is separated by the Royal Military Canal that was built as a defence against Napoleon in 1806. Parts of the different vineyard sites are exposed to the prevailing south-westerly winds but much of it enjoys good protection from a combination of gentle contours and established hedgerows. There is a roughly equal split between Chardonnay and the two Pinots with around 30 per cent of Pinot Noir and 20 per cent of Pinot Meunier. The greatest threat to the young vines has come from the local badger population requiring extra protection for each and every plant. The first vintages, starting with a little wine from 2006 have been produced on a 'swap' arrangement with Ridgeview and are being stored sur lattes prior to release.

Visiting
The vineyards lie slightly closer to Rye than Ashford and are but a short hop to the east of Chapel Down's headquarters at Tenterden Vineyard. A new visitor centre is planned to complement the proposed new winery.

VINEYARD FACTS

- Already a substantial 50 acres (20 ha) with scope for more planting.
- Training is that favoured by many for the Champagne varieties — Single Guyot with VSP (Vertical Shoot Positioning).
- Soils are a clay loam with heavier clays in places.
- Unusually, Pinot Meunier gives the lowest yields of the three varieties here.

HOW TO FIND US

- Kenardington Road, Appledore, Kent TN26 2BE
- Appledore can be reached by turning on to the B2080 where the A2070 meets the A259 on the route between Ashford and Rye. Alternatively follow the B2080 east from Tenterden. From Appledore continue north leaving the B2080 and turning right after half a mile into Kenardington Road. A further half mile on the brow of the hill, after passing Horne's Place Chapel, the estate comes into view on the right.
- In order to visit the vineyards contact Jon Pollard on the number below.

Tel/Fax: 01233 758666

HARBOURNE
Wittersham, Kent

Harbourne are another of Kent's survivors, adapting to the local soils and conditions to produce wines as naturally as possible, taking an essentially organic, non-interventionist approach to winemaking.

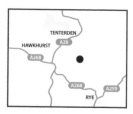

This is a small vineyard owned and run by Laurence Williams. The 3 acres (1.2 ha), first established in 1979, are planted to white varieties Ortega, Müller-Thurgau, Bacchus, Schönburger and Seyval Blanc together with some Pinot Meunier and Blauer Portugieser for reds. As part of a natural approach to viticulture and wine-making no insecticides are used and grass is grown between the rows. A green manure is produced from a mulch of skins and prunings. The vines are also pruned hard to reduce the vigour and yields.

Wine production
The grapes are picked by hand and all winemaking practices are carried out at the winery. The wines are produced as naturally as possible with simple basket presses, a low temperature stainless steel fermentation and natural cold settling. Only very small doses of sulphur are used for stability. The wines produced in any given year depend to some extent on the growing conditions experienced. Regularly produced are a dry white, a medium-dry white and a rosé. More occasional are varietal whites, reds and Traditional Method sparkling wines.

Visiting
Wittersham is south of Tenterden on the Tenterden to Rye road close to Chapel Down. Harbourne are also near the centre of what has become quite an intensive area for wine production in southern England with both new and more established estates but a short distance away. The winery is open most afternoons and weekends and several wines from older vintages are available for sale.

A selection of Harbourne wines

HERBERT HALL

Marden, Kent

The future is sparkling, especially if you happen to have a prime vineyard site in the south-east of England. Herbert Hall promises to add to the thrill and romance of an exhilarating future for English 'fizz'.

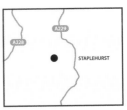

VINEYARD FACTS

- The first plantings (2007) are 10 acres (4 ha), seven of it in a large single block.
- Chardonnay dominates plantings with 20 per cent each of Pinot Noir and Pinot Meunier.
- Soils are a mix of sand and clay but with a gravel bed running through part of the main vineyard.

Target Farm runs to some 350 acres (142 ha) of mostly apples, pears and plums. Although hop production has declined dramatically in the area, respected farmer and horticulturalist Peter Hall also farms 2 acres (0.8 ha) of organic hops here which go into the Duchy Original organic ale. The vineyard part of the new winemaking enterprise (potentially 15 acres/6 ha), Marden Organic Vineyard is a joint venture between Peter and his brother Nicholas. The wine brand, Herbert Hall with its elegant logo is Nick's tribute to their great grandfather who set up a hop garden on the vineyard land back in 1894.

Wine production

There is a mix of different clones amongst the 13,000 vines that have been put in on the sand and clay soils. Nick will oversee both the vineyard and winery operations having studied for two years under Peter Morgan at Plumpton College (see page 64). The new winery will take shape on the south side of Plain Road next to the smaller of the first two vineyard plantings. There are plans to do everything here bar the disgorging with an initial output of 20,000 bottles. Nick's philosophy is to produce a single vintage-dated cuvée that is an expression of this piece of land, something akin to the French concept of terroir.

Visiting

The vineyard lies close to the attractive unhurried village of Marden. The Millennium Lime Tree Walk and newly established wildflower meadows, both initiatives of Peter Hall can be enjoyed by visitors to the area.

Attaching the trellising wires

HOW TO FIND US

- Marden Organic Vineyard, Plain Road, Marden, Kent TN12 9LS
- Like the best Kent villages, Marden has escaped the stresses common on the major arterial routes but is easily reached from London by car or train. From Maidstone take the A229 south through Linton before turning right for Marden.
- Visits by appointment only. There are no plans for a shop as such but sales directly from the winery are a possibility. It is probably a good idea to ask about joining a mailing list now!

Tel: 01622 831550
Email: nmh@herberthall.co.uk
Web: www.herberthall.com

Tending the young vines

HUSH HEATH ESTATE
Cranbrook, Kent

You can't visit this estate but you can drink its produce and if the finest pink English 'fizz' is what you're after you won't be disappointed. Quality is considerably higher than most of the more widely seen rosé Champagnes.

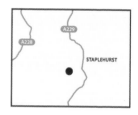

Hush Heath estate comprises 400 acres (162 ha), a mix of mostly apple orchards, fields and oak woodlands. The centrepiece is a fine timber-framed Tudor manor house. This is one of the homes of business guru Richard Balfour-Lynn and his family. Everything has been undertaken with serious intent, helped along with a bit of cash of course. The restoration of the manor house included restoring the original tiles while the garden has had similar attention lavished on it.

The vineyard
Richard Balfour-Lynn planted the first vines in 2002 under the guidance of leading UK viticultural expert Stephen Skelton. Initially just 4 acres (1.6 ha) were established on a gentle south-facing site that had once been given over to producing Bramley apples. Additional planting in 2008 has bought the total planting to 12 acres (5 ha). The new vineyards are on a protected South — SSE facing site. The overall composition of the vineyard is 45 per cent each of Chardonnay and Pinot Noir with the balance from Pinot Meunier. Some leaf thinning is employed prior to harvesting to encourage full physiological ripeness. All the grapes are hand-harvested, typically in mid-late October; the Chardonnay around two weeks ahead of the two Pinots.

Looking across the garden of England

VINEYARD FACTS

- 12 acres (almost 5 ha) are dedicated to nearly 18,000 vines of Chardonnay, Pinot Noir and Pinot Meunier.
- Vines are VSP (Vertical Shoot Position) trained and pruned to a two-cane horizontal Guyot system.
- Soils are composed of Wealden Clay over Tunbridge Wells Sand.
- The best grapes are destined solely for Balfour Brut Rosé.

BIOGRAPHY | Richard Balfour-Lynn

Owner Richard Balfour-Lynn is a highly successful business figure active in the City of London and chairs both public and private companies in the retail, hotel and office provision sectors. From a wine perspective of greater interest is Richard's majority shareholding in English Wines Plc which incorporates the Chapel Down group, the leading commercial wine operation in the UK. While he own properties in London, France and South Africa, it is his impressive Manor House built in 1503 that provides the backdrop to Hush Heath estate.

Despite the clamour for the fine pink sparkling wine the estate is still orientated more towards the production of high quality pure apple juice from roughly equal proportions of Cox Orange Pippins, Bramley Seedlings and Egremont Russet varieties.

A formal garden, oak woodlands and fields are all part of the mix too

Wine production

The wine is made by Chapel Down's winemaking supremo, Owen Elias one of a handful of individuals giving a strong quality-led direction to the English wine industry. Following a gentle pressing only the best part of the juice is retained for a slow cool fermentation. As is not uncommon in Champagne a small amount of a red wine ferment is added to provide the colour. What follows is a classic champagne method (Traditional Method) treatment with up to 2 years on the lees prior to disgorgement.

Visiting

Hush Heath estate is not open to visitors. However close by are Sissinghurst Castle Garden and other vineyards in the Weald of Kent. Should you wish to finish your day's travels with this fine sparkling English rosé, the wine can be purchased online from distributors Bibendum Wine or bought from the likes of Harvey Nichols and the Whole Foods Market in Kensington in London.

HOW TO FIND US

- Hush Heath Manor, Cranbrook, Kent TN17 2NG
- For Cranbrook or Sissinghurst or for other vineyards in the Weald of Kent leave the A21 south of Royal Tunbridge Wells, taking the A262 through Goudhurst.
- Not open to the public.

Tel: 020 7479 9500
Email: info@hushheath.com
Web: www.hushheath.com

The Wines

Balfour Brut Rosé

This is only the wine produced here. The early efforts have earnt high praise and with good reason but there is the potential for still more as the vines age.

2004 vintage

Tasted in January 2007, this highly impressive début bottling was produced solely from very young Chardonnay and Pinot Noir vines. Just 9000 bottles were made. Even this early effort showed a touch of class and a fresh, well-defined ripe fruit-intensity. There's plenty of acidity, a touch of sweetness and good purity. One to retaste if you're lucky enough to have some.

2005 vintage

A warm late September to mid-October made this vintage. 4 per cent of Pinot Meunier was added to the blend in which the Pinot Noir slightly dominated the Chardonnay. Palest copper pink with refined apple, strawberry and a lightly herbal influence. More richness and intensity than 04 with a fine creaminess yet plenty of vigour. Added complexity and plenty of potential. Best kept till 2010 or beyond.

Future prospects

The 2006 vintage was mostly hot and dry but finished a little wet. Highish acidities and good structure are expected to ensure a wine with good ageing potential. In 2007 a weak English summer and outbreaks of downy mildew impacted on yields. High acidities and a greater reliance on Pinot Meunier have also resulted.

LEEDS CASTLE
Broomfield, Kent

The vineyard at Leeds Castle, with just a little over 3 acres of vines, is nothing grand when compared to the castle itself. Yet there was a vineyard here at the time of William the Conqueror and the completion of the Domesday book.

Leeds Castle straddles two islands on the river Len, a tributary of the Medway which it joins at Maidstone. Much of the modern restoration and the refurbished interiors derive from the last private owners, in particular the passion of Lady Baillie for the castle which she came to in 1926. Upon her death in 1974 the castle was bequeathed to the Leeds Castle Foundation.

The Vineyard
The modern vineyard was first planted in 1980 with Müller-Thurgau and Seyval Blanc vines. This was extended a little in 2000 when some Reichensteiner and Schönburger were added. The 3.2 acres (1.3 ha) are south-facing on a gently sloping site with rows a typical 2m apart. One of the biggest threats to an adequate

VINEYARD FACTS
■ 3.2 acres (1.3 ha) of vines are planted on a mix of sand and clayey soils.
■ A south-facing site at around 100m elevation.
■ The grape varieties are Müller-Thurgau, Seyval Blanc, Reichensteiner and Schönburger.
■ Netting is used to protect the ripening fruit from birds.

harvest comes from birds so in the autumn netting is used to protect the grapes from these winged plunderers.

Wine production
The modest grape production is transported down to Chapel Down (see page 28), near Tenterden for vinification and bottling. Whites labelled Dry and Medium-Dry have regularly been produced and there is also a vintage-dated bottle-fermented sparkling wine. All the wine produced is used for events at the Castle or sold from the shop.

Visting
Leeds Castle is of course one of the major tourist attractions of Kent and the south-east generally. There are many reasons for paying a visit besides seeing the iconic castle. The gardens, the aviary with its many exotic birds, the Duckery, the Yew maze, an underground grotto and even a

Black swans on the castle's moated lake

LEEDS CASTLE | Early history

There was a single acre of vineyard at Leeds Castle when the Domesday book was compiled. It was planted by Bishop Odo of Bayeux who shared the same mother as William the Conqueror. At that time the 'castle' was no more than a small wooden fortress. When Bishop Odo fell out of favour with his half-brother, possession of the castle fell to Robert de Crevecoeur who erected the first stone buildings. It became a royal castle in 1278 and remained so until Tudor times, with Henry VIII a regular visitor. It has had a colourful history since then too serving as a garrison, a prison, and a convalescent home as well as a family home.

Acres of netting protect against birds at harvest

golf course are reason enough for some to visit. Dog lovers might want to take in the Dog Collar Museum with hunting dog collars dating back 500 years. Hopefully you'll have time too to take in the vineyard. Conferences, weddings and other special events also bring visitors to Leeds Castle. It is well signposted from almost anywhere in the vicinity but for directions see below. If you intend to stay on in the area there are now three holiday cottages within the castle grounds available to rent.

The Wines

The Leeds Castle sparkling wine is made by Kent's leading winery, Chapel Down. A Traditional Method production is employed with the second fermentation on the yeast lees in the bottle. Vintage-dated, the wine may be drunk when released but should also keep for at least another 3-4 years.

HOW TO FIND US

- Leeds Castle, Broomfield, Maidstone, Kent ME17 1PL
- The most usual approach to Leeds Castle is to exit the M20 at Junction 8 and quickly find the entrance to the castle off the B2163. If coming from Maidstone use the A20. If travelling up from the Weald vineyards in the Tenterden area, join the A274 at Biddenden, continuing through Headcorn before joining the bottom of the B2163 at Five Wents. Another 2 miles brings you to the castle.
- Open daily except Christmas Day and occasional other days (check website for details and prices).
  10am – 7pm (April to end September)
  10am – 5pm (October to end March)

Tel: 01622 765400

Tel (group reservations): 01622 767865

Fax: 01622 735616

Fax: (group reservations): 01622 767837

Email: enquiries@leeds-castle.co.uk

Web: www.leeds-castle.com

MEOPHAM VALLEY
Meopham, Kent

An established source of good quality sparkling wine, this small operation is a good example of a well-run Kentish vineyard showing just what is possible with good vineyard husbandry and competent winemaking.

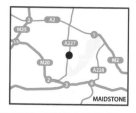

Meopham Valley can be found in the low hills of the Kent Downs tucked away from the Medway towns. It was established by David and Pauline Grey in 1991 after help from Gillian Pearkes (see Yearlstone Vineyards, page 132/3), arguably the established authority on English wine production at the time.

Wine production

The almost 5 acre (2 ha) vineyard is orientated to the south-east on a uniform slope. As well as Chardonnay and Pinot Noir which are used for both the sparkling Brut and Brut Rosé, there is the usual somewhat motley collection of grapes including hybrids which at the time were seen as insurance for cool, wet summers. Other varieties include vinifera Pinot Gris, Madeleine Angevine and Reichensteiner but also hybrids Léon Millet and Triomphe. For Meopham

Valley, maximizing the potential of their fruit means using the winemaking services offered by Owen Elias and his team at Chapel Down. The sparkling wine production has received the most attention and yet again shows the potential for the Champagne varieties in southern England, given the right soils and location. Still wines include a varietal Pinot Gris and a rosé in a medium-sweet style.

Visiting

Lying between the A2/M2 and the M20, Meopham is a good vineyard to visit if making a less hurried dash than most through north Kent. Groups of up to 25 people are also welcomed but it is first necessary to make an appointment. The wines are sold both from the vineyard shop and the local Farmers' Markets at Meopham, Penshurst, Rochester and West Malling.

SANDHURST
Sandhurst, Kent

The vineyard here benefits from being a small piece in an agricultural jigsaw. Having an expert contract winemaking facility close by, has also made it possible to focus solely on producing high quality fruit.

Hoads Farm is owned by Anne Nicholas and is a large estate of 350 acres (142 ha). There are orchards, arable crops, hops and grass land. The first vines were planted in 1988 and the vineyards now cover 25 acres (10 ha). White varieties include Bacchus, Reichensteiner, Huxelrebe, Schönburger and Seyval Blanc while for red there are plantings of Rondo, Dornfelder and Pinot Noir.

Wine production
Christopher Nicholas

VINEYARD FACTS

- 25 acres (10 ha) of vineyard on a sandy loam over Wealden clay.
- The vines are Double Guyot trained with planting densities typical of southern England.
- Some of the production is retained for the Sandhurst label but other grapes are grown under contract for other wineries in the area.

SANDHURST
vineyards
2001
Late Harvest Dessert
ENGLISH VINEYARDS QUALITY WINE PSR
50 cl e   18% Vol

concentrates on producing healthy fruit while the winemaking task is left in the capable hands of the Chapel Down team (see page 28). The range of wines made covers pretty much the full gamut of styles made in England, including dry and medium-dry whites, rosé, red but also sparkling wine and a dessert wine. Due to contractual arrangements only part of the wine produced from the vineyards ends up being bottling under the Sandhurst label. These include Oak Dry, Bacchus Dry and Medium-Dry whites and a Vintage Brut sparkling wine. A varietal Pinot Noir is a promising new development earning critical praise from both the first two vintages, 2003 and 2004. An example of the dessert wine was made in 2001 from late-harvested Huxelrebe grapes.

Visiting
If you're looking for more than a self-guided tour then a booking is necessary. For a small charge there will then be a guided tour

B&B accommodation in a 16th century farmhouse

concluding with a tutored tasting of the wines. There is also the opportunity to purchase the wines at the farm shop.

HOW TO FIND US

- Hoads Farm, Crouch Lane, Sandhurst, Kent TN18 5PA
- The A268 links the A21 to Rye, and may be joined from the A229 or the A28 from either north or south. Between the A229 and the A28 it passes through Sandhurst. Crouch Lane is just beyond the village on the left if travelling from west to east (on the right just before the village if coming from Tenterden or Rye).

Tel & Fax: 01580 850296
Email: ca.nicholas@btinternet.com
Web: www.sandhurstvineyards.co.uk

SURRENDEN
Little Chart, Kent

A small plot of the classic Champagne varieties was planted here in 1986 making these the oldest surviving plantings in the UK. The small production is dedicated to sparkling wine.

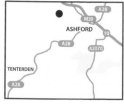

Martin and Tessa Oldaker both undertook planting projects in 1986. Tessa's garden became celebrated on TV while Martin's daring vineyard was bubbling under. Both lie within the original confines of Pluckley estate that was the domain of the Dering family.

Wine production

The wines have long been made at Stanlake Park (formerly Thames Valley Vineyards, see page 86) by Vincent Gower. Surrenden's provocatively labelled Traditional Method sparkling wine, MQC (Mieux que Champagne) is a

VINEYARD FACTS

- 3 acres (1.2 ha) planted to the three Champagne varieties in 1986 and 1987.
- Greensand soils with some chalk content too.
- Unusually the vineyard faces north, on the reverse slope of Pluckley Hill.
- Training and pruning were also established along Champagne lines.

vintaged example, the wine only returned to Surrenden after all the winemaking processes, including lees ageing, disgorging and bottling have been carried out. Hot years like 2003 bring the kind of sugar levels and ripeness that bring wider recognition.

Visiting

Both the vineyard and the 3 acre garden developed by Tessa Oldaker are included

A view across the vineyard

within the NGS (National Gardens Scheme) by which there are limited openings to the public for charity. For walkers the Greensand Way walk passes along the top of the vineyard.

HOW TO FIND US

- Walnut Tree Farm, Swan Lane, Little Chart, Ashford, Kent TN27 0PS
- The vineyard and gardens are between Little Chart and Pluckley which lie just below the M20, slightly north, and west of Ashford. Travelling from Ashford take the A20 Maidstone Road, turning left for Little Chart before crossing the M20.

Tel: 01233 840214
Fax: 01233 840703
Email: martin@surrenden-vineyard.co.uk

A successful harvest at Surrenden

THROWLEY
Throwley, Kent

A small north Kent vineyard making an impact well beyond its small size. Chardonnay and Pinot Noir grapes on chalky soils allied to expert winemaking help them punch above their weight.

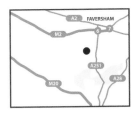

Like Meopham Valley Vineyard, Throwley is a small north Kent vineyard making a name for high quality sparkling wine. Also like Meopham, Throwley is situated in the North Downs of Kent and benefits from a warm local mesoclimate and predominantly chalk soils.

Wine production

Current owner Duncan Wilson has enjoyed plenty of recognition within the UK for his small output which has always been contract made given the small size of the vineyard and a lack of winemaking facilities. The vintage-dated Brut sparkling wine is based on roughly equal parts

The year's new growth

VINEYARD FACTS

- A small widely spaced vineyard of slightly less than 4 acres (1.5 ha).
- It is south-west facing with mostly Chardonnay and Pinot Noir grapes on chalky soils.
- The early ripening Ortega is also grown for a still dry white wine.

Chardonnay and Pinot Noir and is given a Traditional Method elaboration with around two years on the lees. It has achieved consistent success and should be tried from a vintage like 2001. An aromatic dry white is made from the Ortega grapes that are harvested well ahead of the Champagne varieties, usually around a month sooner. Throwley also made still wines from the Pinot Noir (red and rosé) and Chardonnay grapes (white) in the

very hot vintage of 2003. Total production ranges from a meagre 2000 to 5000 bottles per year.

Visiting

The vineyard is not open for visiting but this part of Kent is not far from Faversham, Canterbury or Ashford. A designated Area of Outstanding Natural Beauty, this is indeed a very pretty part of the North Downs with fine churches and houses dotted amongst the gently undulating low hills.

HOW TO FIND US

- The Old Rectory, Throwley, Faversham, Kent ME13 0PF
- Not open to the public but the village of Throwley with an attractive church and village green can be reached off the A251 that runs between Faversham and Ashford.
- For sales outlets visit the website or use the contacts below.

Tel: 01795 890276
Email: duncanm.wilson@virgin.net
Web: www.throwleyvineyard.co.uk

DENBIES WINE ESTATE
Dorking, Surrey

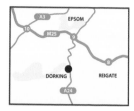

Denbies claim to being England's largest vineyard looks set to run and run. Although now surpassed by larger estates such as Nyetimber none exist as a single entity of 265 acres (107 ha).

Background

Formed from the Denbies and Bradley farms just north of Dorking, it is nestled in a chink in the North Downs. As a single continuous parcel it offers an extraordinary vista of vines when approached from any direction, be it by foot, car or train. To make the most of a visit to the winery be sure and view it from the fabulous panorama afforded by Box Hill which rises steeply immediately beyond the pretty Mole river, just east of Denbies estate.

As a wine estate Denbies dates from 1984 when Adrian and Gillian White took advice from Professor Richard Selley. A bold and ambitious undertaking it gave the UK wine trade press sceptics plenty to ponder, and this well before the string of hot years enjoyed over the past decade or so. Current direction comes from the next generation of the White family in the shape of Christopher White.

The vineyard

The composition of Denbies vineyards has evolved substantially over the past 20-odd years. From a plethora of obscure varieties there has been some grubbing up of the least successful. 94 ha are currently in production with new planting restricted to

VINEYARD FACTS
■ England largest single vineyard: 94 ha of 107 ha are currently in production.
■ Most grapes are machine-harvested but those for sparkling wines are picked by hand.
■ Spring frost can be a problem but only in lower, flatter vineyards.
■ Hi-tech recycling sprayers are used to reduce residual spray and help protect the environment.

infilling of rows. Despite a certain consolidation there are still plenty of names that will be new to most, to try and get your tongue around. Müller-Thurgau, Seyval Blanc, Schönburger and Reichensteiner

Denbies vines are nestled in the North Downs near Dorking.

figure strongly in the leading blended whites. In 2005 Ortega was added and in 2006 more Bacchus was added, a smart move from a quality perspective. All of the fruit is estate grown, coming immediately from around the winery. What you can see is what you get. The hillside vineyards are the most exciting for quality and include the plantings of Chardonnay, Pinot Noir and Pinot Meunier for the top sparkling wines.

Frost is a major consideration, without protection the potential reduction in yield doesn't bear contemplation. On the slopes at least, it is not a problem. On the flatter, lower lying slopes where it is, frost busters are employed to encourage air circulation. Frost risk starts with budbreak in early to mid-April and continues until the beginning of June. Where possible mechanical harvesting is used to bring in the grapes. However, the higher slopes including all the Pinot Noir and other grapes for fizz, are harvested by hand.

Wine production

Winemaker Marcus Sharp who has been here 10 years and in charge of wine production since 2003, considers the wines as either aromatics, sparkling or rosé/red. In fact around half of Denbies production is dedicated to the aromatic still whites which include the long-established Surrey Gold. This wine epitomises the Denbies style which is all about consistency and drinkability. It is a great commercial success, and

Fuel oil burner used to protect vines from late frosts

The Wines

2007 Bacchus Vineyard Select

Bright, ripe and pungent, this a Bacchus that offers plenty of typical nettle and gooseberry character as well as a hint of green pepper and mineral. Round, supple and fruit-intense with balanced acidity. Best with 2-3 years' age.

2006 Schönburger Vineyard Select

In this variety the berries turn from green to pink as they ripen and this is a pristine, varietal example. Enticing hedgerow and pear scents precede plump, well-concentrated fruit on a marginally off-dry palate.

2006 Ortega Vineyard Select

Denbies Ortega is both barrel-fermented and aged in oak. Aromatic with spiced melon and guava it is also denser, fuller and with more breadth than the Bacchus. Likely to keep for perhaps 3-4 years.

Rose Hill (rosé)

Now this needs to be drunk really young. Always drink last year's vintage. But from the pale cherryish colour to herbal and floral scents, and the cool red fruit and herbal flavours, this can make delicious summer drinking if served lightly chilled.

Denbies distinctive winery building viewed from the vineyards in late summer

delivers classic English herbal and floral scents together with balance and freshness in a negligibly off-dry style. Juniper Hill, a Bacchus/ Schönburger blend, also deserves its following with the unusual contrast of floral, green fruit with a riper, more exotic character but more exciting are the new Vineyard Select single varietal aromatics from Bacchus, Ortega and Schönburger, three of the top varieties grown in England. All display excellent varietal fruit character and intensity, well worth contrasting with the same varietals made by other leading English producers such as Chapel Down or Three Choirs.

While Denbies is not dedicated solely to sparkling production like other industry leaders such as Nyetimber or Ridgeview it is nonetheless taken very seriously. Marcus Sharp has increased the sparkling range which includes the more everyday Whitedowns Cuvée from Seyval Blanc and a sparkling rosé from Pinot Noir grapes. Encouragingly too, through the premium Greenfields Cuvée he expresses a desire to make an English sparkling wine, albeit from Champagne varieties. After all, to ape Champagne is one thing and some are doing this well enough but to produce a high quality sparkling wine with an intrinsic English (or Surrey) characteristic drawn only from the downland chalk is something else.

Yet there seems the potential for this Surrey giant to focus still more on the high quality sparkling output. Despite the modest production of Greenfields, with an enhanced structure and concentration this smartly presented wine could be honed into an iconic English wine like the Nyetimber cuvées. A 2007 Blanc de Noirs cuvée tasted from a sur lattes sample amply demonstrated a fine ripe underlying fruit quality and impressive structure, suggesting another Denbies wine to get your hands on in the future, perhaps released in time for those 2012

The Wines

2006 Redlands

Comprised of Dornfelder and Pinot Noir in equal measure. With a good ruby colour this is a most attractively perfumed red with floral and red cherry fruit but none of the greeness or harshness sometimes associated with English reds. It is balanced and accessible with good length of flavour and fine subtle tannins.

2004 Greenfields Cuvée

Half of this blend is from Pinot Noir, over a third from Chardonnay with the balance from the other principal Champagne grape, Pinot Meunier. Three years ageing on its lees has added complexity and while it hasn't the vibrancy or structure of a top Champagne it has a ready drinkability with a fine floral/herbal lift.

2004 Rosé Cuvée

This is entirely from Pinot Noir and includes some of the best fruit Denbies has to offer. With salmon-copper hues it offers up floral scents, cherry/berry fruits and lightly bready hints. A touch off-dry, it displays the characteristic softness of all the Denbies sparklers. A lovely pure red fruits flavour together with a dash of English herbs and spice provides lots of immediate charm and appeal.

BIOGRAPHY — Adrian White

Adrian White purchased Denbies Estate in 1984 as a pig and cattle farm. The south-facing slopes being of little grazing value were considered instead for a vineyard but only after the similarities of soil and climate with Champagne had been pointed out by a local Dorking resident, no less than Dr Richard Selley, Professor of Geology at Imperial College, London. By creating one of Europe's largest privately owned vineyards, Adrian White's brillance was to foresee not only the benefits that the economies of scale would ensue but also the added value of educating visitors and selling the wine in-situ. Christopher White, one of Adrian's sons, now oversees day to day operations.

Row upon row of vines in England's largest vineyard

celebrations. The appointment of the hugely experienced John Worontschak as Operations Director in 2008 should further enhance Denbies' reputation.

Visiting

With a staggering 300,000 visitors per year this a major tourist attraction by any measure and the concept and focus as a 'wine experience' is fundamental to Denbies' commercial success. While lacking the intimacy of a small family run vineyard Denbies nonetheless provides an excellent starting point for those new to English wine, or indeed, wine per se.

HOW TO FIND US

- Denbies Wine Estate, London Road, Dorking, Surrey RH5 6AA
- Off the A24, just north of Dorking.
- Close to the M25 and A3 from London
- Regular train services from London to Dorking.
- Denbies is 15 minutes walk from Dorking station
- Open: (Wine & Gift shop) Monday-Friday: 10-5:30 (closes 5pm January-March only)
- Saturdays: 10-5:30, Sundays: 11:30-5:30 (all year round)

Tel: 01306 876616
Fax: 01306 888930
Email: info@denbiesvineyard.co.uk
Web: www.denbiesvineyard.co.uk

The Wines

Surrey Gold

A blend of Müller-Thurgau, Bacchus and Ortega might not sound very enticing but this is fast becoming a consummately crafted English blended white, a sort of English equivalent of Houghton's HWB. The fusion of herbal and floral (particularly hedgerow) scents combined with excellent balance and even a certain delicacy and elegance underpin its deserved popularity.It drinks well young but can also be kept for at least two years

Juniper Hill

With some Bacchus thrown in this hasn't the singularity of Denbies new varietal Schönburger but is well-balanced and offers both the 'green fruit' of the Bacchus component and a more exotic flavour as well as good definition and intensity. Drink from the most recent vintage for the maximum fruit and freshness.'

Coopers Brook

A blend of Chardonnay and Reichensteiner this unusual blend combines a herbal aromatic intensity with a lees-given influence. While it doesn't have the class of a good white Burgundy there is plenty of flavour and a structure that ensures it will keep for at least 3-4 years.

IRON RAILWAY
Merstham, Surrey

Iron Railway is a small landholding with vineyard tucked into a cutting in the North Downs where an old horse-drawn iron railway linked Coulsdon and Merstham to the Thames at Wandsworth in the early part of the 19th century.

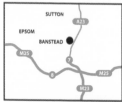

'The (rail) Way through
    the Woods.
They shut the (rail) road
    through the woods
(almost one hundred and)
Seventy years ago....
You will hear the beat of
    a horse's feet...but
there is no road,
    through the woods."

Just a vineyard instead (apologies to Rudyard Kipling). Located in the North Downs just above the M25, this vineyard occupies the cutting left by the old horse-drawn iron railway that linked Coulsdon with Merstham. In 1803 a railway built by the Surrey Iron Railway company between Wandsworth and Croydon was opened. Two years later an extension to Coulsdon and Merstham made it possible to transport stone from the Merstham chalk quarries to the wharves at Wandsworth. However it had been dismantled by 1840s. More recently owner John Dicken, a retired

The vineyard sign reflects an industrial past

headteacher took his interest in gardening and horticulture well beyond a regular allotment by developing the site and vineyard.

Wine production
The first plantings were of Madeleine Angevine (1982/1983) with the other varieties added later. The wines are made by Alexander Carr Taylor at the Carr Taylor winery near Hastings. Whites are produced under Dry, Oaked,

VINEYARD FACTS

- 2.5 acres (1 ha) of vineyard first planted in 1982 and 1983 as part of a 7 acre (2.8 ha) site.
- The site is relatively flat at around 450 feet (137m) above sea-level.
- The vines are spur pruned and include Phoenix, Orion, Madeleine Angevine for whites and Rondo and Triomphe for reds.

Medium and Medium-Sweet labels. There is also some sparkling wine. There are no plans to expand the vineyard but there is a desire to get riper grapes and improve the quality.

Visiting
The vineyard is not open to the public and visits are strictly by appointment only. The wines can be found in local Farmers' Markets as well as at country shows and fairs.

HOW TO FIND US

- London Road North, Merstham, Surrey
- The vineyard can't be visited except by appointment but lies close by the A23, north of Merstham. Coming north on the A23, and soon after crossing the M25 near Junction 7, continue past Harp's Oak Lane entering the one way system. The vineyard can be seen from an access road that runs alongside the A23 here.

Tel: 01737 551829
No Email or Website

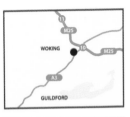

RHS GARDEN WISLEY
Wisley, Surrey

The Royal Horticultural Society describes this garden as their flagship. As well as being a wonderful garden to visit, it is an important centre for research and trialling. Now growing grapes for wine has added a further dimension.

VINEYARD FACTS

- A small vineyard of just over half an acre (0.235 ha).
- Planted to just two of the newer crossings, Phoenix and Orion, that have been bred for disease resistance and ripening potential.
- Fairly typical planting densities with 2m between rows and 1.5m between plants.

The 60-acre (24-ha) Wisley estate, mostly woods and farmland, was gifted to the RHS in 1903. It made it possible for the Society to expand beyond its original leased garden in Chiswick. Selections of the best new introductions of flowers, fruit and vegetables are made from the trial fields. The vineyard, planted in 2004 and the first in the more than 200 year history of the society, was established at the suggestion of Simon Ackeroyd. It is essentially an experimental vineyard intended to show garden lovers that grape growing for wine production is possible in southern England, given the right varieties and location. Besides the small vineyard, more than 100 different cultivars (varieties) of vine are grown.

RHS Wisley's white wine

Wine production
The vineyard is in the care of Alessandra Valsecchi, the senior supervisor of the Fruit and Trial department, who is supported by the department's head, Jim Arbury. Alessandra undertook a trip to New Zealand to gain a better understanding of cool climate viticulture but preparation and planting required the whole team's involvement including Jonathan Keyte. The first wine, a dry white, is being made for Wisley at Plumpton College (see page 64) under the direction of Peter Morgan. A blend of both varieties, it is given a straightforward, low temperature stainless steel vinification. The bottles are available to purchase in the RHS shop.

Visiting
Located just outside the M25 between Cobham and Woking, this famous garden includes a plant centre, a gift shop with an extensive book collection, several cafés/restaurants and Gardening and Science libraries. Group visits to Wisley must be booked in advance. There are also educational opportunities for horticultural training at Wisley.

HOW TO FIND US

- RHS Garden Wisley, Woking, Surrey GU23 6QB
- The garden is just off the A3 below Junction 10 (Wisley Interchange) on the M25. Follow the brown tourist flower signs from either the M25 or A3. By bus, there is the 515 from Kingston and a shuttle from Woking station in the summer months.
- Open: Mon-Fri: 10am-6pm (Nov-Feb: 10am-4:30pm) Saturdays, Sundays & Bank Holidays: 9am-6pm (Nov-Feb: 9am-4:30pm)

Tel: 0845 2609000
Tel: (group bookings): 01483 212307
Fax: 01483 211750
Email: info@rhs.org.uk
Web: www.rhs.org.uk

The vineyard was planted in 2004

PAINSHILL PARK

Cobham, Surrey

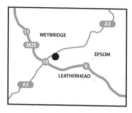

The small vineyard at this 18th century landscape garden has only recently been re-established. But it is a unique example of a historic vineyard restored in the exact same location, albeit 250 years after the original was planted.

VINEYARD FACTS

- The vineyard, first planted in 1740 was replanted in 1992.
- The site of less than 2 acres (0.73 ha) faces south on a steep slope and is planted to Chardonnay, Pinot Noir and Seyval Blanc.
- The modern training is Single Guyot with Vertical Shoot Positioning.

Painshill Park is the story of a quite extraordinary conversion of acres of mostly scrubby, unpromising Surrey countryside into a romantic European-inspired park by Charles Hamilton in the mid-18th century. The ornamental pleasure garden part of the park included a grotto, a Roman temple, ruins, a Turkish tent, a large lake maintained by a large water wheel, and even a Hermitage for a time. Even after it was relinquished by the honourable gentleman, successive owners largely maintained its appearance. In fact Painshill Park only went into serious decline after World War II. After its sale in 1948 it was split up, including detaching the mansion from the park. When the Painshill Trust took over the extant 158 acres (64 ha) in 1981 it was in a state of extreme neglect but they set about restoring the Grade I landscape. The receipt of the Europa Nostra Award in 1998 gives an indication of the extent of the progress made.

The Vineyard

The replanting of the vineyard took place between 1992 and 1994, after several other restoration projects within the park had taken priority. Consultancy was sought from a contemporary expert, Stephen Skelton. Given that the white wine was compared to Champagne (see below) it was decided to replant with Chardonnay and Pinot Noir along with some Seyval Blanc, the latter for its perceived dependability at the time. After the site was cleared the vines were trained up poles as in the original vineyard but with a wider spacing and a Single Guyot training.

The original vineyard and wine production is best described by Charles Hamilton himself in a letter to a friend:

"The vineyard at Painshill is situated on

The vineyard in the exact location as it was in 1740

The vintage sparkling brut

BIOGRAPHY   The Hon. Charles Hamilton

The Hon. Charles Hamilton (1704 – 1786) was the ninth son of the sixth Earl of Abercorn. He was educated at Westminster and Oxford and was both a painter and a garden designer. During two Grand Tours (1725 and 1732) he studied in France and Italy. Much of the inspiration drawn from these travels, which must have taken in the classical work of Poussin and the fabulous landscapes of Claude, were funneled into his one great creation: Painshill. He acquired the lease to the land at Painshill in 1738 and created a romantic garden designed to stimulate the senses and emotions of the visitor. Both an ornamental pleasure garden and an open, naturalistic parkland were developed. According to Sir John Parnell, writing in 1763, he had even delayed building his residence until the garden was perfected. Having run out of money he sold the estate in 1773.

the south-side of a gentle hill, the soil gravelly sand. The first year, I attempted to make red Wine. It was so very harsh and austere, that I despaired of ever making red Wine fit to drink; but through that harshness I perceived a flavour something like that of some small French white Wines, which made me hope I should succeed better with white Wine. That experiment succeeded far beyond my most sanguine expectations; for the very first year I made white Wine, it nearly resembled the flavour of Champaign; and in two or three years more, as the Vines grew stronger, to my great amazement, my Wine had a finer flavour than the best Champaign I ever tasted; but such is the prejudice of most people against any thing of English growth, I generally found it most prudent not to declare where it grew, till after they had passed their verdict upon it.

The surest proof I can give of its excellence is, that I have sold it to Wine-merchants for fifty guineas a hogshead"

Wine production
Today the vineyard is managed by Mark Ebdon. The biggest problem besides getting the grapes fully ripe,

Along with the follies, much of the planting has been restored

has been defending both plants and fruit from the local wildlife. Badgers, deer, rabbits and birds have all proved troublesome. The grapes have so far been made into a rosé, a white as well of course as some sparkling wine. These are made for the Painshill Trust by Vince Gower at Stanlake Park (see page 86) with the sparkling wine undergoing a Traditional Method bottle-aged fermentation.

Visiting
Painshill Park also has facilities for wedding receptions and corporate events. Painshill Park's own wine is served by the glass in the Tearoom while bottles can be purchased from the gift shop.

HOW TO FIND US

- Painshill Park, Portsmouth Road, Cobham, Surrey KT11 1JE
- Exit the A3 at Painshill junction, the first north of Junction 10 on the M25, joining the A245 in the direction of Cobham following the signs. The nearest trains are Cobham and Stoke d'Abernon and Weybridge stations .For buses use the Kingston to Guildford 515 service.
- Open daily from 10:30am until 6pm (March to October) and 10:30am until 4pm (November to February). Closed Christmas and Boxing Day only.

Tel: 01932 868113
Tel (events): 01932 584286
Tel (bookings): 01932 584284
Email: info@painshill.co.uk
Web: www.painshill.co.uk

BOOKERS VINEYARD
Bolney, West Sussex

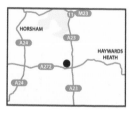

You no longer need to visit mainland Europe to experience the pleasure of visiting a small family estate making quality wines. Expect a personal touch and fine examples of red, white and sparkling English wines.

Background

The Bolney Wine Estate formed a part of the Butting Hill One Hundred and was how this land was registered in the Domesday book. Fast forward to 1972 and Bookers had its beginning as an wine entity but progressed from only 3 acres (1.2 ha) of vineyard to just 7 acres (2.8 ha) 20 years later. All was to change from the nineties and in the last decade in particular. In common with other up and coming English wine enterprises the growth which was needed to sustain a commercial viability has coincided with more than a decade of higher temperatures and improved wine growing conditions.

The Vineyard

The centrepiece of the estate is an impressive uniformly sloping 15.5 acre (6.3ha) south facing vineyard. Planting, started in 2000 was completed over 3 years and includes Chardonnay and Pinot Noir grapes for the sparkling wines. In addition to the estate plantings of 33 acres (13.4 ha) — not all of it yet in production — Sam and

Tanks of varying capacity enable Bookers to respond to the vagaries of the English growing season

her vineyard manager work closely with two contract growers. This includes restricting yields and improved canopy management in order to maximise fruit quality. For whites there are plantings of Pinot Gris, a little Müller-Thurgau and Schönburger while as well as the Pinot Noir there are significant plantings of Dornfelder and Rondo for reds, and even a few rows of Merlot. With the potential to add further complexity to the sparkling wines, some Pinot Meunier will also be added to the mix. For the future, the glasshouse built directly outside the winery's reception will provide a facility to propagate the best vines from the estate's own vineyards.

Wine production

Bookers recently built winery (2005) has the capacity for 150,000 bottle production per year. There is gleaming stainless steel aplenty of variable capacity — giving added flexibility to cope with different-sized harvests. 100,000 bottles are anticipated for 2012 and this is comparable to many small family estates be it in France, Italy or elsewhere in Europe.

VINEYARD FACTS

- Bolney wine estate comprises 23 acres (over 9 ha) with another 10 acres (4 ha) added in 2008.
- The premium vineyard site of 15.5 acres (6.3 ha) on greensand soils forms the centrepiece for quality.
- Grapes supplies are supplemented by that received from contract growers.
- The percentage of red varieties is unusually high for an English vineyard.

BIOGRAPHY — Sam Lintner

Sam Lintner is the linchpin of Bolney wine estate and the success of Bookers wines. The daughter of Janet and Rodney Pratt, Sam trained at Plumpton College in the mid-nineties and caught the winemaking bug. Her Mum and Dad had actually bought the estate in 1972 — starting with just 3 acres (1.2 ha) — with a view to retirement. For Rodney Pratt who had worked in the city of London doing a short course at Plumpton (see page 64) must have come as a breath of fresh air. But it was Sam who made it possible to dispense with contract winemaking as she then set about transforming the family estate from a hobbyist activity to one of southern England's most respected wineries.

Unusual is the amount of land dedicated to red wine production, now moving towards 50 per cent. The new winery includes three dedicated red wine fermenters. The reds subsequently go into barriques. For the Dornfelder and Rondo grapes which are combined in Dark Harvest this means a spell of 6-12 months in used oak. The grapes for the Pinot Noir red get a shorter spell in barrique. Other wines made by Bookers include the increasingly assured Blanc de Blanc sparkler which gets 30 months on the lees, an aromatic Pinot Gris, while the very small quantities of Merlot (Blackbird) are sold only at the winery.

The style of the wines is characterised by their grace and purity. They are not overmade or too ambitious, rather ample and attractive expressions of increasingly high quality fruit. It is not overstating the case to suggest that these are wines that other smaller or newer enterprises could do well to aspire to.

Visiting

The personal touch, hand in hand with spades of integrity and sincerity, not to mention some finely crafted wines to taste and buy, make this a must visit.

Barriques of both French and American oak, play a part in the ageing of Bookers reds

HOW TO FIND US

- Bolney Wine Estate, Foxhole Lane, Bolney, West Sussex RH17 5NB
- From London use the M25 and M23 continuing on the A23 until the A272. A short distance west of the Bolney flyover ignore the turning to Bolney village but take a right turn into Foxhole Lane, soon after passing the service station on the left.
- The nearest train station is Haywards Heath, 15 mins by taxi.
- Open: Telephone to arrange a tour or tasting.

Winery shop: Monday - Friday 9am-5pm
Tel: 01444 881894
Email: info@bookersvineyard.co.uk
Web: www.bookersvineyard.co.uk

The Wines

2007 Autumn Leaves

A straight Bacchus and another example of how well this variety does in England. The enticing green pepper and Sauvignon-like gooseberry fruit also has subtle hints of passionfruit that are not unusual with this grape. There's plenty of acidity but no danger either of it tiring prematurely.

2004 Bart's Bubbly Brut Rosé

Making a fine pink fizz isn't always taken seriously. Slightly off-dry this is soft and creamy with a fine crushed wild strawberry, brambly fruit complexity which suggests an English purity without any of the defects of weaker, underripe examples.

2005 Dark Harvest

A blend of Dornfelder and Rondo, this is the mainstay of Bookers' red wine production. Soft, juicy and round with plummy, berryish fruit there is not the structure or breadth of a red from more noble varieties but drink it for its delightful balance and purity.

2006 Pinot Noir

Aromatically this is not unlike a skin-contacted Gamay red suggestive of strawberry and raspberry fruit. Round and supple in the mouth, it avoids any harshness and is reminiscent of a good Bourgogne Hautes-Côtes or Yonne red with a cool red fruits intensity.

BREAKY BOTTOM
nr Lewes, East Sussex

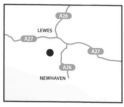

Not far from the sea, isolated and secluded in a fold of the South Downs is an enchanting vineyard and house. Here Peter Hall, one of the pillars of the modern English wine revival, produces handcrafted English sparkling wines.

A stubborn survivor from the first major wave of commercial planting in the late sixties and seventies, Peter Hall has sustained and evolved his small vineyard sometimes in parallel with the industry as a whole, at other times dealing with problems peculiar to his particular location. It took until 1994, when he purchased the farm, before he produced his first sparkling wine — now all of the production is geared towards it. Since then Peter and his wife, Chris, have made steady progress, despite major setbacks including floods. The last and worst episode in 2000 resulted in two and a half years of living in a caravan. He has added stainless steel tanks, a new wine press and most recently, an air-conditioned storage facility for ageing the wines.

The vineyard
The 6 acre (2.4 ha) vineyard, forming part of 30 acres (12 ha) of farm (some of which is leased), is sheltered from the worst of the weather but remains exposed to winds

VINEYARD FACTS
- Mostly Seyval Blanc and Chardonnay vines planted on chalk loam.
- Just 6 acres (2.4 ha) of vineyard but all are pruned by hand by Peter Hall.
- All grapes are hand-picked with help from grown-up family and friends.
- Despite the proximity to the sea, spring frost can be a problem.

funnelled through the downs from the south-west. The first vineyards were planted with Müller-Thurgau, Seyval Blanc and Reichensteiner in 1972 and provided the first crop in 1976. A decade later the balance was changed to become Seyval Blanc dominated, with some Müller-Thurgau. In 2001 some Chardonnay was added, with more in 2004. There is now even a little Pinot Noir and Pinot Meunier but just 8 rows of each.

The vineyards remain susceptible to flooding if planting on nearby fields is not carried out with due care and intelligence. A large population of small snails arrived with the 2000 flood and their predilection for young vines has made it difficult to establish new vines. There is also a healthy and diverse population of birds. Netting proved costly and brought problems of its own (ask Peter about the badgers and pheasants) and so has been discontinued.

Isolated and secluded in a fold the South Downs

BIOGRAPHY   Peter Hall

Peter Hall's immediate ancestry includes French, Irish and English forebears. Having grown up in a large aristocratic pile with a closeness to nature he opted for an agricultural vocation in 1972. He planted his vines before his friend and leading UK consultant, Stephen Skelton did the same at Tenterden. Peter is self-trained as a winemaker, working tirelessly and learning from experience to produce ever better grapes and wines. Resisting expansion and the pursuit of money, he has succeeded in creating a sustainable small vineyard, house and garden that come close to a kind of English Utopia. Peter also has close connections with some of the most respected personalities in both wine producing and wine writing circles.

Wine production

In a year that yields well like 2006 around 20,000 bottles are produced but here as elsewhere in England poor flowering, spring frosts or other problems can severely reduce the amount of healthy grapes that can be made into wine. With the focus now firmly on sparkling wine, still wines are now only likely to appear as one-off bottlings of Seyval Blanc. Alas the Müller-Thurgau is no more. Amazingly a bottling from 1996 still shows plenty of life when first opened as well as a fine bottle-aged complexity that is gently infused with subtle spices.

The small winery, housed in an old barn only lacks for disgorgement equipment so the last stage of making the 'fizz' needs to be completed at Ridgeview. The Breaky Bottom Brut is made each year, with each vintage dedicated to a close friend or relative. Vintages 03, 04 and 05 are entirely from Seyval Blanc but future vintages are likely to include the Champagne varieties. There is real style to these wines, reminiscent of the most elegant Blanc de Blancs examples of Champagne if missing the extra depth and more pronounced yeast autolysis the latter can sometimes show. Setting aside a small amount of sparkling wine, to this is added his own farm produced creme de cassis (also sold as bottled on its own). The Kir Royal tastes a good deal better than many sparkling rosés.

What of the future for Peter Hall and Breaky Bottom? Is there any danger he'll be lost in the new reality of the big professional operations that look set to dominate the industry? No, the obstinacy and character of this man, his ethos, and the quality and individuality of his wines should ensure we are still talking about him in another 20 years.

Visiting

Down the years Breaky Bottom has hosted private music and opera events as well as serving as a unique winery location for topical television on all manner of things wine and food related. In order to make a visit it is necessary to telephone and fix an appointment. The wines, however, may be ordered direct from the winery via the internet or by phone.

The Wines

Breaky Bottom Brut

Both wines are Traditional Method and 100 per cent Seyval Blanc

2003 Cuvée Alex Mercier

Refined hedgerow and elderflower aromas including a slightly wild herb aspect. Fully ripe with a certain elegance and a full, quite luxuriant mouthfeel with delicate pear-like fruit. Not the depth or yeast autolysis of the best Champagne but much, much finer than more everyday examples.

2005 Cuvée Brian Jordan

With a very fine bead, this has greater finesse and elegance than the 03 but is slightly austere with better structure and more of an English purity. The health and balance of this vintage shine through. Delicious, intense and long on the finish. A fine English sparkling wine.

HOW TO FIND US

- Breaky Bottom, Rodmell, Lewes, East Sussex BN7 3EX
- Turn off the A27, just west and south of Lewes, for Kingston, continuing past the village before turning right (signposted Newhaven). Past Iford but before reaching Rodmell look for a turning to the right, into Northease Farm. Follow the farm track up on to the Downs then fork left with sign marked Breaky Bottom before descending to the vineyard.

Tel: 01273 476427
Email: breakybottom@btinternet.com
Web: www.breakybottom.co.uk

CARR TAYLOR
Westfield, East Sussex

One of the more recognisable names in English wine production is but a short hop from Hastings and the seaside. There is ample opportunity for vineyard tours as well as buying wines, fruit wines and other products from the winery shop.

VINEYARD FACTS

- 36 acres (14.5 ha) of vineyard on soils are that are mostly Wealden Clay over a sandstone/ ironstone subsoil.
- Reichensteiner, Schönburger, Kerner, Huxelrebe, Bacchus, Ortega, Wurzer and Chardonnay grapes for whites.
- Black grapes are Dornfelder, Pinot Noir, Pinot Meunier and Seibel.

David Carr Taylor is one of those who contributed to the major expansion in English wine production that occurred in the late sixties and early seventies, having started planting in 1971. He has experienced many ups and downs in the more than 30 years since production began. Following the first commercial crop in 1976, a winery was established on the property in 1982. By the mid-eighties some of the first sparkling wines made in the UK were being produced including the first commercially available sparkling rosé.

Wine Production

Most of the vines are trellised on a wide spaced Geneva Double Curtain system which encourages higher yields. Since 1995 the wines have been made by Taylor's son, Alexander who learnt the ropes from his father as well as gaining experience abroad. Some 50,000 bottles are produced each year, around 20,000 of which are sparkling. Unusually the still wines are bottled without an indication of the vintage, making it difficult to be certain of the wines' freshness. Still wines include Alexis, Vessel IV, 1066 Hastings and Rosé. Sparkling wines are made by the Traditional Method and include a vintage dated medium-dry style as well as non-vintaged dry and rosé versions. Mead and fruit wines are also made.

Visiting

Open for almost the entire year, a visit that includes a tour of the vineyards and a wine tasting, is actively promoted here. In addition to a small café there is a retail shop where the wines are sold along with the fruit wines and other local produce. Booking in advance is required for groups or clubs.

The Sparking rosé, Alexis and Vessel V

HOW TO FIND US

- Carr Taylor Wines, Wheel Lane, Westfield, Hastings, East Sussex TN35 4SG.
- Leave the A21 just north of Hastings, joining the A28 as far as Westfield village. Turn left here at Old Courthouse pub and continue for less than a mile.
- Open: 10-5pm every day except 25th Dec to 1st Jan

Tel: 01424 752501

Fax: 01424 751716

Email: sales@carr-taylor.co.uk

Web: www.carr-taylor.co.uk

DAVENPORT
Rotherfield, East Sussex

Will Davenport has not one but two wine estates. Grapes from both Horsmonden in Kent and Limney Farm near Rotherfield in East Sussex are treated to the same exacting organic standards.

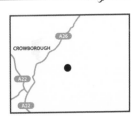

Owner and winemaker Will Davenport is a graduate of South Australia's Roseworthy College, where many leading New World winemakers have studied. He planted his first 5 acres (2ha) of vineyards on the family farm at Horsmonden in Kent in 1991. The vineyard has subsequently been expanded and the original varieties which included Ortega, Faber, Bacchus, Huxelrebe and Siegerrebe have been added to, including some Pinot Noir. In 1993 Will also put in a vineyard on Limney Farm in East Sussex and here the farm's dairy buildings were converted into a winery. Pinot Noir and Auxerrois are planted at Limney, with Double Guyot trellising.

Wine production
The modern facilities help underpin the organic approach to making English wines, helping eliminate the more rustic elements sometimes associated with a more natural approach to winemaking. Natural yeasts are used as is a minimum

Will Davenport in the vineyard

Davenport wines that have been regularly produced include a varietal Bacchus.

Visiting
If you can manage it a visit to Limney Farm will provide real insights to organic wine production in the UK. The wines can be bought via the website.

VINEYARD FACTS
- Organic viticulture, certified since 2000.
- No fungicides, insecticides or weed killers, and no chemical fertilizers are used.
- Use of winter cover crops and green manures are part of the natural approach to grape growing.
- 14.4 acres (5.82 ha) at Horsmonden and 4.13 acres (1.67 ha) at Limney Farm.

amount of sulphur while in the 2007 vintage the wines were bottled completely unfiltered for the first time. This included a Pinot Noir (Diamond Fields) that is a blend of the 06 and 07 vintages, and was last made in 2001. Horsmonden Dry is a long-standing, flagship white from a selection of the best of the Kent vineyard fruit. The Limney Estate sparkling wine comes from the farm's Pinot Noir and Auxerrois grapes and gets more than two years on the lees. The 2005 vintage is an almost equal blend of the two varieties. Other

HOW TO FIND US
- Limney Farm, Castle Hill, Rotherfield, East Sussex TN6 3RR
- The best approach is to make for Crowborough on the A26 but visits are by appointment only so phone ahead for detailed directions.

Tel: 01892 852380
Fax: 01892 852781
Email:
info@davenportvineyards.co.uk
Web:
www.davenportvineyards.co.uk

HENNERS
Herstmonceux, East Sussex

Henners is one of the new breed of English wine producers looking for a quintessentially English expression of Champagne-like quality. Here the stated objective of producing an exclusive sparkling wine of the highest quality looks to be well-grounded.

The future of English sparkling wine is currently being led by just three important wineries in the south-east of the country. However there is a veritable flotilla of smaller craft both ready and well-prepared for the journey ahead. Larry Warr had a career as a race engineer for Grand Prix Formula One teams Stewart and Jaguar before setting up an engineering consultancy involved with high performance engine design. An interest in farming, as well as in turning out a high quality product, were to culminate in planting a vineyard with a view to making world class fizz. Larry's 5 acres (2 ha) of vines (8500 plants) are south-facing with a commanding view of the Pevensey levels towards Pevensey Bay. Study at nearby Plumpton College (see page 64) combined with research into winemaking and viticulture underpin his plans.

Wine production
You won't be able to buy these wines before late 2011 at the earliest. Larry will supplement his own training with expert consultancy advice from the Institut Oenologique de Champagne. The race track attributes of excellence and competitiveness can't be bad for the future of English sparkling wine either. Added to this is the desire to use a significant percentage of reserve wines to add maturity and complexity. There are plans for expansion, nevertheless initial production will be small.

Visiting
Henners is close to the majestic moated Herstmonceux castle and gardens as well as the Observatory Science centre. There are plans for sales and tastings at the vineyard after the first wines have been released.

VINEYARD FACTS

- Vineyard planted after two years search for the best combination of soil, aspect, altitude and mesoclimate.
- South-facing slopes on greensand soils over a sandstone substratum.
- Planted in 2007 exclusively to the three classic Champagne varieties.
- The vines are trained Single Guyot with cane pruning.

HOW TO FIND US

- Church Road, Herstmonceux, East Sussex BN27 1QJ
- Herstmonceux is on the A271, less than 5 miles from the A22 and north and east of Hailsham.
- Not yet open.

Tel: 01580 211134
Email: (from website)
Web:
www.hennersvineyard.co.uk

NUTBOURNE
nr Pulborough, West Sussex

Off the quiet leafy lanes north-east of Pulborough are lakes and vineyards perfect for a stroll. There's also the opportunity to taste the wines made from these vines and take a bottle or two home with you.

Nutbourne Vineyards were first established in 1980 and have now grown to 18 acres (7.3 ha). Bridget and Peter Gladwin have been the owners for more than 10 years. They are near neighbours to the mighty Nyetimber (see page 60) but offer instead mostly the kind of dry whites that are more typical of English wine production over the past two or three decades. Soils are the typical greensand found in the area, the younger chalk deposits having been eroded away.

Wine production

Nutbourne output ranges from 25,000 bottles to more than 50,000 bottles. Sussex Reserve is a dry aromatic style. Both Bacchus and Schönburger are also made varietally, the latter being labelled as Late Harvest Dry. Sussex Oak is another blend but as the name suggests the wine also spends a little time in oak for a slightly broader, softer style. There are also some Pinot Noir and Chardonnay vines.

VINEYARD FACTS

- 18 acres (7.3 ha) of vineyard on greensand soils.
- Mostly planted to Germanic varieties Bacchus, Huxelrebe, Müller-Thurgau, Schönburger and Reichensteiner, for dry white wines
- Also a little Pinot Noir and Chardonnay which go into the Traditional Method sparkling wine called Nutty.

These grapes are added to Reichensteiner for their own 'fizz', Nutty. This is a Traditional Method sparkling wine made with similar competence to that seen in the dry whites. A rosé is also made. All benefit from the winemaking expertise and facilities provided by Chapel Down.

Visiting

Set around Nutbourne Manor are lakes and vineyards in which you're free to wander. At the Windmill shop you can taste and buy the wines.

The restored mill rises behind a newly planted vineyard

HOW TO FIND US

- Gay Street, nr Pulborough, West Sussex RH20 2HE
- Leave the A29 (Stane Street) part way between Pulborough and Billingshurst following signs for the vineyard.
- Open: The vineyard is open May to October. Mon-Fri: 2-5pm Weekends and Bank Holidays: 11-5pm

Tel: 01798 815196
Email: sales@nutbourne vineyards.com
Web: www.nutbourne vineyards.com

NYETIMBER
West Chiltington, West Sussex

Nyetimber broke new ground as the UK's first dedicated sparkling wine operation modelled on Champagne. It is now being transformed from small quality flagbearer into a high quality international brand.

STORRINGTON

There is mention in the Domesday book of 1086 of a Nyetimber manor. From the 12th century it belonged to the Cluniac Priory of Lewes but following the dissolution of the monasteries by Henry VIII it passed briefly to Thomas Cromwell then to Anne of Cleves. A long period of ownership by the Goring family followed before the property was bought in 1919 by John Junius Morgan, nephew of JP Morgan of the American banking dynasty, who devoted much to its care and restoration.

Upon visiting the estate this history doesn't seem to hard to conjure up but the modern era of wine production only began when Stuart and Sandra Moss bought

VINEYARD FACTS

- There are now 260 acres (105 ha) of vines planted, all of it producing grapes by the 2009 vintage.
- The overall composition is half Chardonnay with the balance from Pinot Noir (40 per cent) and Pinot Meunier (10 per cent).
- Vineyards are all in the local area, most on greensand soils like the original vineyards but a small percentage are on chalk.
- 250 pickers will be required at harvest when the vineyards are fully productive.

Nyetimber's original closely spaced vineyards slope gently south towards the South Downs.

BIOGRAPHY Eric Heerema
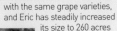

In 2005 Nyetimber's owner and CEO, Dutchman Eric Heerema (47) originally planted up some 15 acres (6 ha) of Sussex downland around his farm with the three Champagne grape varieties. His long-term ambition was to expand the vineyard and build up a world-class sparkling wine business. When he acquired Nyetimber in March 2006, a dream came true with an established vineyard planted with the same grape varieties, and Eric has steadily increased its size to 260 acres (105 ha). "It gives me much pleasure and satisfaction to work with my dedicated team to build the future of Nyetimber. We all share a passion to produce sparkling wine that competes at the highest international level." Eric started his career as a lawyer, followed by asset management activities including venture capital.

The Wines

Nyetimber Classic Cuvée Brut

Vintages produced to date: 1993, 1995, 1996, 1997, 1998, 1999, 2000, 2001

2001

Just over 40 per cent Chardonnay, the balance equal amounts of both Pinots. Fuller, rounder and more savoury than the Blanc de Blancs from the same vintage. Although there is plenty of acidity and a certain firmness it will require less patience. Real persistence and intensity if less singular than the Blanc de Blancs.

1993

70 per cent Chardonnay, the balance from the two Pinots. This has not been recently tasted but after 6 years' age revealed classic bisuity yeasty aromas and good depth and breadth of flavour on the palate. It is possible this wine peaked early but it offered plenty of pleasure as well as showing the potential for both Pinots in the local soils.

Nyetimber manor in 1986. They planted 37 acres (15 ha) to the three Champagne varieties and put the wine writing press in a spin with most hacks writing off their chances of success. But the couple from Chicago had serious intent and although they initially needed to make the wines in Kent, they did so with the help of expert Champagne consultancy. Then they waited to get things right, releasing their first wine, the 1992 Première Cuvée, a Blanc de Blancs style, to great acclaim in 1997. Even now with nearly 16 years age it is rich, creamy and complex (see below). A succession of excellent, much lauded and awarded wines ensued. The Mosses sold up in 2001 to songwriter Andy Hill but the focus on quality was maintained. Continued outside consultancy, together with winemaking from Peter Morgan (now at Plumpton College), then Dermot Sugrue (now at Wiston Estate) underpin current or yet to be released vintages made since the turn of the new millennium.

The subsequent sale of Nyetimber in March of 2006 has brought rapid recent change and a radical new agenda. The new owner, Eric Heerema (see above) also has 'serious intent' and had planted a vineyard the previous year on land near Petworth, but a short drive to the west. Nyetimber presented an ideal opportunity around which to build a much greater enterprise. Seemingly almost overnight, row upon row of new vines went in and the sweep of Nyetimber's vineyard had soon swallowed up 260 acres (105 ha) of West Sussex countryside. As the dust begins to settle the audacity and boldness of this vision take some comprehending. Previously the amount of wine made in a productive year such as 2004 had been as high as 100,000 bottles. In a year or

two, under similar conditions it could surpass 700,000 bottles with profound implications for production, storing and selling of the finished product. The risks are significant but so is the sense of belief by those who dedicated themselves to this new journey. Vineyard management has been entrusted to Paul Woodrow-Hill while the winemaking team is led by the energy and vitality of Cherie Spriggs (see below) and also includes her husband, Brad Greatrix who is likewise, a fully qualified enologist. For the considerable marketing and distribution expertise that the new order demands, Stephen Clark brings 22 years' experience from Champagne Laurent Perrier. It is his intention to see Nyetimber listed in top restaurants everywhere.

The vineyard

The Mosses planted at atypically high densities for the relatively fertile greensand soils with just 1.5m between the rows. The spacing in the new vineyards has been increased and the canopies are opened up, not only to ensure the health and quality of the fruit but also in part to improve the fruit set for the following year. As well as reducing

The 5 bay timbered barn with its crown post roof was built in the late 15th century

the vigour of the vines, to bring the vineyard into balance, the vines are cane pruned and each one is treated individually. All the grapes are both pruned and picked by hand, the selection of grapes being made in the vineyard and not on sugar levels alone. Each vineyard lot is vinified separately, not just one vineyard from another but also parcels within each site. For example, 10 different parcels have been identified from the 'home' Nyetimber vineyards alone. New plantings include the 90 acre (36.5 ha) Netherland vineyard at Tillington. Nearly all the plantings are on the same greensand (Lower Greensand formation) that exists where

the younger chalk deposits have been eroded away. An exception is another vineyard site named after the Roman villa remains near Bignor. Here the vines, being further south, extend on to downland chalk.

Wine production

Nyetimber's existing facilities have been more than adequate until now, with temperature controlled stainless tanks, cold stabilisation and disgorging equipment, and gyro-palettes for the riddling process, only making use of a mobile bottling line from Champagne to finish the process. The recent new plantings will deliver a huge increase in the volume of fruit (especially from 2009) and a substantial new winery is likely to be split across two sites but with a single press centre. A processing capacity for one million bottle production has been reckoned on.

The Nyetimber reputation has been built around the quality of just two wines. The Classic Cuvée is a blend of Chardonnay, with smaller percentages of both Pinot Noir and Pinot Meunier. The Première Cuvée Blanc de Blancs is

Specially equipped machinery is needed to trim the growing vines

BIOGRAPHY Cherie Spriggs

Cherie and Nyetimber's CEO, Eric Heerema share a passion for sparkling wine and a commitment to quality which brought Cherie to Nyetimber in early 2007. After completing a biochemistry degree in her native Canada, Cherie earned a Master's degree at the Wine Research Centre in Vancouver, then a Graduate Diploma in Oenology at the University of Adelaide in Australia. Following her studies, Cherie completed several vintages with top producers from around the globe. Having worked with Nyetimber's existing world-class vineyards, she is looking forward to realising the potential of the new vineyard sites, and building on Nyetimber's formidable reputation.

Nyetimber Manor dates back to the 12th century.

entirely from Chardonnay. Both wines typically spend a minimum of five years on the lees. One of the major shifts in style since the 2000 vintage has been the move to stop the malolactic fermentation taking place. Under Cherie Spriggs a more flexible response is being employed, based on both the vintage conditions and differences between individual batches of fruit. Cherie speaks of the advantage of having greater freedom than in Champagne, such as when to make the cut-off when pressing the grapes. In the 2007 vintage, in addition to the two existing cuvées, she was able to produce Nyetimber's first rosé sparkling wine.

Visting

You currently need an appointment to visit Nyetimber which is working on a special reception facility for guests. Perhaps in the longer term a visitor centre may become a reality. If you just want to buy the fizz and have been frustrated by its relative scarcity over the past few years then clearly all the planting activity provides some hope — at least in 5-6 years or more, once wines from the new vineyards have been made and released.

The Wines

Nyetimber Première Cuvée Blanc de Blancs

Vintages produced to date: 1992, 1995, 1996, 1999, 2000, 2001

2001:
There is a style shift here from early vintages with a more marked austerity apparent when tasted soon after its initial release in 2008. However older vines seem to have added greater depth and there is no loss of purity or intensity. One to cellar if you've got time — 10 years more will do it no harm.

1992: (tasted 14/9/99 and 17/6/08)

The wine that caused a big sensation. Here was a wine that had excellent concentration, balance and complexity and with more than a nod towards quality Champagne with a classic yeast autolysis and elegance of fruit. Retasting this wine after a gap of almost 9 years, what is striking is the richness of fruit on a very full and creamy palate yet it remains vibrant and balanced.

HOW TO FIND US

- Gay Street, West Chiltington, West Sussex RH20 2HH
- Leave the A29 (Stane Street) part way between Pulborough and Billingshurst following signs for Nutbourne Vineyard.

Visits by appointment only.
Tel: 01798 813989
Fax: 01798 815511
Email: info@nyetimber.com
Web: www.nyetimber.com

PLUMPTON ESTATE
Plumpton, East Sussex

Plumpton College plays a key role in turning out competent winemakers who are helping forge the future of the English wine industry. Students gain practical experience on its own wine estate producing white, red and sparkling wines.

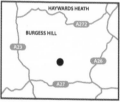

Plumpton College was established as an agricultural college in 1926 and is part of the University of Brighton. Over the past 20 years it has added the role of providing English language winemaking courses in Europe. Courses, usually taken by mature students, run from tasting days through viticultural courses to foundation degrees or a BSc in Viticulture and Oenology. The head of the wine department is Chris Foss, one of the leading lights on the English wine scene. Many of the UK's best winemakers owe at least part of their winemaking education to Plumpton. Established winemakers like Sam Lintner (Bookers) and Mike Roberts (Ridgeview) have benefited while a newer crop of graduates such as Nick Hall (Herbert Hall), Larry Warr (Henners) or Simon Woodhead (Stopham) will also play a part in the future direction of the English wine industry. Students also come from overseas, some taking advantage of the opportunity to improve their English while learning about making wine, resulting in a spreading network of Plumpton graduates.

Harvesting at Plumpton Estate

The vineyard
Plumpton Estate runs to 15 acres (6ha) across three vineyard sites that include the college itself, Ditchling and Rock Lodge,

VINEYARD FACTS

- Three separate sites make up the estate's 15 acres (6 ha) of vineyards.
- There has been some trialling of different trellising systems.
- A wide range of varieties and rootstocks has been studied as befits a college vineyard.
- In the vineyard, as in the winery, students gain first-hand experience in producing wines under local conditions.

near Haywards Heath. Some 60,000 vines are planted on soils that are most clay-chalk and well-suited to making 'fizz' but also includes some sandy loam. The vines are mostly cane pruned to Single Guyot with Vertical Shoot Positioning but with some spur pruned on Geneva Double Curtain and Sylvoz trellising. Viticulture is overseen by Kevin Sutherland and there is on going expansion of the vineyard area, lately at Rock Lodge.

Müller-Thürgau vines in the Ditchling vineyard

BIOGRAPHY Chris Foss

Half-French, Chris Foss was trained in Bordeaux where he also gained his early experience in winemaking. He was hired by Plumpton in 1988 when the college took the bold step of setting up a wine department. His plans for Plumpton, many would argue already largely realised, include making it an international centre for training in cool climate winemaking 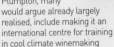 and business across a range of courses. Chris wants to expand the research and development facilities both in terms of production and on the business side of things. He has also gone a long way towards establishing the college as a nerve centre for the industry, providing consultancy and analysis as well as propagating the dissemination of wine knowledge, skills and experience.

Plumpton's Ditchling vineyard, one of three that make up the estate

Wine production

The continued progress of Plumpton's wine department is visually demonstrable in the new Wine Science Centre winery opened in 2007 which includes a lecture theatre, labs and dedicated wine tasting facilities. In the winery the wines are made by the students under the supervision of Peter Morgan who did a short stint at Nyetimber (see page 60). While the winery is run commercially, the need to provide a comprehensive winemaking grounding means many different styles of maturation are encompassed. So while this precludes a more singular focus seen elsewhere, it does ensure that a range of white, red, rosé and sparkling wines, on offer for the wine buying public. Most successful of the wines are a pair of Traditional Method sparkling wines called The Dean (one is in a Blush style). Also made is Cloudy Ridge a blend that includes some of the better varieties used for dry English wines including Bacchus and Schönburger. Small quantities of varietals such as Ortega have also been made. Of two reds, a more ambitious Sutherland's Block Pinot Noir (aged in a combination of used French and American oak) shows potential but wants for more richness and ripeness.

Visiting

There is no cellar door facility but the wines can be bought from the college (see below for details). Tastings are held at the winery, and since September 2008, at the new Wine Science Centre facility.

The Wines

The Dean Brut Non-Vintage

 A blend of 90 per cent Pinot Noir with 10 per cent Chardonnay. It is very fresh, clean and appley with pristine herbal and white flower aromas. This is a good quality, unmistakably English, sparkler with highish acidity.

The Dean Blush Non-Vintage

 This is exactly the same blend as the regular Brut but boasts a pale salmon colour and a slightly more biscuity aroma. Attractive citrus and apple fruit is braced by a firm acidity. From that available in 2008, there is slightly better balance than in the Brut version.

HOW TO FIND US

- Ditchling Road, nr Lewes, East Sussex BN7 3AE
- Leaving the A23 north of Brighton, take the A273 for Burgess Hill, turning at Clayton (B2112) towards Ditchling then continuing on the Lewes Road (B2116) to Plumpton.
- From Lewes head north on the A275 as far as the B2116 which continues west directly to Plumpton.
- Visits can be made by appointment only but the wines can be bought from the college itself between 9-5pm Monday to Friday.

Tel: 01273 890454 (Paul Harley)
Fax: 01273 890071
Email: paul.harley@plumpton.ac.uk
Web: www.plumpton.ac.uk

RIDGEVIEW
Ditchling Common, East Sussex

England's best sparkling wines? — well damn near.
Ridgeview has produced consistently fine quality since
the first vintage in 1996 and it's not resting on its laurels
either with excellent new vineyards coming on stream
and an expanded ageing facility.

First a word about family because it is both
very important here and expanding! Mike
Roberts and his wife Chris have a son and
daughter who are both involved. Son Simon
works with his dad on the winemaking side
of things while daughter Tamara, trained in
accountancy and law, now runs the business
side of operations. Simon's wife, Mardi
directs sales and marketing. A third
generation have recently made their
presence felt. How involved are these little
ones? Well, give it a few years yet but expect
Ridgeview to be a household name by then.

The vineyard
Hills to the south provide some protection
from the worst sea-borne weather and
reduce rainfall locally. The estate itself, on a
limestone ridge over sandstone and clay,
now extends to some 23 acres (9.3 ha) with
new plantings added in 2005 to the south of

VINEYARD FACTS

- Plantings are split fairly evenly between
  Chardonnay, Pinot Noir and Pinot Meunier.
  The amount of Pinot Meunier is exceptional
  by English standards.
- As well as making full use of these three
  varieties, a selection of clones have been
  utilised to maximise complexity.
- All grapes are hand-harvested.
- Trellising at 2m reduces the risk of spring
  frost.

the existing ones. There is an almost equal
split between the three main Champagne
varieties, Chardonnay, Pinot Noir and Pinot
Meunier. The vines are trellised at 2m high,
in part to reduce the risk of spring frost
damage. All the grapes are hand harvested
by a team of pickers based each year around
a core of experienced, seasoned hands. On the
environmental front, the estate is not organic
but operates an integrated vineyard management which includes the recycling of sprays
and old wood is mulched and re-used.

Ridgeview also manage or receive grapes
from a further 70-80 acres (28-32 ha) of
vineyards including an important new site
near Petworth in the vicinity of Nyetimber
on similar greensand sandstone soils.
Some of the grapes are supplied on a 'swap'
arrangement whereby a certain agreed
percentage of the production is returned as
bottled wine to the grape grower. The
balance is channelled into the Ridgeview

Sediment collection prior to 'dégorgement'

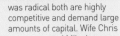

The old wine industry adage about needing a fortune in order to lose it in the wine business has some relevance here, at least the first part of it. For Mike Roberts that money came from the successful MICHAEL Business Systems Plc, a computer company which he ran between 1983 and 1993. While the change in lifestyle was radical both are highly competitive and demand large amounts of capital. Wife Chris and Mike began planting the estate in 1994 and Mike got his start in viticulture and winemaking at Plumpton College. Son Simon has also trained at Plumpton and now shares winemaking responsibilities with his Dad.

cuvées. So when visiting some small growers, especially in the south don't be surprised to be told that 'Mike Roberts makes my sparkling wine'.

Wine production
The Roberts follow the directives for winemaking issued by the Champagne body, the CIVC and take consultant advice from the Champagne Institute and others but enjoy more flexibility than their French counterparts. Thanks to a combination of vineyard site, management and undoubtedly, a decade of warmer years, there is rarely any need to chaptalise. The grapes are whole bunch pressed using a sophisticated, modern Coquard press, and inoculated with Champagne yeasts. The wines are also subject to 100 per cent malolactic conversion and given an inital 8 months on yeast lees in cuve. All of the wines have a total of more than two years development prior to release.

Most people's first instinct when presented with more than one Ridgeview wine is 'Hold on, why all the names, couldn't this be simpler?'. Well no, not really, if you're trying to also market a brand as well as a range of different cuvées. The idea is that

An acknowledgement to Merret

Merret (see box on Christopher Merret) could be England's answer to Champagne or Cava.

Bloomsbury, Ridgeview's signature wine accounts for 60-70 per cent of Ridgeview's production so the wine mostly likely to be encountered but there are several more. As well as Cavendish and the fine rosé, Fritzrovia (also profiled on these pages) there other posh London names to seek out. Belgravia is Chardonnay dominated with the balance almost entirely Pinot Noir. Grosvenor is a Blanc de Blancs style, the 2001 vintage shows what the Roberts can do with Chardonnay grapes alone. Knightsbridge on the other hand, is made only from the black grapes, a Blanc de Noirs style. The 1999 vintage, tasted in 2003 showed less yeast autolysis character than Bloomsbury from the same vintage but was fresh,

The Wines

2005 Bloomsbury Brut

This is a blend of Chardonnay, Pinot Noir and Pinot Meunier (60/25/15). Benefiting from the fine 2005 vintage this is characterised by a fine balance between acidity and a ripe citrusy fruit character. There is already good complexity and some depth as well as a gentle creaminess that promises to build with more age.

2005 Cavendish Brut

A blend of approximately one third of each of the three principal Champagne varieties. With over 60 per cent of the blend from the two Pinots this reveals a fuller, more savoury and red berry interpretation of Ridgeview's fruit. Round and quite full, there is both intensity and good balance as well as a touch of minerality and English hedgerow character. The one to drink first of this trio.

2005 Fritzrovia Brut Rosé

Like Bloomsbury this is Chardonnay dominated but includes more Pinot Meunier (28 per cent) at the expense of Pinot Noir (14 per cent). A classic pale salmon rosé colour. Cool, strawberry, cherry and other red berry hints merge with a lightly herbal character. Has both drive and acidity with a structure that suggests good ageing potential. A really proper rosé style, again the mineral, hedgerow hints adding a touch of class. It perhaps just edges both Cavendish and Bloomsbury for quality in 2005. Deserves more age.

with more of a Pinot savouriness and unexpected refinement. This is still likely to be drinking well if you can find some. More esoteric but also of interest are a sparkling red from Pinot Meunier (made in 2003) and an experimental 100 per cent oak-aged cuvée. Such is the competence of Mike and his family that anything on offer has to be worth a try.

Ridgeview also produce South Ridge for Laithwaites /Sunday Times Wine club in both Brut and Rosé versions. Another Mike Roberts wine, although unlikely to be encountered, is the highly commended Theale Vineyard Founders Reserve. Remarkably this is produced from just 800 Chardonnay vines grown on the edge of an industrial estate near Theale. Although not made in commercial quantities it is yet another indication of the potential for 'fizz' in southern England.

Nyetimber and Chapel Down are not the only two highly competent outfits that are expanding rapidly. Ridgeview's current 80,000 bottle production is set to rise to 300,000 bottles from

---

BIOGRAPHY | Christopher Merret

Who exactly was Christopher Merret (or Merrett) and why do Ridgeview name their sparkling wines after him? Only the inventor of bottle-fermented method of producing fizz that is now responsible for the finest sparkling wines the world over. He presented his work in a paper to the Royal Society as early as 1662. Of course it has been subsequently refined and improved by the Champenoise as the méthode champenoise, now known as the Traditional Method (see glossary) outside La Champagne, but the point is that they (the French) weren't the first, as you may have previously been led to believe. However the French might reasonably argue that Dom Pérignon's work established the basis for world's greatest sparkling wine and a hugely successful industry. It's true England has at least a couple of hundred years to make up but thanks to Ridgeview and others don't expect it to take that long.

---

the 2010 vintage. However, this is still a very modest output compared to Champagne standards. Perhaps as a sign of things to come Ridgeview now have a reseller in Paris. As yet it may offer little resistance to the inward deluge of Champagne, nonetheless it does raise a marker to the swelling stream of progress being made with English sparkling wine.

So let's drink to that.

Visiting

This is a must visit for sparkling wine lovers and is easily reached within a couple of hours from central London, or possibly sooner if taking the train to Haywards Heath or Burgess Hill. If you're making a day of it, visits to Bookers and Plumpton Estate are but a short distance away. The wines can be bought online but are also increasingly widely available in retail outlets.

HOW TO FIND US

- Ridgeview Wine Estate, Fragbarrow Lane, Ditchling Common, East Sussex BN6 8TP
- The best approach is to come from Haywards Heath (from London: M25, M23, A23, A272) on the B2112 before a right turn where it is clearly signposted. However it is also possible to drive north up the B2112 via Ditchling.
- Open: Monday to Saturday: 11am-4pm

Tel: 0845 345 7292
Fax: 01444 230757
Email: info@ridgeview.co.uk
Web:
www.ridgeviewestate.co.uk

SEDLESCOMBE
Sedlescombe, East Sussex

England's first organic vineyard continues to flourish. From a dream of self-sufficiency, commercial wine production along with fruit juices, ciders and fruit wines has proved a more than viable proposition.

Part of Sedlescombe's diverse range of wines

In 1974 Roy Cook found himself with 10 acres (4 ha) of land which he chose to farm organically in an attempt to be self-sufficient. With the realisation that he had south-facing slopes suited for wine production and an awareness of the revival of English wine-making taking place in southern England, the first 2000 vines were planted on just 1.5 acres (0.6 ha) in 1979. The acquisition of other vineyards, including Bodiam Castle and another at Spilstead, converted to organic viticulture, has bought the total holdings to 23 acres (9.3 ha).

VINEYARD FACTS

- All 23 acres (9.3 ha) are now converted to organic viticulture.
- All the grapes are hand-picked and berry selected.
- Spring flowering 'green manure' plants are grown between the vines.
- Winemaking is non-interventionist in order to produce as natural wines as possible.

Wine production

All the wines are certified organic and are given simple, clear and unpretentious labels. Dry White is a blend of the white grapes with the emphasis on a fresh, aromatic fruit character. Bodiam Harvest is a medium- dry style — from Seyval Blanc and Reichensteiner in 2006. An oaked white style is also made. Sedlescombe's red makes use of the hybrid Regent for a bold, brambly red with lots of colour and fruit. Aged in oak for 5 months, it included Pinot Noir in 2005 but was made varietally in 2006. For sparkling there's both a Seyval Blanc based wine, Cuvée Bodiam Brut and a rosé that also includes Seyval but is based on Regent. Both are bottle-fermented Traditional Method styles. Roy Cook has also made wines for Hidden Spring (a Pinot Noir and a dry white in 2007), a small vineyard with a campsite, near Horam.

Visiting

Sedlescombe offer a self-guided vineyard and woodland nature trail as well as the opportunity to taste the organic wines. The shop also includes fruit wines, ciders and other local produce. The vineyard is very close to historic Battle as well as Hastings and Bexhill on the south coast.

HOW TO FIND US

- Cripps Corner, Robertsbridge, East Sussex TN32 5SA
- Sedlescombe Organic Vineyard is on the B2244, just 1.5 miles north of Sedlescombe Village. Coming south on the A21, exit at Vinehall Street taking the B2089 before turning right for Sedlescombe.
- Open every day from Easter until Christmas from 10-6pm and weekends (only) in the winter months from noon until dusk.

Tel: 0800 9802884
Fax: 01580 830122
Email: enquiries@english organicwine.co.uk
Web: www.english organicwine.co.uk

STORRINGTON PRIORY
Storrington, West Sussex

In the village of Storrington is something out of the ordinary: a vineyard run by a canonical order that is intent on making fine English sparkling wine. What's more, if you feel like volunteering for some vineyard work then read on.

VINEYARD FACTS

- 4000 vines planted on a mix of clay and sandy soils with grass between the rows.
- Mostly Chardonnay and Pinot Noir grapes with a tiny amount of Pinot Meunier.
- Vines are trained to Vertical Shoot Positioning on a Single Guyot system.
- Rows run east-west on an elevated south-facing site.

Storrington Priory may not be the only Catholic order to own and run a winery in Europe — Austrian Benedictines have invested heavily in Slovenia's excellent Dveri Pax winery for instance — however it is unusual and rather special. The monastery celebrated 125 years at Storrington in 2007 but the Norbertine order dates back to 1121. Father Paul oversees the running of the vineyard and is supported by a small team of dedicated helpers (take a look at the pictures on their website) and well as people from the local community.

Wine production

The vineyards planted in 2006 are close by the monastery itself and almost entirely Chardonnay and Pinot Noir vines,

Storrington Priory

approximately 55 to 45 per cent. Running east-west with a commanding view to the South Downs, they total 2.5 acres (just one hectare) of vines on soils that are mix of clay and sand. Ernst Weiss who provided the laser-guided planting is responsible for a great many of the new vineyards appearing in the English countryside. 2008 is the very first harvest from Storrington Priory and one of the first wines to be produced from the new sparkling wine facility at Wiston Estate (see page 72) by Dermot Sugrue. Around 5000 to 6000 bottles per year are envisaged with limited scope for expansion. One of the benefits for local residents, besides the opportunity to get involved in helping produce what promises to be a high quality English sparkling wine, is that land given over to vines keeps their village green. In a time when large gardens and green spaces are disappearing under new housing or other developments it would seem one more reason to toast the local priory.

Looking across the South Downs

Visiting

If you want to visit then get in touch with Father Paul but it's quite likely you'll be roped into some hard labour — although expect a cup of tea when you've finished!

HOW TO FIND US

- Our Lady of England Priory, School Lane, Storrington, West Sussex RH20 4LN
- Leave the A24 at Washington, taking the A283 to Storrington. Once in the village, the vineyard and priory are easy to find.
- Contact Father Paul to visit or to offer to help in the vineyard

Tel: 01903 742150
Fax: 01903 740821
Email: whitecanons.storrington @btinternet.com
Web: www.norbertines.co.uk

STOPHAM VINEYARD
Stopham, West Sussex

Not every interesting new winemaking venture in southern England is dedicated to making only sparkling wines. At Stopham dry whites are the major focus with just a nod towards sparkling wine and rosé.

Background

Simon Woodhead, who is heading up the venture, has a lease on a small part of an aristocratic estate that has been family-owned since the 1300s. Simon, a graduate in electronic engineering, fell under the spell of wine while living in Madrid and returned to the UK to do a Foundation Degree in Wine Production at Plumpton College (see page 64). There he met Tom Newham who swapped yacht building for losing himself in a sea of vines. As the project evolves Simon will be more focussed on the winemaking and Tom will take on the vineyard full-time.

Simon Woodhead in his vineyard

Wine production

Two thirds of the initial plantings of 15 acres (6 ha) are to Pinot Gris and Pinot Blanc. The balance of 21,000 vines comes from another Alsace variety, Auxerrois, together with some Bacchus and Dornfelder, plus Chardonnay and Pinot Noir

for the 'fizz'. There is no intention to use any oak, with a cool stainless steel fermentation favoured instead. One advantage of plumping for dry whites is getting a return at least two years earlier than is possible by going down the sparkling route, with its added bottle fermentation and ageing requirements.

Stopham's first wines are expected in 2010 and an old barn and other farm buildings are being converted for the winery operations so all the wine is made on-site. A further 6 ha of planting is planned for 2009.

Visiting

Even if you cannot yet visit the winery, this a very pretty part of West Sussex to tour and an increasingly popular area for putting in new vineyards. The towns of Petworth, Pulborough and Storrington are all certain to have an increasing association with wine production in the coming years.

WISTON ESTATE
Findon, West Sussex

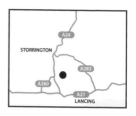

What do get if you combine some of the finest chalk soils in all of England with one of its most talented young winemakers and the best Champagne technology? One of the most compelling new sparkling wine ventures going – not just in the UK but anywhere.

The more than 6500 acre (2632 ha) Wiston Estate is a fine property a little north of Worthing in West Sussex. Owned by Harry and Pip Goring, the imposing Wiston House (dating from 1573) and surrounding lands of Wiston Park have been leased to the Home Office as Wilton Park since 1968. The latter is an institution founded after the end of the second World War to promote the new democracy in Germany and is named after its original location near Beaconsfield. It has evolved into a venue for high-level diplomacy and policy conferences. At Findon Park Farm the Gorings farm 1200 acres (486 ha) which stretch over this part of the South Downs and incorporate numerous south-facing slopes ideal for high-quality viticulture. After considering an approach from a Champagne house, the very first vines were planted in 2006 but with other highly promising vineyard land available, don't expect it to be the last. The vineyard was planted with help from consultant Stephen Skelton. Contact with Nyetimber, with a view to supplying them with grapes, was eventually to result in the hiring of Dermot Sugrue and taking the brave step of doing it all for themselves.

The Vineyard
This being a large estate and farm there are more than 25 full-time employees, many of whom have strong agricultural backgrounds which are being put to use in what promises to be a new era of viticulture in the local area. While much fuss has rightly been made of the leading fizz made to date, such as that from Nyetimber and Ridgeview, only negligible quantities of Chardonnay, Pinot Noir or Pinot Meunier have been grown on chalk. The greensand sandstone seen elsewhere in East Sussex can clearly provide good raw materials but the possibilities from pure chalk remain a tantalising prospect. Champagne experts, Louis Roederer, one high profile visitor to Wiston, were highly impressed with the soil and site analysis made here.

Wiston's first vineyard of 16 acres (6.5 ha), established in 2006, is planted to 55 per cent Chardonnay, 35 per cent Pinot Noir and 10 per cent of Pinot Meunier. Grass is grown between the rows and no herbicides are used. There is good shelter from prevailing south-westerly weather and the vines are trained to Vertical Shoot Positioning on a Single Guyot system.

BIOGRAPHY Dermot Sugrue

University educated in England but of Irish upbringing, the irrepressible and impassioned Dermot Sugrue is another graduate of Plumpton College. He was previously winemaker at Nyetimber where he helped build the winery's considerable reputation. Having worked in Bordeaux for Châteaux L'Eglise-Clinet and Leoville-Barton, and in Champagne for Moet & Chandon, Dermot has also benefitted from working with Champagne oenologist Jean-Manuel Jacquinot and can take the credit for making arguably the finest sparkling wine yet produced in the UK, a 2003 Blanc de Noirs bottling for Nyetimber. The upheaval that followed the change of ownership at Nyetimber presented Dermot with the opportunity to develop the project at Wiston Estate, providing greater scope for his singular vision of what English sparkling wine might be. He started as a consultant in October of 2006 (just five months after the vineyard was planted) before becoming fully immersed in the project a year later.

VINEYARD FACTS

- These are chalk soils, the same as those found in Champagne.
- Planted exclusively to Chardonnay, Pinot Noir and Pinot Meunier.
- A sheltered vineyard site with 22 different permutations of rootstock and clones.
- 26,000 vines on a 16 acre (6.5 ha) slope facing just east of due South.

Wine production

When it comes to producing quality sparkling wines, Wiston has another quality card to play. In Dermot's drive to make the best possible English sparkling wine he has acquired his own traditional Coquard basket press (the same as that still used by a handful of top Champagne houses). This is a remarkable piece of equipment that when in operation additionally requires several people gently lifting the grape marc with forks to maximise the quality of the juice extraction. This is a first for the UK, and only one of four of its type found outside of France. If this were not enough he has also brought in a quantity of oak barriques and demi-muids (600 litre) from Seguin Moreau, Radoux and other top coopers for fermenting and ageing the wines prior to the period on the fine lees in the bottle. Dermot wants Wiston's wines to be different and there seems little doubt he can achieve both individuality and high quality.

In fact 2008 will prove to be a historic year for Wiston Estate. The pace of change has been relentless. In March there wasn't even a winery, only the shell of one which was in the process of being gutted and cleaned up. Although it had previously served as an automotive repair shop for luxury European car brands and was well-proportioned for wine production, significant reinforcement of the structure was required for the arrival of Dermot's new baby — the four tonne Coquard press which would weigh in at more than 10 tonnes when loaded with grapes. By positioning this monster on the first floor it makes it possible for the juice to flow directly to the tanks below without the need for pumping. The latter can have a

Wiston's traditional Coquard basket press is a first for the UK

detrimental effect on quality.

Dermot also travelled far and wide to get the other equipment needed to underpin his vision for the best English sparkling wine possible. In early April, putting on his ambassadorial hat, Dermot managed to squeeze in a tasting of English wines at the massive VinItaly wine trade fair in Verona, in order to promote some of the best existing English wines (Breaky Bottom amongst them, see page 54) to Italian and other international sommeliers. By the end of the month a much needed trip to Beaune in France was made for a van full of the used Burgundian wine barrels detailed above. These barrels are now where some of the juice is destined for, following pressing and settling, via the gravity flow system. Several good Champagne growers also make use of wood for fermentation with the potential for increased complexity and enhanced structure in the finished wines.

An extraordinary amount of work was required in the winery during the summer months, including the momentous unloading of the Coquard press in mid-July, so that all was ready in time for the arrival of the

first grapes in late September. The demanding 2008 growing season also required a particularly

New stainless steel tanks form part of the armoury

fastidious approach in the vineyard in order to ensure the health of the fruit in the face of an ever present threat of mildew.

The first small crop at Wiston was indeed made from the 2008 vintage with a Pinot Meunier cuvée planned for the first release a couple of years hence. A traditional cuvée of all three varieties, a Blanc de Blancs and possibly a Rosé will complete the range. Some grapes are also being supplied from other growers who intend to take full advantage of Dermot's expertise and the new winery facility. Nearby Storrington Priory (see page 70), Jenkyn Place in Hampshire (see page 93), and Tas Valley in Norfolk are among those already committed to using Wiston Estate as their contract winemaker. Despite the small size of this estate relative to Nyetimber or the growing grape supply available to Ridgeview expect Wiston Estate with it privileged chalk slopes and talented winemaker to be challenging for a quality lead over the coming decade.

HOW TO FIND US

- Findon Park Farm where the vineyard is located lies close to Findon, just north of Worthing on the south coast.
- While not yet open to visitors the winery lies close by the A24 between the Washington and Findon roundabouts and there is the potential for a visitor centre in the not too distant future.

Tel: 01903 817996
Fax: 01903 879902
Email: dermot@wistonestate.co.uk
Web: www.wistonestate.com

ENGLISH WINE CENTRE
Alfriston, East Sussex

Not a vineyard, not a winery, scarcely even a grape to be seen. But thanks to its recently retired owner, the English Wine Centre is recognised as a hub of promotional activity and a great place to find lots of the finished product.

Set in the pretty Cuckmere Valley the English Wine Centre was bought by Colin and Christine Munday in late 2007. Both are experienced professionals with a love of food and wine, something the centre's founder, Christopher Ann, was passionate about. Christopher was one of the more important personalities in the English wine industry over the past 30 years. A staunch promoter of English wines long before the current wave of enthusiasm for English wines and local produce, he established the centre in 1972 and also served as director of the English Vineyards Association from 1983-1988. Even more importantly he also launched the English Wine Festival.

Alfriston, East Sussex

Wines
This is still probably the most comprehensive range of English wines in a retail outlet.

The English Wine Centre's online shop is the best choice for most, unless you happen to be touring the vineyards in Sussex or Kent.

Visiting
While the centre is open for wine sales there is much more on offer to anyone

making the effort to track it down. A tour of the centre together with a tasting and a 'Sussex Lunch' can be booked in advance. The tour takes in Walton's Oak Barn, a 17th century edifice that was relocated here (from Epsom) in 1982 and includes a small wine museum. Tours can also be arranged that take in local attractions such as Michelham Priory. The barn serves as a venue for conferences, and wedding receptions are also hosted by the centre. It is likely that the English Wine Festival, held at nearby Glynde Place will continue to bring some visitors to Alfriston for the first time. The festival itself shouldn't be missed by anyone with a serious interest either in English wines or high quality local produce.

HOW TO FIND US

- English Wine Centre, Alfriston, East Sussex BN26 5QS
- Alfriston can be reached off the A27, via the Alfriston roundabout, to the west of Lewes. The A27 can also be used to reach Glynde (for the festival) but instead turning left after travelling just 4 miles from Lewes.
- Open daily from 10am to 5pm (closed between Christmas Eve and New Years day).

Tel: 01323 870164
Fax: 01323 870005
Email:
bottles@englishwine.co.uk
Web: www.englishwine.co.uk

ENGLISH WINE FESTIVAL

- Although no longer held at the English Wine Centre, the festival was an important annual event held here since its inception, in 1975, until 1995. After a brief return the festival now forms part of the Glynde Food & Drink Festival held on the third weekend in September at Glynde Place (2008 is the 34th event).

CENTRAL
SOUTH

Central South

David Moore

Berkshire
1 Stanlake Park

Dorset
2 Furleigh Estate
3 Bride Valley
4 Purbeck Vineyard
5 Sherborne Castle

Hampshire
6 Beaulieu Vineyard
7 Coach House
8 Danebury Vineyard
9 Jenkyn Place
10 Marlings Vineyard
11 Priors Dean
12 Setley Ridge
13 Somborne Valley
14 Titchfield
15 Waitrose Estate
16 Wickham Vineyard

Isle of Wight
17 Rosemary Vineyard

Oxfordshire
18 Bothy Vineyard
19 Brightwell
20 Hendred Vineyard
21 Pheasants Ridge

Wiltshire
22 a'Beckett's
23 Quoins

Avon
24 Mumfords

PHEASANTS RIDGE
Hambleden, Oxfordshire

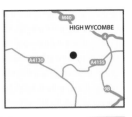

The Gilbeys' small vineyard is part of a wine and food family business that includes two restaurants one in Eton and the other in Old Amersham.

They come from a family of wine shippers so are no strangers to wine production. All the profits from the vineyard are directed towards the local church and associated charities. The site is tended by Michael and Lin Gilbey and local volunteers and the whole enterprise is run very much as a local village enterprise.

Wine production

The vineyard is situated in the heart of the Hambledon Valley between Henley-on-Thames and Marlow and the vines planted on south-west facing chalky soils. Two varieties are planted, Bacchus and Faberrebe and two wines produced. The Gilbeys have just 1.5 acres (0.6 ha) under vine, which they inherited when purchasing their current house. The original vineyard had suffered a number of years of neglect, however the focus now is only on producing the best quality grapes and like many others they will produce no wine at all from the tricky 2007 vintage.

The wines are vinified at nearby Stanlake Park (see page 86). Of the two wines produced, the Bacchus dry white is crisp, clean and cool-fermented. Emphasising the delicate green, floral aromas of the variety is the objective. The Sparkling Brut is characterised by typically English green apple fruit and is marked by its fresh acidity.

The Sparkling Brut

VINEYARD FACTS

- 1.5 (0.6 ha) acre under vine.
- Bacchus and Faberrebe planted on well-drained chalk soils.
- Vineyards tended by both the family and local volunteers and all profits given to the local church and associated charities.
- Wines vinified and aged at Stanlake Park.

The south-west facing vineyard

Visiting

The wines can be purchased direct from the vineyard as well as the local shop. Visiting is by appointment. They are also sold through the Gilbeys' two restaurants.

HOW TO FIND US

- Address: Hambledon, Nr Marlow, Oxfordshire RG9 6SD
- Take the Henley to Marlow A4155. Turn left to Hambleden Village and the vineyard is on the right hand side of the valley after the village.
- Open: Telephone and speak to Michael Gilbey about visiting and wine sales

Tel: 01491 573202
Web: www.gilbeygroup.com

BOTHY VINEYARD
Frilford Heath, Oxfordshire

Richard and Sian Liwicki's small Oxfordshire vineyard is
another valuable Thames Valley address for English wine
enthusiasts to put on their lists of vineyards to visit.

VINEYARD FACTS

- 4.9 acres (2 ha) under
  vine. 6,000 vines planted.
- Sandy, well-drained soils
  ensure an excellent
  environment for the vines.
- Vineyards trained to high
  wire Sylvoz for reds and
  Double Guyot for whites.
- Wines produced from
  home vineyard.
- Trellising ensures good
  levels of photosynthesis
  and sugar in the grapes.
- Modern well-equipped
  small winery.

The vineyard is no flash in the pan and
rather venerable in English vineyard terms
having been founded in 1978 by Roger and
Dorothea Fisher. Indeed viticulture has been
practised here in the Vale of the White
Horse since medieval times. The vineyard is
very traditional and run on similar
lines to many small French family
domains and virtually everything is
carried out by hand, including
pruning and the harvest. The
Liwickis enjoy the help of many
friends and volunteers in the
pursuit of producing the best
quality, well ripened fruit they can
and in this respect are very similar to their
counterparts in some of Europe's more
established wine regions.

The Paradox white

The Vineyard
There are now 4.9 acres (2 ha) which is
planted to an extensive range of varieties.

Whites comprise Ortega, Huxelrebe,
Bacchus, Perle, Findling, Kerner, Albalonga
and Solaris. Red varieties include Regent,
Rondo, Dornfelder and Acalon planted in
2004 which, it is hoped, will produce a first
crop with the 2008 harvest. The white
varieties are trained on a Double
Guyot replacement cane system.
The reds on a Sylvoz single high
wire and trained downwards. The
key is exposing the canopy to
maximum light during the growing
season which will increase the
natural sugar in the grapes. While
the vineyards are very labour
intensive, this viticultural approach will
produce better quality fruit with better and
more intense flavour. An added advantage
is the type of soil here. It is a sandy loam
over sand and is very free draining, ideal for
vines, and low in fertility which helps in
reducing vigour and excess summer growth
of the vines' foliage.

Wine production
Unlike many other vineyards of a
comparable size who contract their
winemaking out, Richard Liwicki makes the
Bothy wines himself. They have a well-
equipped small winery with a Vaslin press,
full filtration equipment and stainless steel
tanks for settling, fermentation and ageing.
A number of wines are made, although as
with most English vineyards this will vary
from year to year depending on how
generous nature has been with the growing

Winter pruning

season. 2008 looks likely to be a difficult year. They produce two white styles, the Oxford Dry which is just that, and the Renaissance which has a little residual sugar and is slightly sweet. In 2007 the aromatic Oxford Dry was vinified from Huxelrebe, Bacchus and Perle, the peachy Renaissance from Ortega and Findling, although this vintage was given a special name. It was labelled Paradox for the year because a rainy July resulted in a fruit set of seedless small berries but concentrated flavours with high sugar levels. The fruit was picked early enough to ensure sufficient acidity and balance in the wine. Both whites are kept on their lees for a short time which adds a little additional weight and gives the wine a richer, rounder texture. A rosé Oxford Pink, was added for the first time in 2007 from a blend of the young vine reds with Huxelrebe and Ortega and is is produced in a crisp dry style. The first red fruit from the 2008 harvest is likely to spend a period of time in small oak which should add extra weight and provide a more rounded structure and a suppleness of the wines' tannins. The Liwickis also offer a number of other

Sterile bottles

BIOGRAPHY   Richard & Sian Liwicki

The Liwickis took on the vineyard after acquiring an interest in the subject and helping out themselves as volunteers. They still enjoy this social element of winegrowing today. They were first and foremost drawn to the potential of the site and its excellent mesoclimate and long ripening season. The fact that the mature vines and low yielding vines produced wines of intensity, depth and quality was a further incentive. They have continued to extract the maximum they can from this site and have won best white wine awards consistently over the last three years in the Thames region.

Bottling

wines on the price list from time to time and these have included Stanlake Park's Brut Superior and Camel Valley's Pinot Noir Rosé sparkling wines.

Visiting

Visits can be made to the vineyard on Fridays and Saturdays between 10am and 5pm from May until Christmas and also Sundays and Bank Holidays between 1pm and 4pm. There are tasting facilities for visitors and the wines can be purchased both at the winery and through their website and are also available locally in good gourmet restaurants. The vineyard is open at other times, although you will have to make an appointment and group tours can also be catered for, again by appointment.

HOW TO FIND US

- Address: Faringdon Road, Frilford Heath, Oxfordshire, OX13 6QW
- Bothy Vineyard is in Central Oxfordshire, in a little hamlet named Frilford Heath which is situated just three miles to the west of Abingdon, or roughly seven miles south west of Oxford. Once you have found Frilford Heath, the entrance to Bothy Vineyard is on the North side of Faringdon Road, between the Dog House Hotel and Oakley Park.
- Open: May to Christmas Friday and Saturday 10am to 5pm and Sundays and Bank Holidays 1pm to 4pm. An appointment is necessary at other times and for tours.

Tel: 01865 390067
Email: office@bothyvineyard.co.uk
Web: www.bothyvineyard.co.uk

BRIGHTWELL
Wallingford, Oxon

Among the top vineyards in Oxfordshire and the Thames Valley, located just to the south of the river outside Wallingford. It has been under its current ownership since 1999.

The original vineyards were planted between 1986 and 1989 and were known at the time as Clapcot. All the fruit was sold on to Chiltern Valley Vineyards. Bob and Carol Nielsen purchased the property in 1999 and their current range of wines has been sold since 2002. The wines are available through a number of local farmers markets and stores as well as at Brightwell's own shop. They can also be found at The Oxford Wine Company.

The Vineyard
Four white varieties are planted, Chardonnay, Huxelrebe, Reichensteiner and Bacchus. Red Dornfelder and Dunkelfelder are also cultivated, the former used in the vinification of both the red and rosé. The flinty, chalk, greensand soils of the Thames Valley are ideal for growing grapes of persistent and intense flavour. The area is a bowl surrounded by hills which benefits the vineyard with lower than average rainfall. 14 acres (5.7 ha) are planted and the vines trained on a Geneva Double Curtain system.

Wine production
The wines are all made at Stanlake Park (see page 86), using the latest modern vinification techniques and equipment. With a facility such as this close by it makes sense for a smaller vineyard to make Harvesting is generally carried out during early October and only on the finest days and of course by hand. Whites are cool-fermented to emphasise their freshness and fruit character, rosé gets a

VINEYARD FACTS
- 14 acres under vine. 20,000 vines planted.
- Six varieties cultivated for red, white, rosé and sparkling wine.
- Vineyards trained on a Geneva Double Curtain system.
- Big vine trellising helps to avoid excess vigour and summer growth.

Autumn colours emerging

short period of maceration on the Dornfelder skins and the fermentation will also be controlled to retain the forward fresh fruit aromas of the wine. In addition to the wines profiled here there is an additional white, Crispin, which is a soft, lightly aromatic, easy drinking blend of Reichensteiner and Bacchus. The Regatta red is a fruit driven style vinified mainly from Dornfelder. Marked by dark berry fruit, it sees a little oak during ageing in cellar.

HIGHLIGHTS | Feature box

Bob and Carol Nielsen took over the running of Brightwell from Carol's father Denys Randolph who first established the vineyard. They have put in a considerable amount of work to bring the property into its current condition with well ordered vineyards, producing crisp, fresh and approachable wines with the help of Vince Gower at Stanlake Park. This approach has been rewarded with the wines being sold not just by themselves but by reputable wine merchants and restaurants. The Nielsens are also notable supporters of the industry and hosted the United Kingdom Vineyards Association awards in 2008 at Brightwell. Bob Nielsen is also the Chairman of the Thames and Chilterns Vineyards Association.

The Wines

Brightwell Sparkling Chardonnay

This comes solely from Chardonnay and is a classic Blanc de Blancs style. Subtle citrus fruit is nicely underpinned by a rich toasty lees character.

Brightwell Bacchus

A 100% varietal example with good, fresh aromatic fruit. The wine is made with just a touch of residual sugar for balance. Drink young and fresh.

Brightwell Oxford Flint

Marked by green, appley fruit and a hint of citrus in the background. This is a dry, almost minerally blend of Huxelrebe and Chardonnay.

Brightwell Oxford Rosé

Made from Dornfelder grapes grown on chalk and flint, gravel soils. There is only a short maceration on the skins although the wine has good colour and a ripe, raspberry fruited character and a little structure.

Early season growth

Visiting

Visitors are very welcome here, and the wine store is on the right hand side of the driveway as you enter the property. The shop is open for sales and tasting Friday, Saturday and Sunday. You can visit at other times, although you will need to make an appointment. Throughout the summer you can also take guided vineyard tours with tastings. The walks will take you through the vines, woodland and lakeside of the estate. Additionally if you wish to stay in the area for a day or two there is a small two bedroom cottage built in a traditional style overlooking the vineyards.

HOW TO FIND US

- Brightwell is just to the south of the river Thames off the A329 between Shillingford and Wallingford.
- Open: Friday, Saturday and Sunday. Telephone or e mail to make an appointment at other times.

Email: wines@brightwines.co.uk
Web: www.brightwellvineyard.com

HENDRED VINEYARD
Wantage, Oxfordshire

Steve and Vivianne Callaghan's recently purchased 9 acre (3.6 ha) vineyard looks set to become one of the more important source of wines in Oxfordshire and a key destination for visitors.

The property is on the borders of the small picturesque village of East Hendred, a few miles to the east of Wantage. They purchased the property in 2006 and have since invested both money and considerable effort. The original Hendred vineyards were first planted in 1972 to Reichensteiner and covered a total area of 3 acres (1.2 ha) by 1976. The then owners, the late Malcolm 'Mac' Mackinnon and his wife Mary, sold their property with the original vineyard. They retained though, part of their land and the current vineyard was planted in 1992 by the Mackinnons and their friend Biaggio Grillo. After Malcolm Mackinnon passed away the vineyard was cash cropped between 2003 and 2006 before the Callaghans purchased it.

VINEYARD FACTS

- 5.5 acres (2.2 ha) under vine. 6,075 vines planted.
- Wines produced solely from home vineyard.
- Vineyards spur pruned and vertically trellised.
- Trellising ensures good levels of photosynthesis and sugar in the grapes.
- Sparkling wine produced and disgorged off-site.
- Modern winery with stainless steel tanks and from 2008 full temperature control.

CALLAGHANS FURLONG DRY WHITE WINE 75cl 11.5%vol

The Vineyard
The vineyard now covers some 5.5 acres (2.2 ha) and is planted to a mix of Madeleine Angevine, Seyval Blanc and Pinot Noir, which is not the early clone. It is grafted onto a low vigour

The Hendred vineyard logo

rootstock, which will undoubtedly result in better balanced flavour in the fruit. The first Pinot harvest will not be until 2009. The soil is ideal for growing top quality grapes, it is greensand over a chalk bedrock which helps to promote natural acidity in the fruit and better balance in the resulting wines. The gentle south facing slope of the vineyard provides not only good exposure to

BIOGRAPHY — Steve Callaghan

Steve Callaghan grew up on the east coast of Scotland and had long wished to own his own vineyard. After a career in the corporate world as the Chief Executive of two publicly listed companies, he has been able to make that life-style change. He and his wife Vivianne made the decision to purchase Hendred and still enjoy the advice of 74 year Sicilian Biagio Grillo. Steve looks after the wines and winemaking, while Vivianne, who is a very experienced

horticulturalist, oversees the vines. It's very much a small hands on "boutique" winery and vineyard.

sunlight but also enables frost to drift easily off the slope. A gully has also now been dug just below the vineyard to help this process and minimise the development of frost pockets in the lower lying vines. As elsewhere, considerable care goes into vineyard trellising and training of the vine canopy, maximising sugar and flavour in the fruit and avoiding any excess green aromas which come with very marked canopy growth.

Wine production

The Callaghans have invested considerably in their small on site winery and will, for 2008, have full temperature control throughout the building. They also now have their own crushers and presses, although bottling is done by hand. For the time being some of the winemaking is done off-site at Stanlake Park (see page 86), particularly sparkling wine, which is made at present from Seyval Blanc. It is anticipated that the Pinot Noir will contribute to the sparkling blend and also provide a little dry rosé. Two whites are currently available Furlong and Burydown. Both were produced in 2007 solely from Madeleine Angevine, although the Burydown will generally have a little Seyval also. Furlong is more typical of an English dry white. It is cold-stabilised and lightly filtered before bottling. The Burydown by contrast has minimal processing and is bottled unfiltered and offers a more oxidative style, not dissimilar to some of the new wave wines now being made in this manner in the Loire Valley.

Visiting

Visitors are welcome at the vineyard most Saturdays between 10 am and 4 pm and there are regular winetastings which are free and notified on the Hendred website. It is advisable to check the site first before visiting because the Callaghans are regularly to be found at the Wantage Farmers' market where wines may also be tasted and purchased. They request that groups of 12 and above make an appointment first. The wines are also available at a number of local stores, County Delicacies in Reading and at the Oxford Wine Company.

HOW TO FIND US

- Address: East Hendred, Wantage, Oxfordshire OX12 8HR
- The property is on the edge of East Hendred, just off the A417 in Allins Lane, which is on the western edge of the village as you approach from Wantage.
- Open: Most Saturdays between 10 am and 4 pm. Telephone or check the website before visiting. Weekly winetasting details are on the site.

Tel: 07771 921210
Email: hendredvineyard @btinternet.com
Web: www.hendredvineyard.co.uk

Harvesting by tractor

STANLAKE PARK
Twyford, Berkshire

Stanlake Park originally began life as first Thames Valley Vineyards and then Valley Vineyards and is now under the committed stewardship of current owners Peter and Annette Dart.

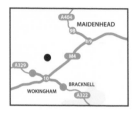

The vineyard remains an extremely impressive source of some of the country's best wine and is an important and very significant contract winemaker for a number of vineyards in the Thames Valley and Hampshire.

The origins of the estate stretch back to 1166 when the property was originally named Hinton Pipard. The current name emanates from the 15th century as a result of a marriage between Elizabeth Thorpe, whose family had inherited the estate and Nicholas Stanlake. Ownership during Tudor times was first by the Bray family and then it passed to the Sandy family by marriage. It is thought likely that Henry VIII would have visited with his love of hunting and the close proximity of Windsor Castle.

The estate was sold to the Aldworth family in 1610 and under their supervision the present manor house was built. Stanlake remained in their family, who had been royalists during the Civil War. After the revolution in the 1680s they accepted the new house of Orange and the clock tower of the stable block has the inscription "Revolution 1688". The estate has continued to prosper in the

VINEYARD FACTS

- 25 acres (10.1 ha) under vine.
- An extensive range of varieties planted.
- Different trellising and pruning methods used to optimise fruit quality.
- Contract winemaking facilities offered to other vineyards.
- Modern well-equipped winery for the production of still and sparkling wines.

ensuing period and was owned in the latter part of the 20th century by the Leighton family. It was Jon Leighton who had the vision of planting a vineyard on the estate in the late 1970s.

Barrels add atmosphere

The automatic bottling line

The new shop and tasting room

The Vineyard

The original small test area of vines was planted by Jon Leighton in 1979. Since that time the vineyard has increased dramatically. There are now over 30,000 vines covering an area of some 25 acres (10.1 ha). The vineyard itself is still referred to as Valley Vineyards. More individual grape varieties are grown here than anywhere else in England. Plantings include, among the white varieties, Gewürztraminer, Ortega, Reichensteiner, Müller-Thurgau, Regner, Scheurebe, Bacchus, Madeleine Angevine, Schönburger, Wurzer and Ehrenfelder. All three Champagne grapes, Chardonnay, Pinot Noir and Pinot Meunier are planted, as well as a number of other red grapes including Gamay and Dornfelder.

In line with the wide range of grape varieties a number of different trellising and training systems are in operation. This makes perfect sense in optimising the light exposure of the canopies and consequently the potential flavour in all the grapes. Unique to the estate are the Stanlake "Bow" and "Ballerina" trellises. They are both based on the New World

Precarious work for a "Cellar Rat"

Smart-Dyson Ballerina system but provide an excellent balance of fruit quality at a reasonable yield in the long and particularly cool growing season here. In order to maintain the quality of the fruit from harvesting into the winery and the commencement of vinification all the grapes are carefully picked and sorted by hand.

The Wines

Brut Superior

The flagship wine of the estate and one of the country's important sparkling wines. Made from a blend of Pinot Noir and Chardonnay, the wine offers impressive weight and intensity with a nice yeasty complexity.

Brut Superior Rosé

This is the top sparkling pink which is also made from Pinot Noir and Chardonnay. The light colour of the wine is achieved after a short period of contact with the grape skins prior to the primary fermentation.

Heritage Brut

This is a softer and more approachable style of sparkling white, more characterised by its crisp fruit than the more complex bready, yeasty notes found in the Brut Superior. Nevertheless 18 months on lees adds depth and intensity.

Regatta

This is a crisp and approachable dry white marked by its fresh and lightly herbaceous fruit, making it a good partner for shellfish. Made from a range of grape varieties and generally including Schönburger and Ortega.

Hinton Grove

This aromatic, off-dry white is a good well-made and reasonably intense blend of Schönburger, Siegerrebe and Wurzer. In 2006 it was particularly fresh and zesty.

The attractive stable block now part of the winery

Wine production

Like Three Choirs (see page 138) in Gloucestershire, Stanlake Park is an extremely important contract winemaking resource for a number of small boutique wineries in the Thames Valley and beyond and is in the very capable hands of Vince Gower. As well as offering their many vineyard clients a complete vinification service, the property is also very important in the provision of sparkling winemaking facilities including ageing on lees and disgorging, which requires specialised equipment including gyropalettes and disgorging machines.

The winemaking facility is in a 17th century reformation barn. Although it is extremely well equipped, the Darts on acquiring the property invested heavily in the best winemaking technology and equipment. While on the outside it may look in stark contrast to the modern winery buildings of the New World in places like Australia and California, this modern facility is capable of processing over 200 tons of fruit a year. All individual fermentations are monitored and carefully controlled both during fermentation and afterwards during stabilisation and ageing.

A wide range of wine is made at Stanlake and released under the estate's own label. In addition to the wines profiled individually there are a number of other bottlings. Sparkling wine is

The Wines

King's Fumé

This has been a well-established style here for many years. A blend of Ortega and Regner, the wine has a lightly aromatic undercurrent, good weight and breadth and quite noticeable oak influence.

Pinot Blush

A fine dry rosé produced from mainly Pinot Noir with a little Pinot Meunier and Pinot Gris. It offers a subtle strawberry fruit character and excellent fresh acidity which lifts the whole palate. Drink young and fresh.

Ruscombe

This is the most important red produced at Stanlake Park. Forward and approachable, it is a blend of Triomphe and Dornfelder with a deep colour and rich, ripe dark berry fruit.

Pinot Noir

Understandably given the climate even in the relatively warm Thames Valley, a varietal Pinot Noir is only made in the warmest years. When it is made traditional Burgundian techniques are used with ageing in new French oak.

The Reserve

The Reserve red is a selection of the very best Dornfelder, Triomphe and Rondo sourced in the vineyard, rather than a barrel-selection. Subtly oaked with some of the typically fruity flavour of these varieties.

a key speciality and will be as significant in the future and Brut Superior rosé both released under the same label, the Heritage Brut is a lighter more forward style, while the Hinton Brut is currently made from German-sourced fruit to see if a more aromatic style will prove popular with consumers. Also made is a small range of varietal whites including Gewürztraminer (labelled Gewurz), Ortega, Madeleine Angevine (labelled simply Madeleine) and a Bacchus. The key to these, and following the approach throughout the white winemaking, is the preservation of the wines' delicate varietal character, something that the best English wines showcase well. A long and cool fermentation assists in achieving this.

Because of the vagaries of the English climate and the varying yield year by year, it has been decided that there should be an additional range of wines for visitors to taste and buy and a number of the excellent wines of Kathy and Gary Jordan from Stellenbosch in South Africa are also available.

BIOGRAPHY — Annette and Peter Dart

Annette and Peter Dart bought the Stanlake Estate in 2005. Previously known as Valley Vineyards they went about re-launching the brand as Stanlake Park Wine Estate. They established a new brand identity, employed a marketing approach to the wine, and added several new varietals to the range. Peter and Annette both have marketing backgrounds and they saw an opportunity to add their marketing expertise to the well-established viticulture and excellent winemaking that had been in evidence for over 20 years. They believe there is a great future for English wine in the UK and beyond; however their immediate priorities are to serve London and the Thames Valley where they have already discovered a strong demand for high quality, authentic, locally produced products.

Visiting

The vineyard is of course open to the public and seven days a week for most of the year. It is only closed over Christmas and on New Year's Day. You can visit Monday to Saturday from 11 am till 5pm and from noon on Sundays. All of the wines are available at Cellar Door prices and there is a 5% discount for Club Members when purchasing 12 or more bottles. This club is well worth considering. As well as the "by the mixed case" wine discounts, there are invitations to exclusive wine tastings in the manor house and a quarterly newsletter notifying members in advance of additional events. Among these are Open Days with free guided tours of the vineyard and winery, promotion weekends, English Wine Week activities and special packages and offers for Christmas.

The manor is a private house and as such is not open to the public. The walled vineyard, Percy's Acre, though is open and a wide range of grape varieties can be viewed. There are also a number of footpaths that you can take for a wander around the estate. A range of snacks can be purchased as well as wines and these can be consumed in the walled vineyard gardens.

Morris dancers performing during English wine week.

HOW TO FIND US

- Address: Twyford, Berkshire RG10 0BN
- Take the B3018 Road out of Twyford or Ruscombe in the direction of Bracknell. Stanlake Park is only a mile from Twyford on the lefthand side. The Vineyard is known as Valley Vineyards.
- Open: Seven days a week

Tel: 0118 934 0176
Fax: 0118 932 0914
Email:
info@stanlakepark.com
Web: www.stanlakepark.com

BEAULIEU VINEYARD
Beaulieu, Hampshire

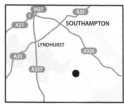

This is one of the country's oldest vineyards, with medieval origins. It was established in the 1950s. Its viticulture has been completely overhauled although its future direction is yet to be finalised by tender.

VINEYARD FACTS

- 4.45 acres (1.8 ha) under vine.
- Four varieties planted on clay loam based soils.
- Vineyards trained to Geneva Double Curtain.
- Wines vinified off site.

The origins of the vineyard go back to 1204 when the Cistercian monks of Beaulieu Abbey planted a vineyard here. Winegrowing was revived at Beaulieu by two of the early 20th century English viticultural pioneers Lt. Col. and Mrs Margaret Gore-Brown in 1957. The vineyard, which was initially planted to just 1,000 vines, flourished under their stewardship and the Gore-Brown name is celebrated with the Gore-Brown Trophy which is awarded to the English Wine of the year in the annual English Wine Awards. The vineyard is now a part of the Beaulieu Motor Museum and was taken over in 1974 by Lord Montagu, who has been an avid supporter of English viticulture for many years.

Wine production

The vineyard itself has been overseen in recent years by Roger Marchbank of the nearby Coach House Vineyard (see page 91) with much effort going into improving the quality of the fruit produced. The long term management of the site is unclear at present

though and a number of tenders have been placed both for the management of the vineyard and the sale and distribution of the wines.

The vineyard covers just under 4.5 acres (1.8 ha). There is a mix of soils and the site is quite difficult to work and is trained to Geneva Double Curtain providing a big vine canopy area which reduces the vigour of the vines. The clay loam top soil is quite acidic and with a relatively low soil pH of just over 6, although some intermixed gravel helps with drainage. Only very typical English white grape varieties are planted and these consist of Bacchus (48%), Müller-Thurgau (24%) as well as 14% each of Reichensteiner and Huxelrebe. Some Seyval Blanc was planted but this has now been replaced by Bacchus.

Two wines are currently sold under the Beaulieu Estate label, although this may change in the future as the management and direction of the vineyard becomes clear. All wine-making is contracted out and there are no on-site vinification facilities. The

Medium-Dry white is made by Roger Marchbank, close by at Setley Ridge (see page 96), whereas the Sparkling white is vinified by Vince Gower at Stanlake Park (see page 86), where there are facilities for bottle lees ageing and disgorging.

Visiting

The vineyard is open although by appointment only. The wines themselves are available for sale in the Motor Museum shop and can also be found locally.

HOW TO FIND US

- Address: Beaulieu, Brockenhurst, Hampshire SO42 7ZN
- Beaulieu National Motor Museum is very easy to find and is well signposted. The entrance is just to the north of the small New Forest village of Beaulieu on the B3056.
- Open: Telephone or email to make an appointment to visit the vineyard. Wine sales are available during the opening hours of the National Motor Museum.

Tel: 01590 612345
Fax: 01590 612624
Email: info@beaulieu.co.uk
Web: www.beaulieu.co.uk

COACH HOUSE
West Wellow, Hampshire

Roger Marchbank's small property is just on the northern fringes of the New Forest. The vineyard is not open to the public so it is best to contact him direct to find out about tasting opportunities and purchasing the wines.

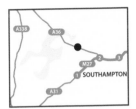

Roger gained his wine-making background at Wickham Vineyard (see page 100), working with the pioneering Australian wine consultant John Worontschak and the Harvest Wine Group. He now makes his wines at Setley Ridge (see page 96), where he helps Paul Girling and also advises at Marlings (see page 94) in both the vineyard and cellar and provides a guiding hand in the running of the refurbished vineyards at Beaulieu Vineyards (see page 90).

Only white and rosé are made

Wine Production
The vineyard, planted 20 years ago, is at a slight southerly aspect and on New Forest sandstone soils. This is important, providing good drainage and therefore reduced vigour, better vine balance and fruit quality. Without a marked slope to the vineyard, training and vertical shoot positioning is important, providing good light exposure to build sufficient sugar levels in the vines prior to harvest.

The principal varieties planted are Bacchus and Reichensteiner and because they ripen at similar times they are harvested together, by hand. A little Dornfelder and Pinot Noir is also planted and a small amount of rosé is also made. As ever with English vineyards yields can vary enormously. Frost and early growing hazards like coulure affecting fruit set after flowering are perennial problems. In a good year a yield of two to three tons to the acre would be considered a good result. Although the vineyard is not open to the public the wines though, are regularly shown at local shows and tastings. Contact the vineyard for more details.

The Wines

White
This is produced, very much like the rosé in a crisp and dry style from a blend of the Bacchus and Reichensteiner. The objective is a pure fruit driven character and the wine works well to match with food.

Rosé
The white is the main wine produced and the quantity of the rosé will depend very much on the generosity of the vineyard. It is generally a blend of varieties and the 2006 was very much a dry and crisp style.

VINEYARD FACTS

- 1 acre (0.4 ha) under vine.
- Bacchus, Reichensteiner, Dornfelder and Pinot Noir planted on well drained soils.
- Both wines vinified at Setley Ridge.
- Vineyard and winemaking consultancy provided for a number of Wessex based vineyards.

HOW TO FIND US

Address: The Coach House, Salisbury Road, West Wellow, Hampshire SO51 6BW
Open: The vineyard is not open to the public, however it is worth telephoning Roger Marchbank to discuss tasting and purchase opportunities.
Tel: 01794 323345
E Mail: roger.marchbank@btinternet.com

DANEBURY VINEYARD
Stockbridge, Hampshire

Owner Ernst Piech's small working vineyard is only open by appointment. The vineyard, was first planted in 1988 and purchased by the Piech family in 1993. The property was originally a famous racing stable.

VINEYARD FACTS

- 5.3 acres (2.15 ha) under vine.
- Auxerrois, Ruländer, Pinot Blanc, Schönburger, Faber Gris, Madeleine Angevine and Bacchus planted on well drained chalky soils.
- Vineyards vertically trellised to optimise exposure to sunlight and improve natural sugar levels.
- Wines vinified at Stanlake Park and then stored and aged on site

The site has a southerly aspect and is located on soils with a beneficially high chalk content, widely found in north-west Hampshire. Indeed Waitrose (see page 102) new vineyards for sparkling wine will be located just a few miles away.

Wine production

The vineyard is surrounded by beech trees which provide an excellent natural windbreak on these somewhat exposed slopes, fencing also helps to guard against damage from the resident deer and rabbit population.

The original varieties planted were Auxerrois, Ruländer, Pinot Blanc, Schönburger and Faber Gris. In 1996 Madeleine Angevine and Bacchus were

The 'Cossack' sparkling white

also added. At around the same time a conscious effort was put into improving the quality of the grapes produced with better training and pruning methods. Double Guyot is now employed which improves light exposure, reduces the potential damage from spring frosts and increases the airflow around the vineyards keeping the vines healthy.

A major investment has also gone into an underground cellar in the chalk bedrock to store and age the wines. With the historical racing connections of the property, the top sparkling wine 'Cossack' is named after the Derby winner from the 1840s which was trained here. The still whites are all made with modern cold fermentation techniques at Stanlake Park (see page 86) to emphasise their crisp, floral delicate fruit character. Dry white varietals are each made from Bacchus, Schonburger and Madeleine Angevine

and there is a blended white labelled simply House White.

Visiting

Visitors are welcome by appointment. There is a tasting room and gardens and a selection of menus designed specially to accompany the wines.

HOW TO FIND US

- Address: Nether Wallop, Stockbridge, Hampshire SO20 6JX
- From Stockbridge take the A30 direction towards Salisbury. After 2 miles out of Stockbridge, take the road to the right sign-posted 'The Wallops'. Follow the road for 1 mile, then take the turning to the right marked by a dead-end sign. Follow this road all the way to the very end.
  Open: Telephone or email to make an appointment.

Tel: 01264 781851
Fax: 01264 782212
Email: info@danebury.com
Web: www.danebury.com

JENKYN PLACE
Alton, Hampshire

Property man Simon Bladon first planted his vineyard here in 2004 and added a second small site in 2005. This is likely to emerge as an exciting, albeit relatively scarce source of some fine sparkling wines.

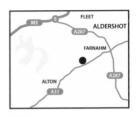

Like so many wine drinkers his view of English wine was at best sceptical. A visit to Nyetimber (see page 60), not to taste wine but for an antique furniture sale, gave him his first experience of the potential quality that could be achieved with sparkling wine on these shores. He thought he was drinking top quality Champagne, in his own words providing him with his personal "Saul on the road to Damascus" moment.

Wine production
What has also proved to be extremely propitious is that two blocks of his land are planted on the same finely drained greensand soil over a limestone and marl bedrock. Greensand is also found at Nyetimber. He has now planted all three

Champagne varieties both in 2004 with further plantings in 2005. A total of 6.8 acres (2.75 ha) are planted and at a plant density of around 1,100 vines to the acre. The slopes are gently south facing and all the natural conditions appear to be in place for the production of exceptional English sparkling wines.

The first two vintages of the Sparkling Brut 2006 and 2007 were vinified by Mike Roberts at Ridgeview (see page 66). In order to give the 2006 a minimum of 2 years in bottle on its lees the first wine will not be available until midway through 2009. As from the 2008 vintage the fruit will be vinified by Dermot Sugrue at Wiston Park Estate (see page 72). It is here he has designed a state of the art

sparkling winemaking facility.

Visiting
Jenkyn Place will not be generally open to the public. Tastings can be arranged by appointment when the wines become available in 2009.

VINEYARD FACTS

- Vineyards first established in 2005. 6.8 acres (2.75 ha) under vine in two separate vineyard sites.
- Chardonnay, Pinot Noir and Pinot Meunier planted at sufficient density to avoid unwanted vigour in the vines growth.
- Vines planted in ideal, free-draining greensand over limestone and marl soils.
- From 2008 wines will be produced in state of the art sparkling winemaking facilities.

HOW TO FIND US

- Address: Bentley, Alton, Hants GU10 5LU
- Contact the vineyard to get directions once you have made an appointment.
- Open: Tel: 020 7736 3102 or email to make an appointment.

Email:
simon.bladon@westella.org

Roses planted at the end of vine rows can warn of potential diseases

MARLINGS VINEYARD
Sway, Hampshire

The vineyard here was originally established 18 years ago. Although Marlings is not open to the public, it is one of Hampshire's fast improving vineyards now owned by David and Lori Balls.

A wide range of varieties are planted on the south facing slopes

When David and Lori purchased the property in 2005 they inherited a vineyard planted to a range of grapes including Chardonnay and Pinot Noir. Both varieties have proved troublesome in providing a reasonable crop and have been largely replanted.

VINEYARD FACTS

- 3.5 acres (1.4 ha) under vine.
- Double Guyot vertical trellising for optimum light exposure and natural sugar.
- 3,500 bottles now produced a year.
- All wines vinified on site.

The well equipped small winery

Wine production

There is now a range of more appropriate grapes including Dornfelder and Triomphe for reds and Seyval Blanc, Reichensteiner, Bacchus and Schönburger for whites. With a vineyard planted to finely drained sandstone soils and a southerly aspect, the quality now being achieved is certainly impressive. The vines are all trained on a Double Guyot vertically shoot positioned trellis.

David trained at Plumpton College (see page 64) and has invested heavily in his own winery, understandably preferring not to rely on others when tank space gets short in abundant vintages like 2006. All the wines are sensibly bottled under screw cap and as well as utilising sophisticated stainless steel tanks he has also given his winery an epoxy lined floor for optimum drainage. Truly an indication of David's commitment.

Visiting

Although the vineyard is not open to the public the wines though, are regularly shown at local shows and tastings, so encountering them will not be difficult, certainly locally.

The Wines

Three Cows White

This was produced from Reichensteiner in 2006 and will have a little Bacchus included in 2007. A full, rounded dry style for drinking within two or three years of the vintage.

Three Cows Rosé

Very good, crisp and fresh style of rosé vinified from Dornfelder, offering vibrant juicy fruit and a relatively deep colour.

Three Cows Red

A blend of Dornfelder and Rondo, roughly 60/40. Good, deep colour and a touch of grip and structure as well as deep colour from the Rondo. A touch of acidity on the finish provides a wine with excellent balance.

HOW TO FIND US

- Address: Mead End Road, Sway, Southampton, Hampshire SO41 6EE
- The vineyard is currently not open for visiting.

Tel: 01590 681606 for all wine sales and tasting enquiries.

PRIORS DEAN
Liss, Hampshire

This small vineyard in East Hampshire is one of the older established in the county, now being two decades old. It is a partnership between the Morley family and a friend Neil Elkins.

VINEYARD FACTS

- 1.5 acres (0.6 ha) under vine.
- Bacchus, Madeleine Angevine and Seyval Blanc planted on chalk rich soils.
- Vertical trellising employed to optimise photosynthesis.
- Wine vinified at Stanlake Park (see page 86).

The steep hillside vineyard

Priors Dean was first planted in 1988. Just one wine is currently produced, a blend of the three varieties grown here. It is a crisp fruit-driven white that has enjoyed notable success in the best English wine competitions.

Wine production

The vineyard is planted on a steep southerly slope at an altitude of 120 to 150 metres and only the white grapes Bacchus, Madeleine Angevine and Seyval Blanc are planted. The soil is excellent for vines, well-drained, with a light loam over a chalky subsoil enabling the vine roots to grow deeply, sourcing minerals and nourishment.

The vines are trained high in order to optimise their exposure to sunlight and achieve as much natural sugar as possible in the fruit before ripening. This also has the benefit of improving the flow of air and reducing the risk of mildews and other maladies. Spring frosts are also less of a problem drifting off the steep slope and below the trellised vines. One final, and crucial benefit in the late summer and autumn when the grapes are ripening is that the fruit is beyond the reach of the local badger population.

Visiting

Visitors are welcomed although an appointment is necessary and you should be aware that access is only available on foot. A small picnic area can be used by prior arrangement.

HOW TO FIND US

- Address: 5 St Mary's Road, Liss, Hampshire GU33 7AH
- The vineyard is located between Alton and Petersfield. You will need to telephone or email the vineyard for directions.
- Open: Tel: 01730 894147 or email to make an appointment.

Email: pamelaelkins@ukonline.co.uk
Web: www.priorsdeanvineyard.co.uk

SETLEY RIDGE
Brockenhurst, Hampshire

Setley Ridge is based in the heart of the New Forest just outside the small town of Brockenhurst. A range of wines is made from grapes grown almost exclusively in the home vineyard.

Paul Girling purchased the property in 1999, having to start virtually from scratch. The vineyard was established 10 years earlier but had fallen into poor condition. There are six and a half acres (2.6 ha) now planted from which he produces dry white and rosé, a red as well as a medium-dry style white and an occasional botrytised sweet white, almost Vin Santo in style.

The Vineyard
The vineyard is planted on lightly sloping New Forest sand and gravel soils which provide excellent drainage and help in optimising ripening. The aspect also helps in reducing the risk of spring frosts, a perennial problem for English winegrowers. Although yields are kept carefully under control, two and half tons to the acre is typically what is expected, the vagaries of the very marginal English climate can often reduce this substantially in difficult years like 2007. Optimum light exposure as ever is all important in the vineyard and Double Guyot, vertical trellising is employed. Throughout the growing cycle, vegetative growth in the vine canopy is also tightly managed to ensure an optimum balance of sugar and flavour at harvest.

VINEYARD FACTS

- 6.5 acres (2.6 ha) under vine, planted to Pinot Blanc, Schönburger, Seyval Blanc, Muscat for whites and Regent and Rondo for reds.
- A small amount of fruit is bought in to supplement winery needs.
- Vineyards mostly trained to Double Guyot.
- Vertical trellising and summer canopy control ensure good levels of sugar in the grapes.
- Extensively equipped winery with some oak used to age the red.

Wine Production
There is a modern well equipped winery with temperature control and stainlees steel tanks for fermentation and assemblage. Paul trained in winemaking at Plumpton College and works with Roger Marchbank, who also makes his own Coach House Vineyard wines here as well (see page 91). The crisp floral whites sometimes have a light chaptalisation, the red very rarely needs to be. A small amount of oak is used to age the red and the level of new wood used has varied as they seek an optimum balance and move towards a more obviously fruit driven style.

BIOGRAPHY — Paul Girling

Before buying Setley Ridge in 1999, Paul Girling background was in surveying and building. When he purchased the property it was in a very rundown state and needed considerable refurbishment. He has constructed his own farm shop and built a new winery. He enrolled like many of his contemporaries at Plumpton to gain a formal grounding in winemaking and has since worked with Roger Marchbank. When he is not making the wines and tending his vines he is also responding to fire calls as a retained firefighter in Brockenhurst. He is married to Hayley who looks after their farm shop selling a wide range of locally grown produce.

A view across the New Forest

Visiting

Visiting and tasting here can be done for its own sake or in tandem with any of the other numerous attractions of the Forest. There is an impressive new farm shop where the wines are available to taste and purchase. A number of other vineyards' wines are stocked as well as a range of locally grown produce.

Vineyard tours are available and other functions and corporate events can be arranged with the vines as an ideal backdrop.

HOW TO FIND US

- Address: Brockenhurst, Hampshire SO42 7UF
- From the M27 take the A337 through Lyndhurst and Brockenhurst in the direction of Lymington. The vineyard is just on the left hand side around 1 mile after you leave Brockenhurst and there is a brown tourist sign to guide you.
- Open: Daily 10am - 5pm.

Tel: 01590 622246
Email: enquiries@setleyridgevineyard.co.uk
Web: www.setleyridgevineyard.co.uk

New Forest pony

The Wines

Setley Ridge Dry White

This comes from Seyval Blanc and offers a fine, delicate aromatic intensity with grassy hints and a touch of slatey minerality underpinned by notes of citrus. Sufficient acidity will enable the wine to age and add a little dimension for three or four years.

Setley Ridge Medium Dry White

Generally an off-dry style, this was a little sweeter in the 2006 vintage. A blend of Muscat and a little Seyval Blanc offering a steely, fresh citrus edge to the aromatic, grapey Muscat.

Setley Ridge Rosé

A crisp fresh example of dry rosé, getting a limited skin contact from the 50/50 blend of Rondo and Schönburger, the latter adding acidity and a little structure.

Setley Ridge Red

A blend of Regent, Triomphe and Rondo. Good weight and and concentration with a not inconsiderable oak influence, particularly in the 2006. Future vintages are likely to offer more berry fruit character.

SOMBORNE VALLEY
Kings Somborne, Hampshire

This recently established and moderately sizeable vineyard operation, owned by Nigel Wolstenholme, is located in the heart of Hampshire's scenic Test Valley, south of Stockbridge towards Romsey.

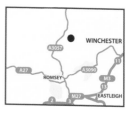

There is a sizeable vineyard holding already with ambitious expansion plans, including an on site winery, as the fledgling English wine industry begins to develop.

Wine production

The vineyard currently has 11.1 acres (4.5 ha) planted to 20,000 vines, a significantly higher planting density than in many other English vineyards. There are also plans to expand this vineyard holding. This makes sense given the significant demand for English wine at present and particularly sparkling wines. A number of major sparkling wine projects are emerging in Hampshire. The soil is excellent for quality grape growing being a loam overlying chalk. It has minimal fertility, which will reduce the vigorous summer growth of the vines' canopy, as well as being well-drained. Trellising and pruning is in line with other well-organised vineyards and the vines are Double Guyot trained. The

Pinot Noir ripening

VINEYARD FACTS

- 11.1 acres (4.5 ha) under vine.
- Two white and three red grapes planted on chalk based soils.
- Vineyards vertically trellised and Double Guyot trained to optimise exposure to sunlight and improve natural sugar levels.
- Wines vinified off site.

grapes now being cultivated are as one would expect of a modern forward-looking operation with sparkling wines in its portfolio. Whites consist of Pinot Blanc and Chardonnay, reds Pinot Noir and Pinot Meunier as well as Rondo. Fruit is also bought in from a number of other growers.

Winemaking is currently being carried out at both Chapel Down and Three Choirs This makes sense, given the level of high tech equipment available for the Somborne vinifications. The longer term plan does include an on site winery. Of the wines, there is a well-priced Estate White, in 2004 produced

from Madeleine Angevine and a crisp dry style. Red and rosé are made from Pinot Noir and there is also an Estate Red from a blend of grapes. Look out also for a Blanc de Blancs sparkling white which was solely from Chardonnay in the bumper 2003 vintage.

Visiting

The vineyard is open for wine sales by appointment and there is a full retail licence.

HOW TO FIND US

- Address: Hoplands Estate, Kings Somborne, Stockbridge, Hampshire, SO20 6QH
- Take the A3057 from Stockbridge to Romsey and in the centre of the village follow the left hand turn into Furzedown Road. Take the first left after leaving the village. The vineyard is at the end of the lane on the right hand side.
- Open: Telephone or email to make an appointment.

Tel: 01794 388547
Fax: 01794 388701
Email: info@sombornevalley.com
Web: www.sombornevalley.com

TITCHFIELD
Titchfield, Hampshire

This small vineyard was first planted in 1991 and is located on a sheltered site close to the Solent between Southampton and Portsmouth and just outside the historic Elizabethan village of Titchfield.

Although the vineyard was planted five years earlier, the first wines only emerged with the 1996 vintage. The site is very maritime by English standards and less than a mile from the waters of the Solent. The Isle of Wight though provides a natural break from the English Channel and the mesoclimate is relatively warm and dry.

Wine production

The vineyard is typically English and quite small with some 2.7 acres (1.1 ha) currently planted. Despite this a fairly wide range of grapes has been established. Owners Colin and Nicola Baker though have ensured they have the ability to produce a comprehensive range of both wines and styles depending on the vagaries of our less than predictable climate. They have also wisely considered varieties that will give them good quality flavour in their grapes and those that will ripen with some ease.

Grapes planted include: Bacchus, Reichensteiner, Auxerrois, Faber, Madeleine Angevine and Chardonnay among whites and Pinot Noir, Rondo, Regent, Dunkenfelder and Pinot Meunier comprise the reds. Everything is done by hand, including the harvest with local volunteers who are well trained in discarding poor quality grapes. Vinification is carried out on site in a dedicated small winery under the direction of Hans Schliefer who also makes the wines at Rosemary Vineyard (see page 104) on the Isle of Wight. Varietal Pinot Noir and Bacchus are produced as well as two sparkling wines Southern Shore and Festival. Dry and medium white as well as red and rosé are also released under the Misty Haze label.

Visiting

Visitors are welcome by appointment. Wines can be purchased from the vineyard and by mail order from the website as well as the Titchfield village off-licence. In the same way as at Three Choirs (see page 139) and Pebblebed in Devon (see page 128), you can also adopt a vine here.

HOW TO FIND US

- Address: Brownwitch Lane, Titchfield, Hampshire PO14 4NZ
- The vineyard is just to the south-west of the village of Titchfield. When travelling from Southampton on the A27 take the right turn onto Warsash Road just before Titchfield. Before the road bears right, turn left onto Common Lane and immediately right onto Brownwitch Lane.
- Open: Telephone for details

Tel: 01489 895773
Email: sales@titchfieldvineyard.co.uk
Web: www.titchfieldvineyard.co.uk

Well supported rows of vines

WICKHAM VINEYARD
Wickham, Hampshire

Well established Hampshire vineyard producing some of the best wines in the county. Ambitious expansion plans will see an increasing range of wines including sparkling as well as still reds, whites and rosé.

Wickham is one of England's older vineyards, originally established in 1984 and now in its third ownership guise with Gordon and Angela Shannon having taken on new partners to develop the project. The original 6 acres (2.4 ha) have now trebled in area and the current output of 25-30,000 bottles a year is likely to increase dramatically in the next few years. As well as being stocked by local restaurants and wine merchants the wines are also sold to Waitrose, the Co-op and the Vinopolis Wine World in London.

The Vineyard
There are now 18 acres (7.3 ha) planted out of a total of 40 acres (16.2 ha) on the property on a mix of clay and gravel soils. There is a southerly aspect and the vines are almost exclusively trained on a Geneva Double Curtain system. Only the Pinot Noir, which responds poorly to spur pruning, is Double Guyot trained. The use of GDC is important in achieving a natural vine balance and therefore good quality fruit, with a low plant density helping to reduce excess vigour. A range of varieties are planted on the property and the vineyards are farmed sustainably.

Wine production
The small well-equipped winery is due to be expanded in two to three years time. It is therefore key for New Zealand trained William Maitland Biddulph to run a tightly managed programme, particularly at harvest time. Stainless steel tanks are all temperature

VINEYARD FACTS

- 18 acres (7.3 ha) under vine. 10 varieties planted.
- Grapes also bought in from contract growers to supplement winery needs.
- Vineyards mostly trained to Geneva Double Curtain to reduce vine vigour.
- Extensively equipped winery with stainless steel tanks and full temperature control.

controlled and monitored manually to ensure both the consistency of the ferments and the quality of the finished wines. Oak is used to age the white Fumé and the Special Reserve red and the wine is regularly tasted prior to assemblage and bottling to avoid an excess of oak character in the wines. As well as the key labels we have profiled here there are also two limited release sparkling wines, a Row Ash Medium white which blends Reichensteiner and Auxerrois, and a fine

Oak barrels for maturing the wine

BIOGRAPHY — William Maitland Biddulph

William Maitland Biddulph is now the full time winemaker at Wickham. Born and educated in Scotland, he has been involved in the UK wine industry for over 25 years. He was initially involved with wine retailing in the employment of Berry Brothers and Rudd Ltd. In 1999 William took up the opportunity to study viticulture and winemaking in Gisborne,

New Zealand, where he stayed for five years having gained employment in the wine production. Since his return to Britain in 2003 he established his own winemaking and grape growing consultancy business. William has assisted Wickham Vineyard for the past four years and took over as winemaker and vineyard Manager in January 2008.

Vintage Selection Dry white which comes mainly from Faber.

Visiting

Visitors are able to take an audio tour of the vineyards before tasting in the shop and there is a nature reserve with an attractive walk. One of the key attractions here is the restaurant. This has long been popular and is now being moved to a different level with a franchise being opened as we went to press by the Michelin starred chef Atul Kochar, famed for his Mayfair based Indian Restaurant, Benares. The new restaurant, "Vatika"

Autumn colours

which means "vineyard orchard" in Hindi, will feature the best of modern British food with a classic Indian slant.

A modern English winery

HOW TO FIND US

- Address: Botley Road, Shedfield, Southampton SO32 2HL
- The vineyard is roughly halfway between Botley and Wickham on the A334, on the left hand side if you are travelling south east in the direction of Wickham.
- Open: Every day including Bank Holidays (except Christmas Day and Boxing Day). Monday to Saturday 10:30am–5:30pm and Sunday 11:30am–5:00pm. The vineyard is closed for the first two weeks in January.

Tel: 01329 834042
Fax: 01329 834907
Email: info@wickhamvineyard.co.uk
Web: www.wickhamvineyard.co.uk

The Wines

Special Release Fumé

This comes from Reichensteiner and Bacchus and gets a short period of oak ageing, very carefully controlled by the winemaker. The oak is in no way overdone, with subtle citrus notes in the background.

Wickham Medium

Although sweeter in style, this is not excessively so and has fragrant zippy quality underpinning its slightly sweet style.

Celebration Rosé

This is generally a slightly off-dry example of the style and is produced almost exclusively from Dornfelder. Fresh, vibrant and immediately approachable.

Row Ash Red

The first, and most approachable of the Wickham reds, dominated by the Triomphe variety and offering lots of easy forward, juicy fruit character.

Special Reserve Red

A level up in quality and depth from the Row Ash red, this is a blend of Rondo and Pinot Noir. The latter adding depth and backbone to the forward, lightly tannic, cedary character of the Rondo.

WAITROSE ESTATE
Leckford, Hampshire

Waitrose are the largest supermarket stockists of good quality English wines and they have established their own site to be planted to provide them with a guaranteed source of supply as demand for English sparkling wine increases.

There is real interest in sparkling wine production in England with several major new investments planned to compete with the likes of Nyetimber (see page 60). Waitrose have been ardent supporters of these wines and recognise that there may well be a significant shortage of supply, not only in available wine but rapidly in the area of land planted for sparkling wine production. Their own market feedback has indicated to them that their market for English wines grew by 90% in 2007. They also account for around 40% of English wine sold through multiple retailers. The focus is to support good local vineyards near their stores as well as having wines available for sale through their website Waitrose Online. As a result of this and having suitable land available to them on their own Leckford Estate property, they have decided to plant from 2009,

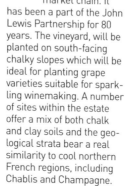

The Waitrose Cup

although the first wines won't appear till 2014. The five year cycle will involve three years after planting before a crop can be achieved and then there will be a further two year period of lees/bottle maturation.

Wine production

The Leckford Estate is large at some 4,000 acres (1.619 ha) so there is no shortage of potential terroirs for the new vineyard. The farm itself is run sustainably and is an important source of produce for the super-market chain. It has been a part of the John Lewis Partnership for 80 years. The vineyard, will be planted on south-facing chalky slopes which will be ideal for planting grape varieties suitable for sparkling winemaking. A number of sites within the estate offer a mix of both chalk and clay soils and the geological strata bear a real similarity to cool northern French regions, including Chablis and Champagne.

Visiting
The vineyard has not yet been planted and is therefore not open to the public. Further details may be obtained from Waitrose in 2014.

BRIDE VALLEY

Little Cheney, Dorset

Bella Spurrier and her husband Steven, one of the UK's top international wine writers and critics, will join the list of future high quality sparkling wine producers when their vineyard is planted in spring 2009.

VINEYARD FACTS

- 20 to 22 acres (8-9 ha) will be planted commencing in April 2009.
- Up to 54 acres (22 ha) of the property is suitable for vinegrowing.
- Soils with a high level of chalk.
- Vineyard includes an ideal south, south-east and south-west facing bowl.
- First wines to be vinified off site.

Many with a knowledge of and enthusiasm for wine will be familiar with the work of Steven Spurrier. He is an internationally recognised wine critic and writer and is a leading figure on the leading UK consumer monthly wine magazine 'Decanter'. He organised the famous "Judgement of Paris" in 1976 when the best California Chardonnays and Cabernets beat their then, far more established French rivals in a blind tasting challenge. Perhaps a similar competition beckons a few years hence when the best in southern England take on the Champenois.

The Spurriers established in the late 1980s that their 200 acre (81 ha) farm had a lot of chalk in the soil. The onset of global warming and the emergence of English sparkling wine spurred them into investigating an Anglo-French joint venture, first with the Champagne house Duval-Leroy and then with the Burgundy merchant Jean-Claude Boisset. An extensive analysis of the soil showed that up to 54 acres (22 ha) were suitable to be planted to vines. Boisset wished to target a £14.99 price for the wine, whereas the Spurriers consider that maintaining top quality at a premium price with a smaller output is the most prudent approach with their young vineyard. While this is not commercially ideal for the volume Boisset require, they will be working with the Spurriers in marketing the wine.

Wine production

The vineyard, the Boissets felt to have tremendous potential, would seem to be ideal. It is a protected bowl, providing a warmer very local meso-climate, and faces south-east, south and south-west. There is also some additionally suitable land overlooking the sea which faces south. There will be 12.3 acres (5 ha) planted initially from which it is planned to produce around 35,000 bottles a year. The wines are to be vinified at Ian Edward's winery at Furleigh Estate (see page 106), with all the necessary equipment for sparkling winemaking in place.

Visiting

The vineyard will not be open for visiting until the first wines are available in 2014.

HOW TO FIND US

- Address: Litton Cheney, Dorset DT2 9AW
- The vineyard is located between Bridport and Dorchester. When the first wines are produced contact the Spurriers for visiting details.
- Open: The vineyard has not yet been planted and is not therefore open.

Tel: 01308 482367

Email: arabella.spurrier @homecall.co.uk

The stunning Bride Valley

ROSEMARY VINEYARD
Ryde, Isle of Wight

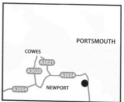

This Isle of Wight vineyard is one of the larger properties in England with a substantial vineyard holding now acquiring increasing vine age since the original planting commenced in 1986.

The property, and vineyard, is a major tourist attraction and as well as producing wines, fruit juice and cider are also made and sold here. Owner Conrad Gauntlett has since purchasing the property established the island's largest vineyard. In addition to this he is ably assisted by winemaker Hans Schliefer. A comprehensive range of wines is offered and the vineyards planted to a wide number of varieties.

The Vineyard

After the original purchase in 1986 the vineyard has been built up to a substantial 30 acres (12.15 ha). The aspect is ideal for growing good quality grapes, being in a sheltered valley, retaining summer warmth and lies gently down a south-facing slope. It also has the benefit of being protected

VINEYARD FACTS

- 30 acres (12.15 ha) under vine.
- Soil is a free-draining clay-silt loam over greensand.
- Vineyards use mainly Geneva Double Curtain trellising.
- Trellising should ensure a balance of good levels of photosynthesis and sugar in the grapes with a control of the vigorous growth of the vines canopy during the summer .
- Wines all vinified on-site.

Rosemary
ENGLISH TABLE WINE
Rosé
MEDIUM DRY
75cl   11% Vol

from south-westerly winds. The soil is good: it is free-draining but sufficiently moisture-retaining for good growth. It is clay-silt loam and is a touch fertile but has some greensand, so desired across southern England. With the sheltered south facing slopes, frost damage is a risk but reduced as it tends to drift directly off the slopes. An extensive range of grapes is planted including Triomphe and Rondo for reds and no fewer than six white varieties. These are namely Seyval Blanc, Bacchus, Schönburger, Orion, Madeleine Angevine and Phoenix. Trellising is generally on high wires and Geneva Double Curtain, which given the scale of the vineyard allows for control of excess vigour.

The sheltered vineyards during mid summer

Wine production

Winemaker Hans Schliefer has a background in large scale winery production (certainly by English standards), and Rosemary is sizeable. To this end there is a dedicated and very well-equipped on-site winery with abundant stainless steel tanks, high quality presses and all the equipment required for stable bottled wine. There is also an automatic bottling line, which is designed to ensure technically correct clean and well-made wines. Of particular interest for the more technologically orientated visitors, the winery is open on certain days during the year for viewing and to see wine-making procedures in action. As with the vineyard walks there are display boards which will guide you through the process. The range of wines produced is extensive and includes dry, medium dry, medium sweet and sweet whites, sparkling white and both a dry and medium red. A range of fruit wines is also produced.

Visiting

Given the nature of the operation here, visitors are most welcome. The property is open seven days a week during the summer and Monday to Saturday in the winter. There are a whole range of vineyard

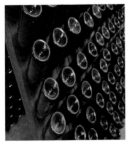

Gaining richness from the lees

BIOGRAPHY   **Conrad Gauntlett**

Conrad Gauntlett made the decision to establish Rosemary Vineyard in 1986 and has developed a very successful operation with lots to attract the wine tourist, although it remains very much a family-run business. He quickly realised that as a vineyard with a large number of visitors there is a need to offer a wide variety of products and keep his customers interested. The working winery visits are an unusual feature and add an additional dimension to the more usual features that English vineyards offer. The key to success here is the provision of a wide range of juices, liqueurs and ciders as well as the wines.

related attractions. If you prefer you can stroll around the vineyard on your own or take an organised tour. For the latter it is likely that booking in advance will be necessary. Strolling on your own offers much though. There are regularly placed explanatory display boards and beforehand you can watch a "Vine to Wine" video. There is a small on-site restaurant the "Vine Leaf Café" which directly overlooks the vineyards and an extensive range of light meals and lunchtime dishes is all prepared from fresh local produce all of which can be washed down with a glass of one of the vineyard's wines. There is an impressive vineyard shop where you can taste and purchase wines as well as a wide selection of Island products. You might also consider your own individually tailored label, a range of designs is available.

Rosemary
ENGLISH TABLE WINE

MEDIUM SWEET
75cle   10% Vol
Produced at Rosemary Vineyard, Ryde, Isle of Wight, UK

HOW TO FIND US

- Address: Smallbrook Lane, Ryde, Isle of Wight PO33 4BE
- The vineyard is located just to the south of Ryde. From the town centre you should take the A3055 south in the direction of Sandown. Turn right into Great Preston Road and Smallbrook Lane is the first turning on the left. Follow this over the railway line and the vineyard is on your right hand side.
- Open: Summer opening hours are Monday to Saturday 10am–6pm and Sunday 11am–4pm. Winter opening hours Monday to Saturday 10am–4pm.

Tel: 01983 811084
Fax: 01983 812899
Email: info@rosemaryvineyard.co.uk
Web: www.rosemaryvineyard.co.uk

FURLEIGH ESTATE
Bridport, Dorset

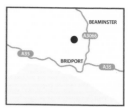

This a very newly established vineyard led by Plumpton trained Ian Edwards and targeting a first "crush" in 2008. It is also likely to become a key source for contract winemaking.

VINEYARD FACTS

- 14.8 acres (6 ha) under vine.
- Five varieties planted on sandy loam soils.
- Different trellising methods used as well as both cane and spur pruning.
- Wines to be vinified on site.

Furleigh Estate is jointly owned by Ian Edwards and Rebecca Hansford. They first planted their site in 2005 and now have a relatively substantial holding of 14.8 acres (6 ha) under vine. They have developed the project further by establishing a purpose-built winery in 2007. Their first commercial crop will be brought in with the 2008 harvest and there are plans eventually to vinify wines for other vineyards. Among these, famed wine writer Steven Spurrier and his wife Bella are planting on their Bride Valley farm in 2009 (see page 103) and it is anticipated that Ian will vinify the wines. Ian is the winemaker and studied at Plumpton College for three years. He also has wine consultancy input from Epernay in France's Champagne region.

The adolescent vines

Wine production

The vineyard is sited on well drained soils near Bridport. Among the red varieties there are holdings of Pinot Noir, Pinot Meunier and the hybrid Rondo variety. Whites comprise Chardonnay and one of the country's more successful varieties Bacchus. A total of 22,000 vines have been established on the 6 hectares giving a relatively high planting density by English standards. The key is the fertility or lack of it of the soil which aids wine quality and flavour. Some thought has also gone into the training methods used for the vines. These vary, depending on the variety and include the low trained vine method found in Chablis as well as Single Guyot. Both spur and cane pruning are employed.

The production of sparkling wine will clearly be very important here, although the still dry white and red wines can be sold earlier while the sparklers gain complexity with lees ageing in bottle. This is being taken very seriously and the top wines will get up to 5 years on their yeast lees. To this end the winery has been equipped with Willmes pneumatic press, temperature controlled stainless steel tanks, oak barrels for both fermentation and ageing, a semi-automatic disgorging line for the sparkling wines and full temperature control has been installed in the ageing cellar.

Visiting

The vineyard will be open for wine sales from summer 2009. Further details can be gained from contacting Ian Edwards at the vineyard if you plan a visit. There are no plans for any on-site refreshments but tasting will be possible as well as wine sales.

HOW TO FIND US

- Address: Salway Ash, Bridport, Dorset DT6 5JF
- The vineyard is just a few miles to the north of Bridport on the B3162 and barely a mile past Salway Ash on the right hand side. Please contact the vineyard in 2009 for final directions.
- Open: Contact us for more details in summer 2009.

Tel: 01308 488991
Email: iemail@btinternet.com

SHERBORNE CASTLE
Sherborne, Dorset

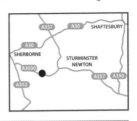

Sherborne Castle is one of Dorset's major tourist destinations and historical landmarks with landscaped gardens as well as the house. The wines produced from their Wake Court vineyard are just one of the reasons for visiting.

The origins of the original castle date from the 12th century, with the first building being a medieval hunting lodge. The ruins of the old castle are in the grounds of the standing castle, which is a 16th century Tudor mansion. It was built by Sir Walter Raleigh in 1594, after his imprisonment in the Tower of London during the reign of James I. Ownership passed in 1617 to the Digby family and has been since then. For those visitors of a historical disposition, it is possible to view the archives of the estate. This includes papers relating to the Digby family as well as to Sir Walter Raleigh.

The old castle was left in ruins by General Fairfax during the Civil War and the new mansion was renamed "Sherborne Castle". The grounds include extensive gardens which were laid out by Capability Brown and there is a range of walks and trails.

Wine production

The wines are produced from the family's own Wake Court Vineyard, just outside

---

VINEYARD FACTS

- Around 3 acres (1.3 ha) under vine.
- South facing vineyard aspect with vines planted on a mix of soils.
- White varieties planted are Seyval Blanc, Schönburger, Bacchus and Reichensteiner. Reds are Pinot Noir, Regent and Léon Millot
- Vineyard trellising is by Geneva Double Curtain.

Sherborne. There are around 3 acres (1.3 ha) of vines from which up to 12,000 bottles are produced depending on the generosity of the vintage. The vineyard is planted on a south facing site with a soil that is a mix of limestone, loam and clay with the vineyards trained to a Geneva Double Curtain.

Three wines are produced as well as a brandy, which is distilled from Sherborne Castle fruit and then aged in oak barrels for 8 years. The varietally labelled Schönburger is lightly aromatic, the Bacchus and Reichensteiner blend crisper and a touch more

mineral. A blended white is also offered, the Special Reserve. Plantings now include red Pinot Noir, Regent as well as the red hybrids Regent and Léon Millot as well as the four white varieties.

Visiting

The house and gardens are both open to the public and wines can be purchased through the gift shop at the castle or through a number of local wine merchants.

HOW TO FIND US

- Address: Cheap Street, Sherborne, Dorset DT9 3PY
- The entrance to the castle is in Sherborne on the eastern side of the town.
- Open: March 22nd to October 30th every day except Mondays and Fridays 11:00am – 4:30pm. Both house and gardens are also open on Bank Holiday Mondays.

Tel: 01935 813182
Fax: 01935 816727
Email: enquiries@sherbornecastle.com
Web: www.sherbornecastle.com

PURBECK VINEYARD
Corfe Castle, Dorset

This is a relatively new name among English vineyards. The property was established in 2000 and there is a four star boutique vineyard hotel and restaurant as well as the vineyard.

Robert and Theresa Steel purchased Purbeck in 2006, the original vineyard being established in 2000. The vineyards produce grapes for the production of both red and white wines and Robert Steel now has his own on-site winery. The vineyard is to be found halfway between Corfe Castle and Dorset's spectacular Jurassic Coastline, now a designated World Heritage Site. A major feature here, and opened in 2007, is the small boutique hotel. There are six rooms, all ensuite, a number with balconies directly overlooking the vineyard, others with lovely views of the surrounding Purbeck hills. All the rooms have been refurbished with the finest contemporary fabrics, fittings and furniture. If you plan to stay it is also worth considering eating in the restaurant with menus created using the finest local ingredients. In the summer you can also have dinner alfresco overlooking the vines.

The Vineyard
The vineyard itself was established in 2000 and there are now 2 acres (0.81 ha) planted and to over 3,000 vines. The soil is good and allows for a vine density of 1,500 vines to the acre which is quite a bit more than many other English vineyards. A small range of varieties is planted including the more classically English Phoenix and Seyval Blanc among the whites with Regent and Rondo

The luxury boutique hotel

representing the reds. Both Chardonnay and Pinot Noir are also cultivated and give some indication of the quality direction that is intended here. The vines themselves are trained to a form of Double Guyot, but with fixed cordons and spur pruning with vertical shoot positioning of the fruiting wood and canopy making the most of the summer sunshine on the vineyards exposed south-facing slopes.

VINEYARD FACTS

- 2 acres (0.81 ha) under vine. Over 3,000 vines planted.
- Relatively high vineyard plant density.
- Trellising ensures good levels of photosynthesis and sugar in the grapes.
- Sparkling wine produced and disgorged off site.
- Modern small well-equipped winery.

The Kimmeridge Bay red

BIOGRAPHY   Robert and Theresa Steel

When they took over Purbeck Vineyard in 2006, the Steels wanted to run a classic, quintessentially English vineyard and the local landscape and spectacular coastline made an ideal backdrop. Robert and Theresa Steel have very wisely looked at the venture as more than just a vineyard producing English wines. Making the wines in their own winery minimises the logistics for them at harvest and the cost of a contract winemaker. Of great importance for their business though is their boutique hotel and restaurant, providing a profitable source of additional revenue to that provided by the vagaries of the English climate in getting a consistent return from their vineyard.

Wine production

Unlike most other small vineyards of this scale the wines here are made on-site. There is a small well-equipped winery, which can cope with all the vineyard's throughput and requirements and Robert Steel makes the wines himself. A number of wines are produced including two blended whites, Kimmeridge Mist and Purbeck Dawn, specifically just from Phoenix and Seyval Blanc. There are also a couple of blended reds, the Kimmeridge Bay which is softer and fruitier, and the Studland Ruby, which is darker and fuller. A single varietal Pinot Noir is also now being produced and a sparkling white, Purbeck Celebration is vinified elsewhere.

Visiting

There is clearly much to appeal to visitors here with a wine shop and full tasting facilities available. The hotel restaurant is open to non-residents who simply wish to enjoy some good food for lunch and sample the wines at the same time in an ideal setting. As is the case in most vineyards, wine tours are available and also some interesting wine-tasting dinners. It could be worth checking in to the hotel and staying overnight to enjoy one of these. The Swanage Heritage Steam Railway chugs along in the valley below the vineyard and you could always consider taking the train to visit. As well as buying the wines at the vineyard, you can also order them over the internet if you have visited and there are particular favourites. A number of local stores also stock them.

Fine dining awaits visitors

HOW TO FIND US

- Address: Valley Road, Harmans Cross, Corfe Castle, Dorset, BH20 5HU
- Follow the A351 from Wareham travel through Corfe Castle and then on towards the town of Swanage. After approximately 1 mile you will enter the village of Harmans Cross signposted on your left hand side. After 500 metres the Purbeck Vineyard is signed on the right hand side of the road. Enter through the gates and park in the designated areas.
- Open: Check the website for opening times and also details of tours and other events.

Tel: 01929 481525

Email: Theresa@vineyard.uk.com

Web: www.vineyard.uk.com

Purbeck Vineyard
Luxury Accommodation & Fine Dining
01929 481525

MUMFORDS
Bannerdown, Avon

Tony and Margaret Cox planted the vineyard here between 1986 and 1989. It can be found just outside Bath overlooking the Avon Valley. Three whites as well as a red and rosé are produced.

Mumfords is the old field-name of the property recorded in ancient tithe maps. The name derives from "Montford", as Simon de Montford owned land in the parish here in 1250 AD.

Wine production

The vineyard now has 5,000 vines planted and covers an area of 3.7 acres (1.5 ha). The vines are planted on a south-facing slope and on an alkaline brash soil over limestone which should provide an excellent growing environment. Trellising is by Double Guyot. Four varieties are planted: Madeleine

Angevine which ripens well here. Kerner, which is a modern German variety, has some Riesling in its parentage. Even more recently created, in 1978, is the Reichensteiner which contributes a very floral, aromatic character. Just one red grape, Triomphe is planted.

The approach is modern and aimed at achieving ripe fruit driven styles and to this end cool fermentations are practised in stainless steel tanks in the on-site winery. Two dry whites are produced, one from Madeleine Angevine with a lightly aromatic grapey character and also a more citrus infused example from Kerner. A medium dry white is also produced, labelled simply Mumfords which is vinified from a blend of the white grapes. A light dry rosé is an aperitif style and the range is completed by the Mumfords Red, again very much a fruit-driven style.

Visiting

The vineyard is open for wine sales by appointment and group visits can be catered for by arrangement.

QUOINS ORGANIC
Bradford-on-Avon, Wiltshire

This newly established vineyard is located close to Bradford-on-Avon on the southernmost limits of Cotswold limestone. The vineyard is not open to the public at present, although the wine can be purchased through a number of local shops.

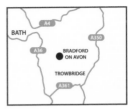

VINEYARD FACTS

- Organic vineyard, fully certified by the Soil Association.
- The vineyard has a southerly aspect and is planted in well-drained limestone soils offering good balanced acidity in the grapes.
- Three varieties planted and vinified separately, Madeleine Angevine, Orion and Rondo.
- All three wines vinified at Mumfords Vineyard.

The first vines were planted here in 2002 on a south facing slope, with a crop providing the first vintage in 2005. Quoins is also one of very few certified organic vineyards in the country, complying with the Soil Association's Organic standards.

Wine production
As a result of the status of the vineyard no spraying of fertilizers or pesticides is used and a natural balance and eco-system are being allowed to develop with the reintroduct-ion of local trees and other flora. A grass cover crop is grown to aid soil nutrition and natural compost used to spray the vines.

The wines are vinified at the Mumfords winery facility (see page 110), which has been certified by the Soil Association as acceptable in the crafting of organic wines. The three varieties planted here are each vinified to produce a single varietal example. There is a crisp and fresh dry Madeleine Angevine as well as an Orion, a new variety, which offers a softer more approachable style with lower acidity. The red Rondo, again from a relatively newly established grape is quite unusual. Most other producers tend to blend it. The grape provides wines with lots of colour and some structure and tannin. Wines from the neighbouring Little Ashley vineyard are also sold by Quoins and they also manage their vineyards. Look for a Madeleine Angevine and a Medium-Dry fruity style produced from Schönburger.

Visiting
Although the vineyard is not as yet open to the public the wines can be regularly encountered at local events and tastings, so it shouldn't be too difficult to find them.

HOW TO FIND US

- Address: Little Ashley, Bradford-on-Avon, Wiltshire BA15 1NF.
- Open: The vineyard is not open to the public. For queries tel: 01225 862334 or email.

Email:
alan@quoins.demon.co.uk
Web:
www.quoinsvineyard.co.uk

The dedicated grape-picking team

A'BECKETT'S
Devizes, Wiltshire

This leading Wiltshire vineyard is located between Stonehenge and Avebury. For anyone planning a day out to visit the two ancient sites, a stop here will be well worthwhile to sample this impressive range of wines.

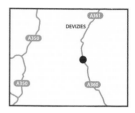

Paul and Lynn Langham established this small Wiltshire vineyard and began planting in 2001. The vineyard is located in the Vale of Pewsey in a hidden valley just to the north of the chalk downs of Salisbury Plain in the village of Littleton Panell and enjoys a particularly good specific, sheltered meso-climate, ideal for quality grape growing. It is considered an important landmark in the renaissance of Wiltshire viticulture and shows the real potential there is when vines are planted on the right soil on a good site.

The Vineyard
With around 5,100 vines now planted, the total vineyard area covers some 4.67 acres (1.89 ha). The vines are planted on

VINEYARD FACTS

- 4.67 acres (1.89 ha) under vine. 5,100 vines planted.
- Vineyards use Double Guyot trellising.
- Trellising ensures good levels of photosynthesis and sugar in the grapes.
- Wines currently vinified off-site.

greensand and chalk, the soils varying from a depth of 3 to 10 feet below the surface. Many of the vines will have to burrow deeply for nutrition and moisture and this low fertility environment provides just the right conditions for keeping canopy growth under control and achieving a better balance in the fruit. In optimising the performance of their vineyard, the Langhams have trained their vines by Double Guyot with replacement cane pruing each spring. A tight control is taken over the growth of the vines' canopy throughout the summer months. They have three white varieties planted: Pinot Auxerrois, Reichensteiner and Seyval Blanc. The reds are made up of Pinot Noir and Dunkenfelder. A little additional replanting was done in 2006 and they are considering increasing their Pinot and adding a little Chardonnay also.

The wine range

Wine production

Given the size of their vineyard and that they are very individually committed to the viticulture, the Langhams have contracted the winemaking out for the time being. However, this is in very good hands, being looked after by William Maitland Biddulph at Wickham Vineyards (see page 100). As a result they are able to benefit from the highly sophisticated modern winery facilities now in place at Wickham. A number of good well-made wines are produced here. First among equals is the Estate Sparkling white, very good in 2006 and made from a blend of Pinot Auxerrois and Seyval Blanc and offering just a touch of yeasty complexity to underpin its crisp piercing fruit. There's a good white Estate Blend made from Pinot Auxerrois and Reichensteiner, and a varietal white Seyval Blanc. The Estate Red blends the red varieties while the Estate Rosé blends a little Reichensteiner with Pinot Noir, providing a very floral and elegant example, particularly in the 2007.

Visiting

The vineyard is open to the public on Thursdays, Fridays, Saturdays and Bank Holidays, between

The Estate Sparkling wine

10.30 am and 5.30 pm. However this is a small working vineyard and it is advisable to telephone first to double check they are open before you travel. Wines can be purchased at the vineyard and organised tours and tastings can be organised for a nominal fee. You can also have nibbles with the tasting if you wish.

You can wander around the vineyard at your own leisure if you prefer. The wines are also available to purchase via the Langhams' website and are available in a number of local outlets in Wiltshire, Berkshire and Oxfordshire. Both quality retail stores and farm shops are supplied, as well as Waitrose. You can also enjoy the wines at a number of local restaurants and they are available in selected Wadworth public houses in Wiltshire, Hampshire, Berkshire, Oxfordshire, Gloucestershire, Somerset, Worcestershire and Herefordshire.

HOW TO FIND US

- Address: High Street, Littleton Panell, Devizes, Wiltshire, SN10 4EN
- From Salisbury/ Stonehenge take the A360 towards Devizes and on entering West Lavington and Littleton Panell continue until you come to the national speed limit signs and turn right straight after the signs.
- Open: Thursdays, Fridays and Saturdays as well as Bank Holidays.

Tel: 01380 816669
Email: abeckettswine@aol.com
Web: www.abecketts.co.uk

The vines are vertically trellised for good light exposure

SOUTH WEST

South West

David Moore

Cornwall
1 Bosue Vineyard
2 Camel Valley
3 Polgoon

Devon
4 Kenton Vineyard
5 Old Walls
6 Pebblebed Vineyard
7 Sharpham Vineyard
8 Yearlstone

Gloucestershire
9 Strawberry Hill
10 Thornbury Castle
11 Three Choirs

Somerset
12 Dunkery Vineyard
13 Oatley Vineyard

**Isles of Scilly
& Channel Islands**
14 St. Martin's
15 La Mare

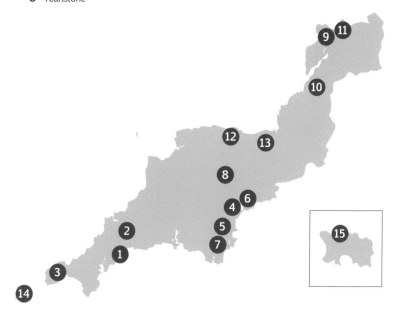

ST MARTIN'S
St Martin's, Isles of Scilly

Established in 1996 by Val and Graham Thomas , this is currently the only vineyard destination available to visitors in the Isles of Scilly. While a very small operation, it is worth the visit.

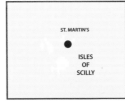

VINEYARD FACTS

- 1.24 acres (0.5 ha) under vine. 2,500 vines planted at a higher than normal density for UK vineyards.
- Eight varieties planted on well drained sand and loam over granite soils.
- Vineyards vertically trellised and Double Guyot trained to optimise exposure to sunlight and improve natural sugar levels.
- Wines vinified on site.

St Martin's is the most southerly vineyard in the South-West. The property was originally a flower farm, one of the major agricultural industries on the islands. The project has been gradually expanded in the intervening years and the wines are almost exclusively marketed to tourists.

Wine production
Having established through their trials that the vineyard was feasible the Thomases, assisted by a joint UK and European grant, expanded the vineyard and in 2004 commenced with their own on site winemaking. The climate here is mild although distinctly maritime, with an average summer temperature a little cooler than southern England. Frost though is not a problem. There is a wide range of grapes varieties planted which are Double Guyot trained. Reds consist of Rondo and Regent, while the whites planted are Orion, Seyval Blanc, Reichensteiner, Findling, Madeleine Angevine and Siegerrebe. The vineyard has a south facing aspect and the soil is good for vine cultivation, a loamy sandy top soil is underpinned by a granitic subsoil encouraging the vines to root deeply for lots of nutrition.

The first vintage was produced in 2000 and yielded just 150 bottles. Output has grown considerably since then and the winemaking is now done in a small on site winery, which Graham Thomas refers to as very basic "cottage industry" in style. This is not necessarily a bad thing, many of France's most characterful regional wines are produced in similar conditions. Three wines are produced a red, a white and a rosé.

Visiting
Although there are no refreshments at the vineyard, there are lots of places to eat very close by.

HOW TO FIND US

- Address: St Martin's, Isles of Scilly TR25 0QL
- From St. Martin's Higher Town Quay, turn right across Pool Green towards English island. The vineyard is on the left about 400 yards from the quay.
- Open: Weekdays 11:00 am to 4:00 pm.
Tel: 01720 423418
Email: grahamw.Thomas@lineone.net
Web: www.stmartinsvineyard.co.uk

The small vineyard has a maritime climate

LA MARE
St Mary, Jersey

This operation is now established as one of Jersey's main tourist destinations and is owned by Trevor Owen. It has a modern winemaking facility as well as a vineyard and distillery.

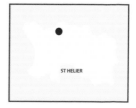

ST HELIER

This is one of Jersey's oldest properties with a number of the buildings dating back to the 1600s with the main farmhouse constructed in 1797. The vineyard was first planted by the Blayney family in 1972. They developed the vineyards and established the Jersey Distillery and Jersey Farmhouse Provision range before selling the property to Trevor Owen in 1997. As well as the vineyards there are fairly extensive orchards and cider is also important here. The farm has been instrumental in reintroducing cider apples to the island and this may prove to be a more successful and profitable crop than the more traditional potatoes that the island is known for. The bulk of the apple crop goes into the production of Jersey Apple Brandy using a century old Calvados pot still.

The Vineyard
The vineyard covers an extensive 25 acres (10.1 ha) making it one of Britain's larger single vineyards. Plant density is very much in line with other properties at around 1,000 vines per acre. The purpose

Modern stainless steel tanks

VINEYARD FACTS

- 25 acres (10.1 ha) under vine. 25,000 vines planted.
- Vineyards use Geneva Double Curtain, Double Guyot and Scott Henry trellising.
- Trellising ensures good levels of photosynthesis and sugar in the grapes.
- Sparkling wine produced and disgorged on site.
- Modern winery with stainless steel tanks, bladder press and gravity fed bottling.

GRAND VIN DE JERSEY
Cuvée de La Mare
12% Sparkling Ale 75cl

is to minimise excess growth in the vines' canopy and produce as much sugar in the grapes as possible. Originally planted using Geneva Double Curtain training, vines are also now trellised by Double Guyot and by the Scott Henry system. The latter method, which involves a split canopy trained both upwards and downwards has proved successful in the new world in improving both the quality of the fruit as well as securing an increase in yield. In the cooler climes of the United Kingdom the gains are less obvious but those beginning to use the system are clearly encouraged. Whites planted include Seyval Blanc, Phoenix, Orion and Reichensteiner. Red grapes are Regent, Rondo and Pinot Noir.

Wine and fine dining

BIOGRAPHY | Daniel de Carteret & Tim Crowley

Daniel was born in Jersey and has lived in New Zealand for the past nine years where he studied for three years before gaining his formal qualification as a winemaker. Daniel then worked in vineyards around New Zealand before returning to Jersey to take over the running of the vineyards and distillery. La Mare's MD Tim Crowley

was born in Cork, Ireland and moved to Jersey over 20 years ago. He took over the running of the estate 10 years ago and has managed its substantial growth since then. That includes a £2m development of a new winery, cognac style distillery, corporate function rooms, visitor centre and food production business.

Wine production

New Zealand born winemaker Daniel de Carteret oversees a modern winery which is extremely well equipped with stainless steel tanks for storage, settling and fermentation, a modern Willmes bladder press, gravity fed bottling as well as a giropallet and disgorger for the sparkling wines. Six labels are now released. These include two sparklers, which unsurprisingly are the flagship wines of the estate, two whites, a red and a rosé. The white Cuvée de La Mare is a Traditional Method wine produced from Seyval Blanc. This grape has proved successful for top sparkling whites, offering relatively neutral base wine but very good acidity, part of the key in this category of winemaking. The sparkling rosé Lillie comes solely from Pinot Noir. Of the two whites, Clos is fresh and fruity made from a blend of mainly aromatic grapes and as such is cool-fermented to preserve its delicate fruit character. The Domaine white, by contrast is a richer, rounder and fuller style vinified from Seyval Blanc and Phoenix and barrel-fermented and

The airy shop and tasting room

aged on lees to add greater weight and a rich texture. The Bailiwick is a fruit dominated red which gains additional depth and structure from ageing in small oak barrels. The range is now completed by a fresh, fruity rosé Perquage.

Visiting

There is a well organised visitor centre which is open between Easter and October from 10 am till 7 pm seven days a week. Thereafter the centre is open in November and December Mondays to Fridays during daylight hours. A restaurant and terrace overlooks the vines making a perfect vantage point to overlook the vineyards and enjoy a leisurely lunch. Extensive guided tours are available

and these take in the vineyards, orchards as well as distillery and a tasting is also included. There is a comprehensively stocked estate shop which includes all the Estate wines, brandies and liqueurs as well as other produce.

HOW TO FIND US

- Address: St Mary, Jersey JE3 3BA
- Head for the Devils Hole in St Mary, and follow our signs. (Ample Free Parking). Bus Route 7 from St Helier.
- Open: 7 days a week Easter to end of October 10am to 7pm and Mon to Fri 10am to 4pm November and December.

Email:
info@lamarevineyards.com
Web:
www.lamarevineyards.com

BOSUE VINEYARD
St Austell, Cornwall

One of a number of good quality vineyards from the far south-west. A small range of grape varieties is planted and modern approachable wines are what visitors will encounter here from the on site winery.

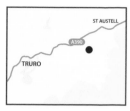

VINEYARD FACTS

- 3.5 acres (1.4 ha) under vine and a total of 3,500 vines planted.
- Vineyard sited on rich, fertile loam soils, necessitating considerable canopy control during the summer.
- The oldest vines now 12 years.
- Vinification and ageing is all done on site.

Background
Paul and Liz Sibley's small vineyard is one of Cornwall's more important wine sources. The vineyard was first established in 1996 with further regular plantings most years up to 2005.

Wine production
The majority of the vines are young at around 4 to 5 years of age. There is a gentle southerly aspect and the loamy soils tend to produce vines with fairly vigorous growth. Sensibly the vine density is low at 1,000 vines to the acre. Guyot training is employed with a mix of cane and spur pruning and considerable effort is expended in the management of the vine canopy during the summer months.

Just four varieties are planted, the white grapes Orion and Phoenix with Regent and Rondo for reds. Spraying is kept to a minimum and the vineyard farmed as much as possible by sustainable means. Vinification is all carried out on site in the Sibleys' own small cellar and the wines vinified to optimise the intensity of the delicate flavours particularly in the whites. The red is also aged in a mix of tank and French oak for between six and nine months. Screw-caps rather than corks are used to seal the wines and ensure consistent quality.

Two whites are now vinified as well as the red and the bountiful harvest of 2006 provided over 5,000 bottles in all. As was the case elsewhere, 2007 was less successful. For the 2008 vintage, a rosé and sparkling wine will be released for the first time.

Visiting
This is an entirely family run operation that is open by appointment only.

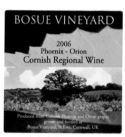

Label showing the southerly vineyard

The dry white

Wines can be tasted and purchased on site and are distributed locally in farm shops, hotels and restaurants.

HOW TO FIND US

- Bosue is just north of the village of St Ewe and a couple of miles south of the A390 St Austell to Truro road. The vineyard is marked on the OS map (Explorer 105) at grid 984 478, north of the minor road between Grampound and Heligan.
- Open: Tel: 01726 843159 or email to make an appointment

Email:
p.sibley@cornwallwines.co.uk
Web:
www.cornwallwines.co.uk

POLGOON
Penzance, Cornwall

This new small vineyard on the outskirts of Penzance may only have been planted in 2004 but its debut 2006 rosé won the Waitrose Trophy for best still rosé in the United Kingdom Vintners Association awards.

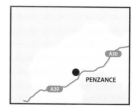

VINEYARD FACTS

- 13 acres (5.26 ha) under vine. 13,000 vines planted.
- Three white and four red grape varieties planted.
- Vineyards vertically trellised and Double Guyot trained to optimise exposure to sunlight and improve natural sugar levels.
- Wines now vinified on site.

When Kim and John Coulson discovered it in 2001, Polgoon was a derelict farm. Since they decided to buy it in 2002, they have set about completely renovating and restoring it. As well as producing wine from their vineyard they also make a grape juice, an apple juice and a sparkling cider, which is produced in the same way as their wines with a second fermentation in bottle.

The well trained vineyard

Wine production
Their vineyard was first planted in 2003 and 3,500 vines were planted on south-facing slopes behind the seaside town of Penzance. The project has evolved dramatically and there are now 13 acres (5.26 ha) under vine with a holding of 13,000 plants with a sensibly low vine density, ensuring that the level of vigorous growth during the summer is kept well under control. The soil is a well-drained sandy loam and relatively low in fertility and the vines trained by Double Guyot which, while more labour intensive to manage than other forms of trellising, ensures an optimum exposure of the canopy to sunlight and consequently achieves greater sugar and flavour in the grapes. An extensive range of varieties has been planted including Seyval Blanc, Bacchus, Ortega of the white varieties and Pinot Noir, Pinot Noir Précoce, Pinot Meunier and Rondo for reds. There is clearly much scope for development here.

Bob Lindo at Camel Valley (see page 122) gave the Coulsons much advice about their vineyards and was instrumental in vinifying the first wines. A new fully functional, modern winery has been established here and winemaker Jeremy Wood has the benefit of equipment that includes a pneumatic press and Speidel stainless steel tanks to keep a tight control on fermentations and ensure optimum temperature conditions for storage and processing. Sparkling rosé, as well as dry rosé, is now being produced and the sparkling wines will spend up to two years on their yeast lees to develop a real autolytic, as well as fruit, character.

Visiting
At present the vineyard is not yet open to the public but this will may change as soon as they increase their production, given the size of their holding. The wines are though, widely distributed locally.

HOW TO FIND US

- Address: Rosehill, Penzance, Cornwall TR20 8TE
- Open: Not open to visitors.
- Tel: 01736 333946
- Email: kim@polgoon.co.uk
- Web: www.polgoon.co.uk

CAMEL VALLEY
nr Bodmin, Cornwall

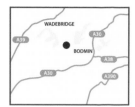

Bob and Annie Lindo's property is the top vineyard in Cornwall, fast establishing itself as one of the country's best sparkling wine sources. Good, well made white, rosé and red are also produced.

The Lindos planted vineyards on their family farm producing their first vintage in 1992. Over the past decade and a half the family have dedicated themselves to producing the best quality grapes they possibly can from their south-facing vineyard site and have developed arrangements with a number of other growers to supply an ever increasing demand. The wines are widely available not just in Cornwall but also further afield on top restaurant and retail wine lists.

The Vineyard
The steep slopes at Camel Valley have a direct, southerly aspect and overlook the Camel River. They tend to enjoy particularly balmy, sunny summers and early autumns, enabling a slow and full ripening of the grapes. A range of varieties is planted and Seyval Blanc works particularly well here, achieving an intense flavour as well as retaining the necessary acidity to provide excellent raw material for sparkling base wine. As winemaker Sam Lindo points out, controlling yield is important, as elsewhere in the wine world to get great flavour in the fruit. However ripening the grapes at all is a perennial problem for English winegrowers. The vineyards are therefore trained to optimise light exposure.

Wine production
The family have invested heavily in their new purpose built on site winery ensuring the optimum quality and balance in their wines. The first run juice at harvest can be cold settled at low temperature, capturing

VINEYARD FACTS

- 16 acres under vine. 20,000 vines planted.
- Grapes bought in from contract growers to supplement winery needs.
- Vineyards mostly trained to Single Guyot.
- Vertical trellising ensures good levels of photosynthesis and sugar in the grapes.
- Gyropalettes used for automated sparkling wine riddling.
- Extensively equipped winery with stainless steel tanks and full temperature control.

Visitors enjoy tasting the wines on the terrace

BIOGRAPHY | Bob Lindo

After leaving the RAF, Bob Lindo made the brave decision to plant his family vineyard to vines in 1989. From the outset he was determined to concentrate on producing wines of regional character and distinction and at all times focussing on achieving the finest quality in the grapes he has been growing. He is modest about the success that Camel Valley has enjoyed, winning international awards and having wines served to HM the Queen at the banquet for the State Opening of Parliament. Bob also takes considerable pride that his son Sam, who has taken on the winemaking reins, should become the "UK Winemaker of the Year".

all the delicate aromas that characterise the best English wines. Reds are also cold macerated prior to fermentation to emphasise their soft juicy fruit. Expensive bladder presses are used and juice quality for the sparkling wines is comparable with top examples from elsewhere. As well as their Cornwall Brut, the family also produces a 100% sparkling white from Pinot Noir and from the sparkling pressings, Atlantic, a white which is a rounder style and better suited to food.

Sam Lindo is very much the hands-on winemaker at Cornwall's most important winery facility at Camel Valley. While contract winemaking is less a priority here, the Lindo's have been instrumental in creating some excellent wines.

Visiting
The old stone building which now houses the airy shop and tasting room was originally home to the winery. It's now a very important tourist destination for the county and around half the Camel Valley output is sold through the vineyard shop. Regular guided tours are offered and also once weekly winemaker led

vineyard and winery tours on Wednesdays from April to October. There are also a number of self-catering cottages overlooking the vines if you care to stay.

HOW TO FIND US

Camel Valley vineyard is approximately 2 miles north of Bodmin off the A389 to Wadebridge. Follow brown **Vineyard** sign one mile to vineyard.

Opening times
- All year round Monday to Friday 10am-5pm
- Saturdays: Easter until end October
- Sundays: Bank holidays only
- Christmas: Closed Christmas Eve until 2nd January

Tel: 01208 77959
Email: info@camelvalley.com
Web: www.camelvalley.com

The Wines

Vintage Cornwall Brut

This comes from Seyval Blanc, Reichensteiner and Huxelrebe and gets 15 months' ageing on lees in bottle. Subtly aromatic but offers impressive weight and a touch of yeasty, bready complexity.

Vintage Sparkling Pinot Noir Rosé

A 100% varietal example, with quite deep salmon pink colour and good intensity. Vibrant, subtle raspberry fruit ensures a wine with much better depth and verve than many a pink Champagne.

Camel Valley Bacchus

Good, fresh example of this aromatic and characterful white, produced in a completely dry style. The subtle, grassy notes of the wine are underpinned by a fine, mineral and citrus quality.

Camel Valley Rosé

A dark and intense rosé made from a mix of Pinot Noir pressings as well as around a quarter Dornfelder adding additional colour and vibrancy. Real purity and depth for the style.

KENTON VINEYARD
Kenton, Devon

A newly established vineyard, close to Exeter, showing all the signs of making some of the best wines in Devon from sheltered south-facing slopes. Characterful red, white, rosé and sparkling wines are all made.

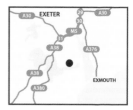

Matthew and Jo Bernstein first planted their vineyards in 2003, having looked for the ideal location for a couple of years. Their scenic property was originally an old Devon farm and is to be found on the western side of the Exe Estuary nestled into the lower slopes of the Haldon Hills. Their wines differ from a number of others, being made from their own single estate fruit. Everything is done on site with the exception of bottle ageing and disgorging the sparkling white, which is carried out at Three Choirs (see page 139).

VINEYARD FACTS

- 8 acres (3.23 ha) planted at the end of 2007.
- Vineyards trained to Guyot and Scott-Henry.
- Vertical trellising ensures good levels of photosynthesis and sugar in the grapes.
- Wines all produced on-site with temperature control for fermentation and assemblage.

The Vineyard
Matthew Bernstein takes the growing of his grapes very seriously and studied at Plumpton College in Surrey prior to establishing the vineyard. Site selection was obviously crucial, with south-facing slopes, well-drained sandstone soils and a particularly warm and sunny mesoclimate, with good drying breezes blowing in from the Exe and crucially relatively frost free after mid April. Vine trellising is, as everywhere in England, crucial to quality. Guyot training is employed as well as Scott-Henry and considerable care taken through the growing cycle to maximise the light exposure on the vines' canopy.

Wine production
The new winery was constructed at the same time as the vineyard was established. Matthew has invested heavily in modern

The airy, well laid out tasting room

The Bernsteins decided on a lifestyle change in the early part of this century. They decided they wanted to settle in Devon for family reasons and because the area provided a combination of good wine quality and a good local market in which to sell the wines, an important consideration in the UK. Matthew enrolled at Plumpton to take the two year-long course in viticulture and winemaking, and then spent 18 months scouring the West Country, for a suitable site, before finding the near derelict estate farm that is now home to Kenton Vineyard. He is a committed student of his subject and reads as widely as he can to optimise the potential of his site.

Kenton's well-sited vineyards

stainless steel vinification equipment to optimise the fresh and fragrant character he can unquestionably achieve in his wines. A cool room, which will help with both maintaining the character of the whites as well as helping the red through its malolactic is high on his priorities.

Visiting

The vineyard and winery are now fully open to the public from the end of May to the end of September and around 2,000 visitors called in during 2007. There is a large vineyard shop where you can taste the wines and then take in the views over the vines from the sunny terrace. If you prefer you can consider a self-guided tour taking in the Vine Trail through the vineyards, or you might prefer to take a guided "meet the winemaker" tour which is available on Sundays during the summer.

- Address: Helwell Barton, Kenton, Devon EX6 8NW
- If you are travelling south from Exeter turn inland off the A379 just south of Starcross, opposite Cockwood harbour. Take the first left (opposite the entrance to the golf course), and continue on this road for about 2 miles. At Black Forest Lodge Cross take the right turning (signposted Kenn) and the vineyard is on your right after 800 metres.
- Open: End of May to the end of September between 12am - 4pm. On Thursdays and Sundays between 11am - 5pm.

Tel: 01626 891091
Email: info@kentonvineyard.co.uk
Web: www.kentonvineyard.co.uk

The Wines

Kenton Vintage Brut

Produced from Ortega and Auxerrois this is a forward, fruit-driven sparkling white aged for nine months on lees in bottle. Fresh green apple fruit is the dominant character, rather than a more evolved bready, yeasty character.

Kenton Ortega

Very good, fresh and lightly aromatic dry white produced solely from Ortega in 2006, offering depth and impressive fruit intensity. Dry white has also been released as Estate White, although Ortega is always the key component.

Kenton Estate Rosé

Made from Pinot Noir, this is a fresh, intense rosé with marked red berry fruit character. Good fresh, zippy acidity provides not only a couple of years fresh fruit but a little structure and grip.

Kenton Estate Red

A blend of Rondo and early Pinot Noir, a red of upfront bright berry fruit and good grip and supple tannin from the Rondo. Indeed the variety can produce earthy, rustic notes in some producers' wines but not here where ripe, spicy and approachable fruit characters are key.

OLD WALLS VINEYARD
Bishopsteignton, Devon

This is a further indication of the potential for quality wines from Devon. Old Walls is located a few miles inland from the English Channel and north of the River Teign.

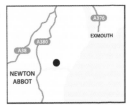

There is evidence of a vineyard on the site here from over 2,000 years ago. No doubt the Romans at the time were aware of the need for south-facing vineyards with well-drained soils. Far more contemporarily the Dawe family is following in the Roman traditions. They have though farmed the surrounding land for over 90 years, so their site is nothing new to them. Father and son Ken and Paul Dawe look after the vine growing and winery between them, while Lesley Dawe, along with the help of her daughter Lisa, looks after the Tea Rooms and wine shop. The name of the vineyard comes from what remains of the "old walls" of the 13th century Bishops Palace of Bishopsteignton. Ken Dawe is involved with the local project which intends to preserve this ancient monument for future generations.

The Vineyard

The vineyard itself was first established in 2002 and there are now 8 acres (3.24 ha) planted and to around 8,000 vines. The soil is good and well drained and balanced with reasonable but not excessive fertility. It is a typical red Devon sandstone and the vine density of just over 1,000 vines per acre will allow for good control over the growth of the canopy during the vigorous summer months and avoid potential green flavours in the grapes. Trellising and training is Double Guyot, which is quite labour intensive but enables the canopy to be trained upwards with good light exposure. An extensive range of grapes is planted. The whites consist of Reichensteiner, Bacchus and Auxerrois, while the reds planted are Regent, Rondo, Dunkelfelder and Pinot Noir Précoce.

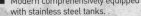
Red, white and rosé are made

VINEYARD FACTS

- 8 acres (3.24 ha) under vine. 8,000 vines planted.
- Vineyards uses Double Guyot training.
- Trellising ensures good levels of photosynthesis and sugar in the grapes.
- Modern comprehensively equipped winery with stainless steel tanks.

BIOGRAPHY   Ken and Lesley Dawe

Ken and Lesley Dawe decided in 2002 that they could add to the potential of their farm by planting a vineyard. This decision was made easier for them by the particular characteristics of their land with well-drained soil, crucially low in fertility and a steep south facing aspect to the land. Both these factors crucial in contributing to the character of their terroir. This is very much a family venture, in the same way as you will find in small domains in many of France's wine regions, with both their son Paul and daughter Lisa working with them.

The steeply sloping vineyard

Wine production

Old Walls differs from many other smaller English vineyards in that they make their wines themselves. To this end they are helped by winemaker Hans Schliefer. They have an extremely modern well-equipped small winery and have invested heavily in their equipment. This includes a full range of stainless steel equipment to produce 26,000 bottles, a crusher and de-stemmer, pneumatic press, plate filter, variable capacity tanks, a bottle steriliser and rinser, 8 head bottle filler, semi automatic corker, capsule shrinker, labelling machine, neck freezer, corker & wire muzzler. Very few other operations of this size are equipped to this level. While good quality wine is undoubtedly "made in the vineyard", a careful control of all the wine making processes improves the potential of the wine in the bottle. Of the wines pride of place goes to the Quality Sparkling Brut, coming from Auxerrois and Pinot Noir Précoce and this has been joined by a sparkling rosé. There are two reds, one a varietal Rondo, whereas the Palace Red blends Regent, Rondo and Dunkelfelder. There is also a rosé from Pinot Noir Précoce and a dry white from Bacchus and a medium dry style produced from Reichensteiner.

Visiting

The vineyard and winery are both open to the public. There is both a wine shop and Tea Rooms here to attract visitors. A comprehensive range of light snacks can be enjoyed with a glass or two of Old Walls wine. This includes morning coffee, a snack lunch or afternoon tea. A number of vineyard and winery tours can also be undertaken which can cater for both individuals or for larger groups. Visitors should be aware that the weather conditions will affect the suitability of a vineyard tour and the vineyards themselves are steep and will not be suitable for anyone of limited mobility. In the modern winery you will be able to view the various processes involved in making the wine. There is also a large meeting room on site that can host 30 people and this would make an excellent alternative for small business conferences.

HOW TO FIND US

- Address: Old Walls Vineyard, Old Walls Road, Bishopsteignton, TQ14 9PQ
- From A380 follow directions to Teignmouth on A381. Continue for approx. 2 miles, passing Jacks Patch Garden Centre. Take next left into village. Continue to Ring Of Bells and turn right. Follow road to small crossroads; Whidborne Manor is on the left.
- Open: Wednesday – Sunday (inclusive) 10:30am – 4:00pm. Open Bank Holidays.

Tel: 01626 770877

Email: enquiries@oldwalls vineyard.co.uk

Web: www.oldwallsvineyard.co.uk

PEBBLEBED VINEYARD
Topsham, Devon

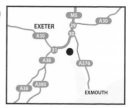

This fine Devon vineyard operation is run on organic principles and is in the process of partial conversion to biodynamic farming. It is not just one vineyard but three which adds a real logistical challenge each harvest.

Geoff Bowen's passion for viticulture began with a community vineyard project at his neighbours' Gail and David Leeder's property, Eden. This vineyard is still very much active today. Since 2002 he and his wife Anna have developed three further vineyards, with his original Ebford Vineyard now certified as organic by the Soil Association. It is named after the deep pebblebed ridge that stretches across large tracts of east Devon.

The Vineyard
There are now three separate vineyards covering a total of 22 acres (8.9 ha), which makes this one of the larger holdings in the south-west. The Ebford and Clyst St George sites are near Topsham, while the West Hill vineyard is near Ottery St Mary. Unquestionably the organisation of the three separate sites is a challenge, however there are undoubted advantages. Some varieties will be better suited to different sites and the perennial risks of disease and frost damage in the marginal English climate can be reduced. Different parcels can be vinified separately and in the longer term individual cru bottlings will also be possible.

The Ebford vineyard is the first Geoff planted in 2002. It is now certified as fully organic and the 8 acres (3.25 ha) planted to a mix of Pinot Noir Précoce, Seyval Blanc, Madeleine Angevine and Rondo. The soil is a sandy loam with underlying sand, marl and pebblebeds and the vines are Double Guyot trained. 6 acres (2.4 ha) are planted at

VINEYARD FACTS

- 22 acres (8.9 ha) in total under vine. Three separate vineyard sites.
- Organic farming practised with some biodynamic experimentation and one vineyard certified organic by the Soil Association.
- Vineyards trained to Double Guyot.
- Black plastic covers used between vine rows to warm the soil.
- Wines vinified in an extensively equipped winery with stainless steel tanks and full temperature control.

Vertically trained vines attracting the sunlight

BIOGRAPHY   Geoff Bowen

Geoff Bowen has a background as a hydrogeologist (studying rocks and groundwater) which has provided him with a very solid base in becoming a successful viticulturalist. Along with a number of others he built up an environmental consultancy in which he sold his interest in 2004 in order to devote most of his time to Pebblebed. He has wisely so far concentrated on his vineyards, having the wines vinified for him at Yearlstone. He is a Trustee with the Devon Wildlife Trust and a Director of the Devon Environmental Business Initiative.

West Hill to a mix of Pinot Noir Précoce, Seyval Blanc, a little Rondo and a small experimental area of Cabernet Sauvignon and Merlot. The soil has thinner pebblebeds and is a touch more acidic but with a good mineral content. At Clyst St George 8 acres (3.25 ha) are now planted and will be fully organic by 2009/10. The vineyard is a mix of Seyval Blanc and Rondo.

The Brut Rosé — enjoy it with fresh oysters

Wine Production

The wines are all currently made by Juliet White at her well equipped winery at Yearlstone (see page 132). Facilities include a cool room to keep grapes and wines fresh and aid reds through malolactic fermentation. A brand new bottling line has also been installed with bottling under screwcap. Cool fermentations ensure consistently fresh and attractive white and rosé styles. The Dry White is a blend of Seyval Blanc and Madeleine Angevine, the Rosé vinified from Rondo, Madeleine Angevine and Seyval Blanc. A 2006 red produced from Rondo will be released in late 2008. A Sparkling Rosé is also made, a blend of Rondo and Seyval Blanc, the grapes picked around a week earlier for the base wine.

The dry Rosé

Visiting

There is now a new tasting cellar in Topsham which was opened in late May 2008. You can taste Pebblebed wines as well as guest wines with a range of cheeses and meat tapas. Vineyard tours are also possible, although you will have to make a specific appointment. Like Three Choirs in Gloucestershire (see page 139), there is a new scheme whereby customers can "adopt a vine" with their own name plate and follow its progress through the year. This will be of real interest for those who wish to see how a vineyard really works. You will also get a tailored vineyard tour and wine tasting and free membership of the "Friends of Pebblebed". The cost is £15 and includes discounts on wine purchases. If you want to spend a few days in the area, there are holiday lets available at Pebblebed House in Topsham, just above the cellar. Vineyard tours and tastings can be incorporated as you wish. See www.pebblebedhouse.co.uk for further details.

SHARPHAM VINEYARD
Totnes, Devon

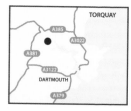

Sharpham is one of Devon's very best vineyards, with excellent wines and spectacular views. It was first planted to vines in 1981 by the late Maurice Ash with advice from Gillian Pearkes, original owner of Yearlstone (see page 132).

The estate, which comprises some 550 acres (222 ha) in all was purchased in the early 1960s and the Ash family moved the property towards sustainable farming and banned hunting. The estate is recorded in the Domesday book with the earliest reference being in 1088. Construction of the current Sharpham House began in 1770 by a naval captain who had received a considerable sum with a share of the bounty for a captured Spanish vessel during the Seven Years War. It provides a very impressive backdrop to the vineyards which overlook a curve in the river Dart, just below Totnes.

The Vineyard
The vineyard is south facing and over three-quarters is planted to Madeleine Angevine which ripens particularly successfully here, with cool moderating breezes drifting up the River Dart. A number of other varieties are also planted including Pinot Noir

Some of the finest whites from the South-West

and Pinot Gris and grapes are also bought in from other vineyards, notably in Suffolk. Much consideration is given to effective vine training and the vineyard has now been moved over to the Scott-Henry trellising system, ensuring optimum, light exposure for the vines' canopy.

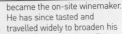

BIOGRAPHY — Mark Sharman

Mark Sharman took over the running of Sharpham Vineyard in 1988. He very quickly realised the need for some training and enrolled on the first ever Viticulture and Oenology course in the UK at Plumpton College (see page 64). The 1989 Vintage was made with Mark assisting the contracted winemaker. Then in 1990 the farm's straw shed was converted into a winery and he became the on-site winemaker. He has since tasted and travelled widely to broaden his knowledge. The UK wine world was initially surprised by his wines, especially the Beenleigh Red, a blend of Cabernet Sauvignon and Merlot, which won best English red wine on a number of occasions. The whites have been consistently and justifiably in the awards for many years.

Wine Production

There is a modern well-equipped winery on site with stainless steel vats for fermentation and storage and a surprising number of oak barrels, used in the production of the barrel-fermented Sharpham white, as well as the juicy, lightly-oaked Sharpham red and more densely structured Beenleigh Bordeaux blend. Base wine for the new vintage sparkling white is vinified at the winery and then bottled and aged on lees at Three Choirs winery (see page 139), for a minimum of two years prior to disgorging. 2005 was a blend of Pinot Noir and Pinot Blanc and the base wine for 2007 is a potentially very impressive blend of Pinot Blanc, Auxerrois, Pinot Gris, Pinot Meunier and Pinot Noir. A 2005 Pinot Noir also showed good potential as did the white Dart Valley Reserve 2006 white, a blend of Phoenix, Madeleine and Bacchus, along with a 2007 fresh, intense Bacchus.

Visiting

There is a small shop with catering in the summer from fresh local produce. The property is also an excellent source for local cheeses produced solely

Vineyards overlook the Dart

from estate milk. Regular guided vineyard tours are offered and you can also undertake your own trek around the estate before tasting. One of these is a must if you are visiting during the summer.

HOW TO FIND US

- Address: Totnes, Devon TQ9 7UT
- Follow the brown tourist signs from the A381, Totnes to Dartmouth road. Take the marked lefthand turning just outside Totnes.
- Open: Monday to Saturday 10am-5pm March 1st – Christmas Eve and every day in June, July and August.

Tel: 01803 732203
Email: info@sharpham.com
Web: www.sharpham.com

The Wines

Sharpham Estate Selection

This is 100% Madeleine Angevine with very good, fragrant, delicate green fruit and underlying citrus intensity. Drink young and fresh on its own or with seafood.

Sharpham Barrel-Fermented

Again solely from Madeleine Angevine, with a nice balance of restrained green fruit and subtle oak. With good natural acidity, the wine gains weight and dimension from going through the malolactic fermentation.

Sharpham Rosé

A short period of skin contact prior to fermentation gives this fresh, crisp rosé lots of attractive fresh berry fruit. Coming from Dornfelder, the wine will develop nicely for two or three years.

Sharpham Red

A blend of Dornfelder and Rondo, the latter adding colour. A three day cold soak prior to fermentation and ageing in oak provides a wine with good depth and concentrated dark berry fruit.

Beenleigh Red

A blend of Cabernet Sauvignon and Merlot, this has a touch of Loire leafiness as well as a cedary backbone. Grown on well-drained steeply sloping stony soils in polytunnels, which crucially keeps the vine vigour and leaf growth under control. Production is tiny though, generally only two barrels a year.

YEARLSTONE
Bickleigh, Devon

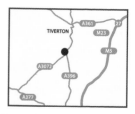

One of the older of the current English vineyards and Devon's oldest. It overlooks the river Exe with spectacular views over the river valley and the quiet and picturesque village of Bickleigh.

The property was planted in 1976 by the late Gillian Pearkes, a pioneering English viticulturalist of her time. The very marginal climate and the consequent problems of achieving a nicely ripened crop from her original vineyards led current owners Roger and Juliet White to replant with a lower vineyard density enabling them to achieve a finer balance of subtle, aromatic and delicate fruit aromas. A small, well made range of white, rosé and red wines are produced along with a fine sparkling brut.

The Vineyard
The original vineyard is mainly planted to Madeleine Angevine with some Pinot Noir and Pinot Gris as well as a little Pinot Blanc. The Devon red sandstone subsoil

Steeply sloped south facing vineyards

VINEYARD FACTS

- 7.5 acres (3 ha) under vine on well-drained red Devon sandstone soils.
- 2 vineyard sites.
- Fruit bought in to supplement winery needs.
- Contract winemaking offered to a number of small local vineyards.

offers excellent drainage and the steeply sloped vineyard has a southerly exposition. Replanting continues, not only to optimise balance in the vineyard, but also because vines in our country can often struggle to provide a viable crop for more than 30 years or so. The English climate is less than propitious for cultivating those very old vines found in warmer regions. Crops here are low anyway, often only two tons to the acre (that's low). A second site, the Quarry Vineyard was planted to red Dornfelder and white Seyval Blanc in 2003. The Seyval providing excellent acidity for sparkling wines.

As with all marginal climates viticulture is crucial. Careful management of the vine canopy ensures optimum exposure of sunlight during the growing cycle. This not only provides for nicely ripened grapes at harvest but also helps in warding off mildews and other malevolent vine infections.

BIOGRAPHY   Juliet White

Food scientist Juliet and former BBC journalist Roger White purchased Yearlstone in 1994. With her scientific background it made perfect sense for Juliet to study winemaking at Plumpton College and Yearlstone is now one of Devon's winemaking landmarks. Her wines took 8 out of 65 awards at the 2007 English wine competition of the year. Roger manages the vineyards and if you are tasting with him he'll be happy to chat about England's chances of beating the All Blacks at rugby or retaining the Ashes from the Aussies. He says his biggest gamble was purchasing Yearlstone with a bridging loan. Juliet reckons hers was marrying Roger!

Wine production

Juliet trained in oenology at Plumpton College, England's increasingly well-regarded academic resource of viticulture and vinification (see page 64). She also makes wines for a number of other local vineyard owners. While top winemakers can generally rely on the quality of their own freshly harvested grapes, it can sometimes be a touch more challenging from fruit bought in by their clients. The Whites' winery though is now very well equipped, with stainless steel tanks and full temperature control along with a cool room which not only aids chilling operations but can also be used to hasten the reds through malolactic fermentation. Among Juliet's recent additions are a membrane press ensuring excellent first run juice, vital for top quality sparklers and a new state of the art bottling line. As elsewhere, the wines, with the obvious exception of the Sparkling Brut, are bottled under screwcap ensuring both their freshness and consistency. As well as the wine covered in the notes, look out for the No 1, a blend Huxelrebe and Reichensteiner and the floral No 2 from Madeleine Angevine.

Yearlstone
ENGLISH REGIONAL WINE
THE YEARLSTONE CODE
1 - ZINGY, GRASSY DRY WHITE
2 - SOFT AND FLORAL DRY WHITE
3 - DELICATE DRY ROSÉ
4 - LIGHT FRUITY RED
5 - AROMATIC DRY WHITE
6 - BARREL AGED DRY WHITE
THE WINEMAKERS
JULIET WHITE - ENGLISH WINE IS LIGHT AND FRESH WITH WONDERFUL AROMAS - MAKING IT PERFECT AS AN APERITIF OR WITH LIGHT SEASONAL ENGLISH FOOD.
YEARLSTONE VINEYARD SITS ON STEEP RED DEVON SANDSTONE SLOPES ABOVE THE EXE RIVER VALLEY - WHY NOT PAY US A VISIT?
ROGER & JULIET
WWW.YEARLSTONE.CO.UK
ESTATE BOTTLED AT YEARLSTONE VINEYARD, BICKLEIGH, DEVON EX16 8RL
CONTAINS SULPHITES
12% vol   2006   75cl ℮

The back label information

Visiting

Visitors can enjoy panoramic views of the vineyards while enjoying a light lunch in the Terrace Café. There are regular guided tours of both vineyard and winery and groups can also be accommodated.

HOW TO FIND US

- Address: Bickleigh, Devon EX16 8RL
- From the M5 southbound take exit and the A361 towards Barnstaple. Take the A396 south towards Bickleigh and Exeter. Just before you reach Bickleigh there is a right hand turn up a steep lane to the vineyard from which you are directed by a brown tourism signpost.
- Open: Every day May to October — check website for further details.

Tel: 01884 855726
Email: info@yearlstone.co.uk
Web: www.yearlstone.co.uk

The Wines

Yearlstone No 5

This is a varietal Siegerebe, not dissimilar to a Gewurztraminer, with a very aromatic quality. It's essential to drink it as young as possible to benefit from these spicy as well as fragile aromas.

Yearlstone No 6

Arguably the best of the whites. A fine blend of Pinot Gris, Reichensteiner and Madeleine Angevine. An impressive weight and minerality here. The wine benefits from a limited period in small barrels adding both depth and structure. This is less obviously aromatic than the other three whites, which readers should be aware of.

Yearlstone No 3

A fresh and immensely enjoyable rosé, a blend of Pinot Noir, Madeleine Angevine and Seyval Blanc. The white grapes no doubt add a floral and fresh edge to the structure and soft grip of the Pinot Noir. Enjoy this as an aperitif or with food.

Yearlstone No 4

Produced from Rondo and Dornfelder this has a typically full, juicy almost brambly fruit character. Soft and approachable with excellent underlying acidity holding everything together.

Sparkling Vintage Brut

From 100% Seyval Blanc. Classic Champagne method vinification with whole bunch pressing and only the first 50% of the juice used. Good fruit purity and depth with additional complexity offered by 15 months on lees.

DUNKERY VINEYARD
Minehead, Somerset

Derek and Valerie Pritchard's vineyard is in the heart of the Exmoor National Park. Wines can be bought direct from the winery and an interesting range of other items are available through their mail order operation, Exmoor Excellence.

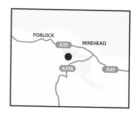

The vineyards at Dunkery are now of quite considerable age and were first planted in 1984. That process continued until 1993. The Pritchards have a number of other projects, among them Exmoor Excellence a mail order business from which they sell not only the Dunkery Vineyard reds and whites but also wines from a vineyard in the Saar in Germany which they purchased in 1988 and worked until 2001. They grew Riesling on steep sloping vineyards and the

Newly bottled wines

early wines they produced were vinified under the supervision of Bernd Philippi of the great Koehler-Ruprecht property in the Pfalz. A range of other high quality goods is also available including local artist Susan Ferguson's watercolours.

The Vineyard
The vineyard area now covers a total of 4 acres (1.62 ha) across two different sites with 4,000 vines planted. The original vineyard is just 1 acre (0.4 ha) and is extremely steep and must be worked entirely by hand with equipment in back packs. The plant density is higher than is normally the case in England and the vines trained by Double Guyot. While labour intensive this will give better fruit. The

VINEYARD FACTS

- 4 acres (1.62 ha) under vine.
- Well-drained Devon sandstone soil of low fertility.
- Vineyards trained to Double Guyot.
- Trellising ensures good levels of photosynthesis and sugar in the grapes.
- Modern well-equipped small winery.

site has the enviable position of being frost free and during the summer and autumn has cooler than normal nights, which builds acidity in the wines. The second 3 acre (1.2 ha) site is less sheltered and flatter although planted on the same Devon sandstone soil which is excellent for vine growing with good

A view of the winery

BIOGRAPHY **Derek and Valerie Pritchard**

Derek Pritchard was originally a research physicist, later spending 14 years designing and developing commercial computer systems. At the end of that period he and his wife decided that they wanted to live on Exmoor. They still wished to drink fine wine every day so decided to grow and make their own. Since the mid 1980s they spent a lot of time in Germany, Luxembourg and France learning about vines and wines, and importing vines and equipment to supply other English and Welsh vineyards; they discovered and introduced many new vine varieties into the UK. Between 1988 and 2001 they owned and worked vineyards on steep slopes in the Saar Valley, growing Riesling wines; German TV made a half-hour documentary about them in 1991.

drainage and low fertility. It also catches the sun all day and initially, rather than using a Guyot training approach in this site Derek established the vines on a Sylvoz trellis with the aim of maximising light exposure for the vines' canopy. He has begun to move everything back to Double Guyot because of the local badger population. Whites planted are Reichensteiner, Madeleine Angevine, Kernling, Orion and Merzling, reds Rondo, Regent, Dornfelder and Dunkelfelder. A little Chardonnay and Pinot Noir was also planted for sparkling wines and a rosé, although this has since been grubbed up. The harvest generally takes place between late September and early November.

Wine production

There is a modern, very well-equipped winery. It is located at the "small vineyard" and is actually partly dug into the hillside. Processing is kept to a minimum and the wines are bottled, all with some ageing. The harvested grapes are crushed and de-stemmed and then very gently processed in a rubber membrane press. Fermentation and ageing of the whites takes place in stainless steel after a short period of skin contact. The wine is kept on lees for a

time in tank before bottling to give extra weight and a richer texture. The reds are all aged in a mix of American and French oak barrels.

Two dry whites are made, a Madeleine Angevine and a Reichensteiner. A medium sweet white still available for the time being, comes from a blend of Senator, Phoenix and Chardonnay. The wine is best served chilled and is quite German in style with a low alcohol,

The 6-head bottle filler

of around 8.5 per cent. There is also a 'blanc de noirs' Pinot Noir bottle-fermented sparkling wine, 'Exmoor Brut'. The rosé, available in July 2008, was a 2006 vintage vinified from Pinot Noir which is intended to be a good food wine. Expect this to come from other varieties in future. There are two older reds which include a Pinot Noir and a blend including Pinot Noir. Of the more recent vintage reds, the first is a varietal Rondo, aged in barriques as well as a more

typically English blend of Regent and Dunkenfelder. Both are aged in barriques for up to eight months.

Visiting

Visits can be made to the vineyard and wines can be purchased and tasted at the winery. It is though necessary to make an appointment first. There is a licence for retail wine sales and free tastings can be arranged for groups and tours provided. The wines are also widely available locally in Somerset and Devon in shops and on restaurant wine lists. Derek Pritchard regularly attends local shows and fairs and details of these are maintained on the website.

HOW TO FIND US

■ Wooton Courtenay, Minehead, Somerset TA24 8RD
■ The vineyard and winery are open by appointment and located in the beautiful Exmoor National Park, near the village of Wootton Courtenay. It is close to Minehead, Porlock and Dunster.
■ Open: By appointment. Telephone Derek Pritchard for details
Tel: 01643 841 505
Email: Derek@exmoor-excellence.com
Web: www.exmoor-excellence.com/dunkery/

OATLEY VINEYARD
Bridgwater, Somerset

Iain and Jane Awty planted their vineyard near Bridgwater in 1986 from which they produce two crisp dry white wines. "Leonora's" comes from Kernling and the more approachable and softer "Jane's" from Madeleine Angevine.

The Awtys' vineyard is located on a south-east facing slope at 30 to 70 metres above sea level between the Quantock Hills and the Bristol channel is planted to just the two white varieties.

Wine production

Some thought has gone into where they have planted their vines. The Madeleine Angevine is earlier ripening and has

The south-east facing vineyard slopes

been established on their more easterly and cooler plots. The later ripening Kernling to the west of the vineyard, where there is more warmth and the risk of spring frosts can be reduced.

Different pruning methods are used for the two varieties. The Kernling is Guyot trained and the vines pruned by replacement cane each year. This is more labour intensive than spur pruning but the variety responds best if pruned this way. In the lower lying sections of the vineyard the Madeleine Angevine is easier to manage and is spur pruned with the vines trained upwards from older laid down wood. The vines can then be efficiently hedge trimmed, keeping growth under control, important in the relatively fertile soils here.

The Oatley whites

Of the two wines the "Leonora's" bottling has a firmer structure with higher acidity and is likely to keep a year or two longer. Additionally although the Kernling grape has a lightly pink skin, a clean cool fermentation avoids any colour pick up from the skins.

Visiting

Visitors are welcome, although you will need to contact them to make an appointment and get directions. Wines can also be supplied for special functions with personalised labels.

HOW TO FIND US

- Address: Cannington, Bridgwater, Somerset TA5 2NL
- The vineyard is located just to the west of Cannington off the A39 on Oatley Lane. Contact for specific directions.
- Open: Tel: 01278 671340 or email to make an appointment

Email:
wine@oatleyvineyard.co.uk
Web:
www.oatleyvineyard.co.uk

STRAWBERRY HILL
Newent, Gloucestershire

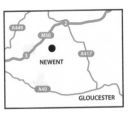

One of Gloucestershire's more recently established vineyards, Strawberry Hill is notable not just for growing the more typical Germanic origin grape varieties but also some of the French classics, albeit with the aid of glasshouses.

VINEYARD FACTS

- A range of varieties planted including 1 acre (0.4 ha) under greenhouse glass.
- Vineyard is sited on rich, Devon sandstone soils.
- The vigour of the vines under glass necessitates considerable canopy control during the summer.
- No sprays or pesticides are used in the glass vineyards with a natural ecosystem having been developed.

Tim Chance began planting vines in 1999 and in 2002 established a number of more classic French varieties under glass. The vineyard has been added to each year since the first vines were planted and now comprises Chardonnay, Pinot Noir, Cabernet Sauvignon and Merlot, grown under glass, as well as the more established English varieties.

Wine production
Just over one acre (0.4 ha) is planted to these varieties and they enjoy a growing season which is between four and six weeks longer than the normal cycle. Greater growing season heat ensures good sugar levels in the fruit, indeed this is still a case of trial and error with Chardonnay having reached a potential natural alcohol of close to 16%. A late harvest example is being considered. The other challenge is the vigorous growth of the vines, particularly in the relatively rich Devon sandstone soils. Drainage though is good, which helps in achieving a balance of sugar and acid in the fruit.

The wines are made by Martin Fowke at nearby Three Choirs, (see page 139) where there is a state of the art modern winery facility. Varietal Siegerrebe and Orion whites are fresh and approachable. There is also a well made fruit-driven red, Montpelier that comes from Regent and Rondo. At present the English style wines would appear to offer just a touch more than the Chardonnay, Pinot Noir and Cotswold Classic produced from Merlot and Cabernet Sauvignon. Two sparkling wines are also made, Classic Sparkling from Orion and the Premier Cuvée from Chardonnay and Pinot Noir. The small range is completed by a Pinot rosé. It will be interesting to see how the wines develop in the coming vintages.

Visiting
Strawberry Hill is open by appointment and visits and tastings as well as tours can be undertaken.

HOW TO FIND US

- Address: Newent, Gloucestershire GL18 1DQ
- The vineyard is found just to the north of Newent, off the B4215. Take the Three Ashes lane turn around a mile north of Newent and then turn left into the Scarr. The vineyard is just off Orchard Road which is on the left side of The Scarr.
- Open: Telephone 01531 822 669 or email to make an appointment

Email: enquiries@strawberryhillvineyard.co.uk

Web: www.strawberryhillvineyard.co.uk

Warm climate plant growing is part of the ethos here

THORNBURY CASTLE
Thornbury, Gloucestershire

Thornbury Castle is now a country house hotel owned by the Von Essen hotel group. There is a vineyard on the hotel estate, with records suggesting the presence of a vineyard here for the past 500 years.

VINEYARD FACTS

- A total of around 2.5 acres (1 ha) under vine in both the Thornbury Castle and the leased St Augustine's Vineyards.
- Six varieties planted in varied soils.
- Just one wine produced, a blend of all the grapes grown.
- Wines vinified off site at Three Choirs Vineyard with access to state of the art winemaking equipment.

There is a fascinating history here. The original castle dates back to 924 AD, when it was a Saxon manor. It was granted to the Earls of Stafford by William the Conqueror and remained in the Stafford family until the latter part of the 20th century, apart from two short periods during the reigns of Richard III and Henry VIII when the dukes at those times were both beheaded for treason. After this the castle was transformed into a luxury hotel. The Thornbury Castle wine is now made for and distributed amongst the Von Essen hotels.

Wine production

The walled and protected vineyard at Thornbury Castle itself is currently just 0.5 acres (0.2 ha). It is of some considerable age being originally planted in 1976 and the vines are gradually being replanted and re-trellised from Geneva Double Curtain to Double Guyot which should add to the quality of the fruit. A further 2 acres (0.8 ha) are leased from the nearby St Augustine's vineyard. There are permeable soils at Thornbury Castle and a mix of loams and clays with interspersed rocks at St Augustine's. Müller Thurgau and Phoenix are planted at Thornbury and Müller-Thurgau, Reichensteiner, Kernling and Madeleine Angevine at St Augustine's. Just one wine is produced, a medium dry white from a blend of all the fruit from the two vineyards. The wine is vinified in the very capable hands of Martin Fowke at Three Choirs (see page 139). In this way there is the opportunity to have access to all the state of the art vinification equipment. The wine is made with full temperature control for fermentation and stabilisation and there is a cool room to ensure the freshness of the fruit after harvesting.

The Thornbury Castle white

Visiting

The wines are exclusively marketed by the von Essen hotel group and Thornbury Castle is the place to try them. If you feel like splashing out this will hardly be a hardship. Thornbury is a sumptuous and luxuriously appointed hotel and as a resident you will have the opportunity to stroll amongst the vines at your leisure if the whim takes you. If you are visiting other hotels in the Von Essen group you may also encounter the wine.

HOW TO FIND US

- Address: Thornbury Castle Hotel, Thornbury, Nr Bristol BS35 1HH Go to the Thornbury Castle website for extremely detailed directions to find the hotel from all directions.
- Open: Wines can be tasted and vineyards visited by hotel residents.

Tel: 01454 281182
Email: info@thornburycastle.co.uk
Web: www.thornburycastle.co.uk

THREE CHOIRS
Newent, Gloucestershire

This is one of the largest and best established of England's vineyards and is a major Gloucestershire tourist destination. Three Choirs cultivates a wide range of typically English grape varieties and in addition Pinot Noir.

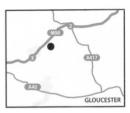

VINEYARD FACTS

- 75 acres (30.3 ha) under vine, planted with a southerly aspect.
- Warm mesoclimate and crucially lower than average rainfall.
- A small amount of fruit bought in from contract growers.
- Extensive range of vine varieties cultivated.
- Modern well equipped winery providing contract winemaking and sparkling wine production facilities.

The property was established in 1973 with just half an acre (0.2 ha) of vines, simply as an experiment. This has expanded dramatically over the years to today where 75 acres (30.3 ha) of vines are cultivated, all on the same single estate home vineyard. Because of the size of the output here a number of arrangements are also in place with contract growers as well.

Quality across the range is good to very good and a modern winery provides not only for all Three Choirs' needs but also offers contract winemaking for around 30 to 40 other small growers, both local and further afield.

The Vineyard

The Three Choirs single-estate is planted on well-drained sandstone soils, most of which enjoys a southerly aspect. The mesoclimate of the vineyard is significant in both its warmth and low rainfall. As a result the approach is very much one of sustainable viticulture. Hand harvesting is the norm and the vineyards managed as naturally as possible without recourse to pesticides and therefore encourage a natural eco-system.

An extensive range of varieties is now planted after monitoring the results of continuous trials over the last three decades. Although there are no plans to increase the current holding of 75 acres, a small amount of the vineyard is being re-planted, including an increased holding of Pinot Noir. Most is the earlier ripening Pinot "Précose" although a little is the traditional later ripening Pinot, found in France. Of the other red varieties Dornfelder is important for its fruity character, the hybrid Triomphe for its fruit and colour and the newly approved Rondo for both colour and tannin.

Winemaker, Martin Fowke would like to

The view over the vineyard from the restaurant and hotel

BIOGRAPHY | Martin Fowke

Martin Fowke is both the winemaking chief at Three Choirs and a director of the vineyard. After studying agriculturing and horticulture at Cirencester and then business studies, he took on the role of vineyard manager here in the late 1980s. He has travelled extensively, working in winemaking in Australia, after which he took control of winemaking operations and vinegrowing at Three Choirs. He has since worked and managed vintages in Chile, Argentina and Bulgaria while remaining committed to his position at Three Choirs. 2008 has proved very successful for him having been given the accolade of Winemaker of the Year Trophy at the 2008 UKVA awards. It will also be his 20th vintage and he looks forward to the next 20 as exciting new developments in the English wine industry evolve.

The Wines

Reserve Bacchus

This is a good, fresh example of varietal Bacchus, one of the best in the country. Good, floral elderflower character is underpinned by subtle citrus notes and refreshing and not overwhelming acidity. 2007 offers lots of potential.

Reserve Siegerrebe

This is a rich, spicy and impressively intense, grapefruit scented white from a variety crossed between Madeleine Angevine and Gewurztraminer. It's an early ripening variety and the wine will be best young and fresh.

Willow Brook

A good aromatic off-dry white with nicely balanced acidity providing some backbone and structure. It's a blend of Siegerrebe, Seyval Blanc, Reichensteiner and Orion.

Premium Selection Rosé

Off-dry rosé style with attractive, forward fresh strawberry fruit. The colour and vibrant summer fruit come from Triomphe, the fresh backbone from the addition of Seyval Blanc. Drink young and fresh.

Premium Selection Red

This is a blend of Triomphe, Rondo and Regent. The wine gets a five day cold soak prior to fermentation and offers good tannin and a soft supple structure as well as attractive dark berry fruit.

The vines are trained by Geneva Double Curtain

see more Bacchus planted for the quality and intensity of its fruit. The variety can be very erratic in its crop here though, while 2006 yielded 12,000 bottles, 2007 produced just 1,000. Madeleine Angevine has also proved successful, although not as a single varietal. It is consistently used in the Reserve Coleridge Hill blend, a crisp, lightly floral dry white and in the top medium style here, the Reserve May Hill, along with Reichensteiner and the rich and distinctive Huxelrebe. Early ripening Siegerrebe provides excellent quality, albeit at a relatively miserly yield. Seyval Blanc, which is almost completely organically grown, Reichensteiner, Müller-Thurgau and Huxelrebe are used in creating the well-priced off dry white Premium Selection. Off-dry styles will often benefit from the addition of a little Schönburger, a spicy aromatic crossing of Pinot Noir and Muscat.

Wine production

As well as producing its own extensive range, Three Choirs is an important winemaking resource for approaching 40 other vineyards, among them Astley and Strawberry Hill Vineyards (see separate entries). With gyropalettes on site they provide important ageing and sparkling wine disgorging options for a number of vineyards.

The modern, purpose built winery is fully equipped with air, temper-

The scenic view from the hotel

ature and humidity control, stainless steel tanks, modern bladder presses and crucially a cool room, which preserves those delicate, floral aromas in the whites. A warm room is also used to usher the reds through the malolactic fermentation.

The whites are gently pressed, to extract the best free run juice and avoid any bitter phenolic components. The juice is then cold settled for 24 hours prior to fermentation, which is generally in tank and cool, with an appropriately selected yeast strain. The Seyval Blanc, which provides good zippy acidity and Triomphe used to make the rosé are pressed together and then they get a little skin contact prior to fermentation. The reds are all de-stemmed at the crusher in order to ensure a fresh, juicy forward fruit character and avoid any bitter green tannins. A proportion of the wine is then aged in a mix of new and used oak. In addition to the wines profiled here, a Reserve Late Harvest white and Four Oaks, a special selection red are also available for sale at the cellar door.

Visiting

On arrival you will find a well laid out small and airy shop as well as a first-class restaurant and if you feel like staying amidst the vines there is an eight bedroom hotel equipped to a high standard. As we went to press a number of small chalets were also being completed right in the heart of the vineyards. Self-guided tours can be taken which include the vineyards, winery and a tasting experience. Indeed visitors are taken very seriously with around one third of the wineries sales accounted for through their shop. Group tours can also be catered for by arrangement and a range of private and corporate functions are available. An additionally interesting feature is the option for visitors to adopt a vine which will bear their own nameplate and provide them with compli-mentary wine. There is also a small micro brewery "Whittington" on site al-though most of the output is sold to the on-licence trade locally.

Sparkling wine, important here as elsewhere

The Wines

Pinot Noir Précose

This is likely to become an increasingly important red here. Again a five day cold soak is employed and the wine is full of subtle restrained red cherry fruit. A top barrel selection of the 2006 vintage showed real potential.

Classic Cuvee Brut NV

This is a blend of Reichensteiner and Seyval Blanc with lots of acidity for the base wine. Offers more fresh, forward fruit than secondary yeast derived flavours although it gets at least 15 months in bottle prior to disgorging.

Reserve Brut Vintage

This is a more serious and structured sparkler produced from a blend of Seyval and Pinot Noir with a longer period on lees. The 2004 offered more complex bready characters, underpinned by a lifted minerally backbone.

HOW TO FIND US

- Address: Newent, Gloucestershire GL18 1LS
- From Gloucester take the A40 west and then the B4215 to Newent. From Newent head north on the B4216 in the direction of Dymock and the vineyard is around 3 miles on the right hand side.
- Open: The vineyard is open Monday to Sunday 9am to 5pm. The restaurant is open for lunch between 12 noon and 2pm and in the evening between 7pm and 9pm. Contact the vineyard for details about the hotel.

Tel: 01531 890223
Email: info@threechoirs.com
Web: www.threechoirs.com

MIDLANDS
& THE NORTH

Midlands & North

David Moore & Neville Blech

Derbyshire (DM)
 1 Renishaw Hall

Herefordshire (NB)
 2 Beeches Vineyard
 3 Broadfield Court
 4 Frome Valley
 5 Lulham Court

Leicestershire (DM)
 6 Chevelswarde
 7 Welland Valley

Nottinghamshire (DM)
 8 Eglantine

Northamptonshire (DM)
 9 Fleurfields
 10 New Lodge

Shropshire (NB)
 11 Ludlow Vineyard
 12 Wroxeter Roman

Staffordshire (DM)
 13 Buzzard Valley
 14 Halfpenny Green

Warwickshire (DM)
 15 Welcombe Hills

Worcestershire (NB)
 16 Astley Vineyards
 17 Rose Bank
 18 Tiltridge Vineyard

Yorkshire (DM)
 19 Leventhorpe

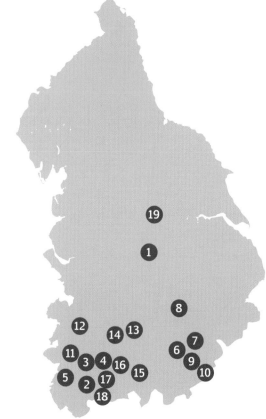

FLEURFIELDS
Brixworth, Northamptonshire

Bill and Flora Hulme made the decision to plant their vineyard during a holiday in Tuscany. They believed their south-facing meadow would provide just the right growing environment for vines.

2004 was their first harvest and they now make three wines: a still white Fleur Fields, a sparkling white Champs d'Amour and a sparkling rosé Champs d'Amour Rosé which includes an assemblage of all the red grapes grown here.

Wine production
The vineyard, which was first established with 1,000 vines in 2002 is planted to a mix of mainly Seyval Blanc along with Phoenix and a small range of red grapes. Beneficial to the development of the vines is the location on a south facing slope, overlooking the

Rows of well trained vines

VINEYARD FACTS

- 5 acres (2 ha) under vine.
- Seyval Blanc, and Phoenix planted on well-drained loamy soils.
- Vineyards vertically trellised and Double Guyot trained to optimise exposure to sunlight and improve natural sugar levels.
- Wines vinified at Three Choirs.

Pitsford Reservoir. The soil is also key in helping the quality of the wine. It is a light, loamy well-drained with a high ph of around 8 which provides for good fresh well balanced flavours in the grapes. Vines are trained to Double Guyot with vertical shoot positioning, exposing the fruiting canes and canopy to as much sunlight as possible. The site covers 5 acres (2 ha) and there are 5,000 vines planted, 4,000 to white varieties and 1,000 to reds.

The first vintage in 2004 produced just 800 bottles. The potential though is good in a warm and benevolent year. In 2006 over 4,500 bottles were produced, the majority sparkling. Indeed with Seyval Blanc planted and the character of the soil, sparkling wine is a very logical route. The variety, being more neutral than many English grown grapes.

Visiting
The vineyard is open by appointment for wine sales, tours and tastings.

HOW TO FIND US

- Address: Hill Farm House, Brixworth, Northamptonshire NN6 9DQ
- The Fleurfields Vineyard is found off the A508 south of the village of Brixworth on the right hand side if you are travelling south.
- Open: Telephone or email to make an appointment.

Tel: 01604 880197
Email: info@fleurfields.co.uk
Web: www.fleurfields.co.uk

NEW LODGE
Earls Barton, Northamptonshire

Joyce Boulos-Hanna's small vineyard covers slightly less than one acre (0.4 ha) and produced its first wine only in 2008 although planting first commenced in 2000 with a first crop harvested in 2006.

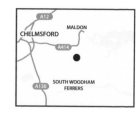

The Saxon village of Earls Barton has seen many industries. A cornmilling community at the time of the Domesday book, the late 18th century brought ironstone quarrying and bootmaking. Only very recently though has it had its own vineyard.

Wine production
The first planting amounted to around 200 vines of which half each were Bacchus and Phoenix. The overall holding of Phoenix has been increased, and with some additional Seyval Blanc planted, there are now some 400 vines being cultivated. There no current plans to grow any red varieties. The vineyard area now covers 0.57 acres (0.23 ha) and the vine density is wisely kept on the low side. The soil is a crumbly loam over iron-stone providing good drainage, although quite fertile. To this extent the vines are trained by Double Guyot, which is very labour intensive but provides good canopy light exposure with vertical shoot positioning.

The first vintage in 2006 has now been accorded Regional Wine status as of April 2008 and the sole wine will be available during the summer of 2008. The year was generous as elsewhere in the country and 1,000 bottles were produced. Winemaking is currently contracted out to Tony Skuriat at Eglantine Vineyard (see page 165). The 2006 white vinified from all the varieties is a fresh, zesty and well made lightly aromatic white. The approach is typical of the style with a long cool fermentation to preserve delicate flavour and early bottling.

Visiting
The project is very new although visitors to the vineyard are welcomed by appointment. The intention is to sell locally to the on and off licence trade as well as to visitors.

VINEYARD FACTS

- 0.57 acres (0.23 ha) under vine.
- Bacchus, Phoenix and Seyval Blanc planted on well-drained loamy soils.
- Vineyards vertically trellised and Double Guyot trained to optimise exposure to sunlight and improve natural sugar levels.
- Wines vinified at Eglantine Vineyard.

HOW TO FIND US

- Address: Earls Barton, Northampton NN6 0HF
- The vineyard is just off the A4500 on the outskirts of East Barton on the right hand side of the B573 Northampton Road if you are travelling north.
- Open: Telephone to make an appointment to visit.
Tel: 01604 811311

WELCOMBE HILLS
Stratford upon Avon, Warwickshire

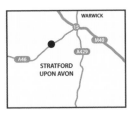

The Gallimores' property sits on land that was once part of William Shakespeare's personal estate near Stratford-upon-Avon. The wines are available in a range of local stores and farm shops, although they are not currently available through the vineyard.

VINEYARD FACTS

- 1.75 acres (0.71 ha) under vine.
- 8 varieties now planted in all, planted in clay soils.
- Vineyards trained by both Double Guyot and Geneva Double Curtain.
- Wines vinified at Three Choirs.

You can though "adopt a vine" in a similar manner as found at Three Choirs (see page 139) and Pebblebed in Devon (see page 128). This will be of particular interest to those who wish to take a more academic interest in a working vineyard, while at the same time enjoying beneficial discounts on their wine purchases.

Wine production
Planting first began in 2001 with an initial half an acre (0.2 ha) planted to Pinot Noir, Dornfelder and Bacchus. The total area now cultivated amounts to 1.75 acres (0.71 ha) and also includes Auxerrois, Pinot Noir Précoce and Chardonnay. The vineyard itself is planted on well-drained clay-based soils, with a southerly aspect and minimal risk of frost, a godsend for any English vigneron. All the initial vines have been Double Guyot trained, with the obvious advantages of light exposure for the canopy and fruiting canes. A small area of Sauvignon Blanc, Bacchus and Seyval Blanc has also been established and trellised with a Geneva Double Curtain as an alternative and may prove more beneficial to a number of the varieties in the clay based soils.

At present the wines are all made under contract by Three Choirs, which makes perfect sense given the size and scale of the vineyard and the equipment needed to vinify wines from such a diverse number of grape varieties. Both Pinots are produced, the Précoce a little lighter than the Pinot Noir and both are marked clean cherry fruit. There is also a rosé from Dornfelder (named after Charles II's defeat at the Battle of Worcester and his subsequent retreat) from a mix of the red grapes. These are joined by a white, floral and aromatic Bacchus and two sparkling wines, a Blanc de Noirs and an unusual sparkling Bacchus aged on lees for 12 months.

Visiting
The vineyard is not yet open to the public but for those who would like to experience it, there is the opportunity to take part in the vine harvest.

HOW TO FIND US

- Address: Snitterfield, Stratford upon Avon, Warwickshire CV37 0QB
- Open: Not generally open however email for details of how to adopt a vine.

Tel: 01789 731071
Email: chrisgallim@hotmail.com
Web: www.welcombehills.co.uk

ASTLEY VINEYARDS
Astley, Stourport-on-Severn, Worcestershire

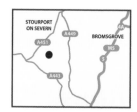

Established in the 1970s, Astley is one of the oldest commercial vineyards in the UK that is still in production. It was, for a short while, also the most northerly vineyard in the world.

Situated within half a mile of the western bank of the river Severn, near Stourport-on-Severn, 45m above its flood plain and terraces, the vineyards at Astley were established in the 1970s by Michael and Betty Bache who planted Kerner and Madeleine Angevine at the time. Whilst most of the grape growing then could be described as experimental, the first real commercial vintage did not take place until 1983. The current owners, Jonty Daniels & Janet Baldwin, who bought the property in 1993 and increased the number of varietals planted, have continued with an eye for quality rather than quantity by deliberately restricting yields.

The Vineyard
Wines are produced from a single 5 acre (2 ha) vineyard site with no bought-in grapes. The objective is to achieve a consistency of production which endeavours to emulate the traditional goal of the winemaker that a wine should reflect a specific geographical location or terroir. This terroir is based on deep, free-draining soils derived from the Triassic red sandstone underlying the vineyard. Vineyard

VINEYARD FACTS

- Free-draining sandy loam derived from the Triassic red sandstone with a thin band of undulating clay.
- 5 acres (2 ha) of low-yielding vines planted at a density of approximately 700 per acre.
- Vine training with Double Guyot except for the Kerner vines.

management is aimed towards producing low-yielding crops that accentuate the vineyard's site and varietal characteristics with 3,500 low-density vines. Yields are generally under 3 tons to the acre. Husbandry is based on an overall pest management approach that limits chemical intervention and, wherever possible, adheres to natural controls rather than industrial ones. Grape varieties: Kerner, Madeleine Angevine, Siegerrebe (especially for late harvest), Phoenix, Bacchus and various small parcels, some experimental.

Wine Production
All the wines, from dry to sparkling, are of English Vineyards Quality Wine psr ("produced in a specific region") status, the highest level of the English quality wine

BIOGRAPHY | Jonty Daniels

Jonty Daniels grew up on top of a hill with an Alsatian dog and film stars (his father was a stills cameraman in the British Film industry of the 1930s and 40s). Things looked bright until he succumbed to agriculture and experienced a meteoric rise to obscurity in farm management both academic (Bristol University) and practical (600 acres of Hertfordshire arable).

Homelessness forced the purchase of Astley! Jonty and his partner, Janet Baldwin, bought the vineyard property in 1993 paying just one pound for the business. Since the purchase, they have striven to constantly improve and upgrade the quality of the wines produced and are confident that the business is worth a lot more than that now!

scheme. The wines are made at Three Choirs (see page 139).

At present, Astley only produces white wines although there are plans to plant Pinot Noir as an additional source of grapes for producing sparkling wine or a still rosé. In the range of whites, apart those shown in the Wine Box, they have in a dry style, Madeleine Angevine — as dry aromatic, "Triassic" (Siegerrebe) — as off- dry, Foundation (mainly Madeleine Angevine) — as medium dry, Old Vine Kerner — as medium, Severn Vale (68 per cent Kerner, 20 per cent Schönburger, 9 per cent Madeleine Angevine, 3 per cent Siegerebbe) and as sweet, Late Harvest (Siegerrebe).

HOW TO FIND US

- Address: Astley Vineyard, Crundle Lane, Astley, Stourport-on-Severn, DY13 0RU
- Open all year: 10am - 5pm daily (Tuesdays & Wednesdays by appointment only). Sunday: Noon - 5pm.
- Off B4196 between Holt Heath (on A443 north from Worcester) and Stourport-on-Severn; on the opposite side of the road to the sign for Astley church.

Tel/Fax: 01299 822907

Visiting

Informal guided tours can be arranged for groups of 12-20, by appointment. There is a self-catering holiday apartment on site.

The Wines

Astley "George Eckert" Vintage Brut 2004

100 per cent Kerner — gentle bubbles, although a little bit austere and very dry on the attack, it smooths out to give a more rounded fruit-driven perception at the finish.

Astley Phoenix 2006

Single vineyard, single low-yielding varietal wine with good aromatic fruit and nicely balanced acid.

Astley Veritas 2007

The first wine they have ever made without having to chaptalise — 100 per cent Kerner, very full in the mouth, hints of grapefruit and gooseberry and a complex finish. Still a little young – will age well. Very fine.

Astley Reserve Fumé 2006

A blend of Madeleine Angevine and Kerner fermented separately, this has light green apple fruit, with a restrained grassy undercurrent somewhat dominated by oak.

Welcome to Astley

ROSE BANK
Fernhill Heath, Worcestershire

A new vineyard venture situated on the outskirts of Worcester with stunning views of Worcester Cathedral and the Malvern Hills.

Richard and Rita Tomkinson's venture began back in 2003, when the land behind their house was put up for sale by a neighbouring farmer. This south-facing slope proved to be the perfect environment for cultivating vines. Starting from scratch, with the help of volunteers, family and friends, the former banker has now planted some 1,500 vines. The first commercial crop was harvested in 2006 with the first wines (around 2,500 bottles) coming on sale in 2008.

Wine Production

Currently, three wines have been produced — Madeleine Angevine, Phoenix and a Phoenix and Reichensteiner blend, Fern Hill. Future plans are to produce a sparkling wine and a rosé. The wines are made by Martin Fowke at Three Choirs, (see page 139). The Phoenix is aromatic and quite fruity and grapey, but nevertheless finishes dry with some complexity and length.

Visiting

To buy a bottle direct from Rose Bank Vineyard or to organise a guided tour of the grounds, call Richard and Rita. The vineyard is open most Saturdays from 9am. until 5pm, other days strictly by appointment. Otherwise Rose Bank wine is also available from the Worcester Wine Company, Bromwich Road, Worcester.

Rose Bank's Fern Hill blend

TILTRIDGE VINEYARD
Upton-upon-Severn, Worcestershire

Tiltridge Farm is situated in the Severn Valley between the Malvern Hills and the attractive town of Upton-upon-Severn. The wines are marketed under the Elgar label in order to have a label that emphasises the Worcestershire location.

In the past Tiltridge Farm was a Council property run by tenant farmers. When the last of the family died in 1982 and finding the farm to be in a poor condition, the Council decided to sell it. Peter and Sandy Barker bought it and spent the next 18 months doing necessary renovations. They planted their first vineyard in the spring of 1988 and the second vineyard a year later. The first commercial crop was picked in 1991 and the vineyard has been open to the public since 1992.

Wine Production
On average, about 3,000 bottles a year are produced, but there are large seasonal variations as the harvest is very dependent on the weather conditions. The wines are made at Three Choirs (see page 139) and marketed under the Elgar label. Many of the images used on the labels

were researched & provided by the Elgar Birthplace Museum.

Seven different wines are currently produced. Elgar Dry 2006, (a blend of Seyval Blanc, Schönburger and Huxelrebe) — crisp and dry with slight goose-berry tones. Good acidity and length. Cello 2006 (Schönburger) is more aromatic than the Elgar Dry. Still a little tight but should age well. Variations 2005 (Seyval Blanc) — six months in old oak barriques which adds some subtle complexity and good length. Enigma 2005 (Huxelrebe) is a little dryer than medium sweet, with good body and should go well with cheeses. They also produce a medium dry rosé (Sonata), a medium dry white blend (Elgar Medium Dry) and a medium dry Huxelrebe (Dorabella).

Visiting
A shop and tasting room is open on site and bed & breakfast accommodation in the farmhouse is also available.

VINEYARD FACTS

- Total area under production — 1.5 acres (0.6 ha) at an altitude of about 35m above sea level, sheltered from westerly winds.
- Vines are grown on clay loam by the Double Guyot system and pruned back to two replacement canes each winter.
- Grapes grown: Schönburger, Huxelrebe, Phoenix & Seyval Blanc.

HOW TO FIND US

- Address: Tiltridge Vineyard, Upper Hook Road, Upton-on-Severn, Worcestershire WR8 0SA
- Shop open Monday-Friday 9a.m. – 5p.m.
- From the centre of Upton turn down New Street at the Midland Bank. After 1/2 mile bear left up a bank and the vineyard shop is located on the left after a further 1/2 mile.

Tel: 01684 592906.
Fax: 01684 594142
Email: Info@elgarwine.com
Web: www.tiltridge.com.

BROADFIELD COURT
Bodenham, Herefordshire

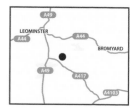

Nesting in a picturesque spot of North Herefordshire countryside, Broadfield Court combines wine production with hosting private, social and corporate events.

Broadfield Court Estate is referred to in the Domesday Book "Radulophus de Todeni tenet Bradfelde" and has survived as a private farming estate to the present day. With just over 1000 acres, this farming estate provides a beautiful and tranquil setting for conferences, business meetings, wedding receptions and private functions.

Keith James founded the vineyard in 1971 with an experimental 50 vines. The following year he added 500 Reichensteiner vines and an expansion programme continued until 17 acres (6.88 ha) of Broadfield's south-facing slopes were covered in vines.

The Vineyard
When developed in 1971, it was described as the best vineyard site in Britain. The vineyard area has subsequently been somewhat rationalised with some of the varietals, notably the Müller-Thurgau, being grubbed up due their age and poor productivity, thus reducing the area of productive vines to 10 acres at present.

VINEYARD FACTS

- 10 acres (4 ha) of south-facing slopes on heavy loam currently producing wine from 10,000 vines.
- No bought in grapes from elsewhere.
- Grape varietals: Reichensteiner, Huxelrebe, Seyval Blanc, Madeleine Angevine, Pinot Noir.

Some vines are grown in polytunnels. At one time the vineyard had its own wine production facility, but it has now been found to be more economical to have the wines made at the state of the art facilities at Three Choirs (see page 139) in dedicated vats.

View of the court from the Court Café

Experimental polytunnel

Wine Production
Five white, one rosé and one sparkling white are made from estate fruit. Broadfield Estate is their entry level wine — a blend of Madeleine Angevine, Reichensteiner and Müller-Thurgau. Broadfield Court is a sweeter wine which should go excellently with cheeses and savouries. On the drier side, the Madeleine Angevine has a nice earthy taste of hedgerow and spice, and there are two other dry whites made from Reichensteiner and Huxelrebe. The Rosé, a blend of Pinot Noir and Reichensteiner, is rose scented and delicate. The range is completed by a sparkling wine made from Seyval Blanc, lively and with good acidity. Wines from Broadfield Court are marketed under the label "Bodenham English Wines".

The wines may be found in various local shops and hotels.

Visiting
Broadfield specialises in the hosting of corporate events and private and public social gatherings. Wine production, outdoor activities and training, field sports and cultural entertainment are also on the agenda. There is a gift shop within the Court Café, which serves home-grown or locally sourced produce chosen to complement the wines. They also welcome coach tours and other group holiday specialists for wine-tasting tours without meals. There are musical, craft and garden events as well.

BIOGRAPHY Alexandria James

Keith James's daughter-in-law, Alexandria, runs the vineyard, café, shop and corporate events whilst husband Mark continues to farm the rest of the estate. Alexandria was born in Shropshire and educated at Lawnside in Malvern. She went to the Webber Douglas Academy of Dramatic Art and then on to the Royal Shakespeare Company for five years and also worked in film and television. She met and married Mark James and they now live with their three children on the estate at Broadfield Court. Alexandria's ethos is to encourage her visitors to come and relax and enjoy the local food and wines that are produced on the estate. In 2000, she left all this behind and trekked the jungles of Borneo. It was her experiences out there that made her understand what is important in life and she hopes that is brought to all her guests that visit the vineyard.

HOW TO FIND US
- Broadfield Court Estate, Bowley Lane, Bodenham, Herefordshire, HR1 3LG.
- Opening hours: 10:30am to 4pm (winter) and 10am to 4:30pm from Easter through the summer.
- From Hereford: Follow the A49 for 8 miles, turn right onto the A417. Follow the A417 for about 2 miles, turn left at Murco Garage onto Bowley Lane travel 1 mile and Broadfield Court is signposted to your right.
- From Leominster: Follow the A49 for 4 miles and turn left onto the A417. Brown tourist signs indicate the way from the A417 and A44.

Tel: 01568 797483 or the Court Café on 01568 797918 (lunch bookings).
Web: www.broadfieldcourt.co.uk

Four of the seven wines made under the Broadfield Court label

BEECHES VINEYARD
Upton Bishop, Herefordshire

Beeches is one of the few remaining original Georgian farmhouses in Herefordshire with a small, family-run vineyard attached. The house has some interesting features including a cold store and large vaulted cellar.

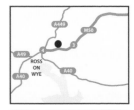

VINEYARD FACTS

- Grapes grown: Madeleine Angevine, Seyval Blanc, Triomphe d'Alsace, Regent and Rondo.
- Total area under vine: 0.75 acres (0.3ha).
- Number of vines: 540.
- Guyot training for vines.

Ikka Boyd began the vineyard in 1991 with the planting of the Madeline Angevine, Triomphe d'Alsace and Seyval Blanc vines, producing a first harvest in 1994. The vines were planted on rough ground not suitable for farming. Rondo and Regent varieties were added and the vineyard now produces a dry white, a rosé and a light red. Ikka's daughter, Karin Wilkins, has now taken over the management of the vineyard after finishing her career in the City to have a family and after several years of living in Europe and Asia.

Wine Production

Three wines are produced, a Beeches Dry White (100 per cent Madeleine Angevine) a Beeches Rosé (52 per cent Seyval Blanc, 48 per cent Triomphe d'Alsace) and a Beeches Red (40 per cent Rondo, 60 per cent Regent). The Dry White is dry and pungent, with good length

on the finish — a good food wine — the Rosé is fruity but with a dry finish and tones of red berry fruits, whilst the Red, although light, has good brambly fruit on the nose with some pluminess on the palate and a reasonably complex finish. The wines are made just a few miles away by Martin Fowke at the Three Choirs Vineyard, Newent, Gloucestershire (see page 139).

Visiting

Visitors are welcome to Beeches by prior appointment only. It is necessary to make contact to see how you may be able to be accommodated. There are regular tasting events and paid lunch functions in the summer months. There is also the possibility of visitors joining in the harvest in late summer when the owners are happy to host a buffet lunch for pickers.

Harvesting the grapes

Karin, the manager

HOW TO FIND US

- Ikka and John Boyd, Beeches, Upton Bishop, Ross-on-Wye, Herefordshire HR9 7UD.
- From the centre of Upton Bishop take the B4221 in the direction of Newent, after a short distance take the first fork left. Beeches is about 200 yards up this road on the left hand side.

Tel: 01989 780 214 (John Boyd), 0777 090 8391 (Simon Wilkins).

Email: info@ beechesvineyard.com.

Web: www.beechesvineyard.com.

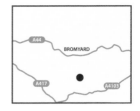

FROME VALLEY
Bishop's Frome, Herefordshire

Wine has been produced in Herefordshire since medieval times and Frome Valley vineyard maintains this tradition. Surrounded by Herefordshire's hopyards and cider orchards, white and red grapes are grown in 4 acres (1.6ha) of vineyard.

The vineyard was established in 1992 by David and Clare Longman who ran it until 2005, when the present owners, Jeanie and Ian Falconer took over. The vineyard lies just south of Bromyard in Worcestershire, although the exact location of the property is in Herefordshire.

Jeanie Falconer in the model vineyard

Wine Production
Several types of wine are produced, which consistently achieve English Quality Wine status. The wines are made at Three Choirs. (See page 139). The following wines were tasted: Madeleine Angevine 2007 —

VINEYARD FACTS

- 4500 vines planted on 4 acres (1.6ha) of clay soil, in a gentle south-facing slope.
- Includes a small model vineyard which shows various methods of training vine varieties.
- Vine varieties are: Bacchus, Huxelrebe, Reichensteiner, Schönburger, Madeleine Angevine, Seyval Blanc, Chardonnay, Pinot Noir, Rondo and Früburgender.

dry, with rounded fruit and good complexity on the finish: Paunton Medium Dry 2006 — a blend of Huxelrebe and Reichensteiner, this is aromatic on the nose, with good, grapey, fruity flavours: Huxelrebe 2006 — here there is a hint of petrol à la Alsace Riesling, but a good dry finish, and Schönburger 2005 — very dry on the palate but with good tangy fruit. Other wines produced are Paunton Medium, Paunton Rosé (90 per cent Pinot Noir, 10 per cent Schönburger), Bacchus and sparkling Seyval Blanc. Wines can be found at sundry shops, restaurants and bars in the region.

Visiting
Small, organised visits of up to 30 persons are welcome which includes a tour of the demonstration vineyard and main vineyard. No entrance charge, but a small charge is made for groups, which includes a guided tour and light refreshments.

HOW TO FIND US

- Frome Valley Vineyards, Paunton, Bishop's Frome, Herefordshire, WR6 5BJ.
- Open: April to October, Wednesday to Sunday and Bank Holiday Mondays, 11.00 a.m. to 5.00 p.m.
- Travel via the B4214 from Bromyard. Just past Munderfield Stocks, look for lane to your left. Follow for a mile and a half. From the south, turn right in Bishop's Frome, follow signs to the industrial estate. When clear of the village, fork left (before crossing the river). Proceed for another mile.

Tel: 01885 490768
Email: Jeanie@fromewine.co.uk
Web: www.fromewine.co.uk

LULHAM COURT
Madley, Herefordshire

Lulham Court vineyard is to be found in the beautiful Wye Valley at Madley, between Hereford and Hay-on-Wye as part of a mixed-crop family farm.

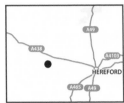

Phil Pennington established the vineyard in 1979 with the planting of Müller-Thurgau grapes with a further planting of Seyval Blanc and Reichensteiner grapes in 1984 and 1986. The vines are now well established and the vineyard produces a Seyval sparkling wine and some crisp, typically English dry and medium-dry wines. Wine has been produced here since 1984.

Wines Produced
In addition to the wines featured in detail here, the estate also produces a medium wine (Reichensteiner, Müller-Thurgau and Seyval Blanc) and a sparkling wine (Lulham Sparkling Brut Celebration Wine), made from 100 per cent Seyval Blanc. The wines are made at the Three Choirs facility in Newent, Gloucestershire (see page 139).

VINEYARD FACTS

- 2,800 vines planted on a 3 acre (1.2ha) site of red loam.
- Vines trained with both Single and Double Guyot systems.
- Grapes grown: Müller-Thurgau, Reichensteiner, Seyval Blanc and Regent.

HOW TO FIND US

- Phil Pennington, Lulham Court Vineyard, Lulham Court, Madley, Hereford, HR2 9JQ
- Off the A438 Hay-on-Wye to Hereford road between Bridge Sollars and Madley, contact the vineyard for full directions.

Tel: 01981 251107
Mobile: 07768 400004
Email: phil@lulhamcourt vineyard.co.uk
Web: www.lulhamcourt.co.uk

Lulham Court's Old Buildings

The Wines

Reichensteiner 2005

A crisp wine, with tones of iceberg lettuce on the palate and with medium length to the finish. Ideal for summer salads, light fish and white meats.

Medium Dry Müller-Thurgau/Reichensteiner 2004

A quaffable and easy drinking wine — more dry than medium. Hints of quince and stone fruits, with nice length and a good balance between fruit and acidity.

Müller-Thurgau 2004

Powerful aroma on the nose with plenty of crisp acidity and a long, aromatic finish. Conventional wisdom is that Müller-Thurgau no longer produces quality wines, but this is maybe the exception to prove the rule.

Rosé 2006

Fairly dry wine made from a blend of Regent and Seyval. Lacks a little generosity of fruit, but there is plenty of backbone here.

Visiting
There are no visiting facilities as such, but visits may be arranged by appointment only.

LUDLOW VINEYARD
Clee St Margaret, Craven Arms, Shropshire

Mike Hardingham's vineyard is located in Clee St Margaret, in spectacular rural scenery on the lower slopes of Brown Clee Hill, near Ludlow in South Shropshire.

The vineyard was established in 1995, but the first commercial vintage was not until 2003. The vineyard produces small quantities of wine now, and will be in full production by 2010. Mike also makes cider at the farm and sells English brandy, but plans to build a distillery, when he would be able to vinify his wines which are currently being made at Three Choirs (see page 139).

Wine Production
Currently four wines are produced. Clee Mists is a dry, oaked wine, made mainly from Madeleine Angevine grapes with a little Seyval Blanc. It is quite fruity with a little sweetness on the finish which would make it more medium than dry. Clee Blossom has a medium, fruity style, made mainly from Madeleine Sylvaner and Madeleine Angevine grapes, with hints of pear and quince. It would be a good accompaniment to spicy foods or even a nice bit of Shropshire Blue cheese. Clee Sparkling Brut

VINEYARD FACTS
- The site is probably the highest in the UK at around 200 metres.
- 8,000 vines planted on 10 acres (4 ha) of heavy loam on clay soil.
- Single Curtain vine training to be expanded to Double Curtain Guyot.
- White varieties - Madeleine Angevine, Phoenix, Seyval Blanc, Madeleine Sylvaner, Kernling, Ortega, Solaris.
- Red varieties — Rondo, Regent, Triomphe d'Alsace.

is fresh, grassy with elderflower and floral notes on the nose — with a light, soft mousse on the palate and a pleasant finish, whilst the Clee Sunburst Sparkling Brut Rosé, has a little fruit on the nose, and whilst dry, has some weight with nicely balanced red berry sweetness on the finish.

All wines and ciders are available at the Ludlow Vineyards stall in the Farmers' Market in Ludlow

Single Curtain training

(2nd and 4th Thursday of each month), as well as Ludlow's regular market each Friday.

Visiting
As the vineyard is in a remote location, it is not open to the public, but visitors are welcome by appointment in the summer. You can, however, order by telephone and deliveries are free within the local area.

HOW TO FIND US
- Address: Ludlow Vineyard, Wainbridge House, Clee St Margaret, Craven Arms, SY7 9DT
- Off the B4364 and B4368 — telephone for exact directions.

Tel: 01584 823356.
Web: www.ludlowvineyard.co.uk

WROXETER ROMAN
Wroxeter, near Shrewsbury, Shropshire

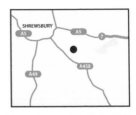

Wroxeter Roman Vineyard is steeped in history. Four generations of the Millington family have worked the soil of Glebe Farm here for the last 50 years.

David Millington founded the vineyard after visiting California's wine growing region. Glebe Farm, which was considered an agricultural liability, was attracting considerable attention from archaeologists digging for further evidence of the Roman occupation in and around Wroxeter. A link between California's viticulture and Glebe Farm being a possible Roman vineyard site inspired David to plant a vineyard to supplement the farm's meagre income. He took expert advice over a two year period from Gillian Pearkes, who was considered an authority on vine growing in England, visiting her Yearlstone Vineyard (see page 132) repeatedly. The vines were planted in 1991, with five varieties all grafted on a range of American root stocks.

A new agricultural adventure has been recently started by the Millingtons in the growing of olive trees and they claim to be the biggest growers in the UK with over 1,000 trees. They will be producing their own olive oil in 2009, but in the meantime hope to have an edible olive crop in 2008.

The Vineyard
The vineyard is situated by a scheduled monument alongside the ancient Roman city of Uriconium (Wroxeter) near Shrewsbury. Lying on a sandy, sheltered plateau near the River Severn, the vineyard is planted to

VINEYARD FACTS

- 9 acres (3.64 ha) of vines approximately 180 feet above sea level.
- Approximately 11,500 vines in all, trained by the Double Guyot system.
- Grapes grown: Dornfelder, Regner, Madeleine Angevine, Reichensteiner, Solaris, Rondo, Regent and Phoenix.
- Over 1,000 light hours received during the growing season to aid ripening – one of the highest in the country.

varieties and rootstocks selected for vigour, suitability of the site and consideration of the variety grafted onto it. Detailed attention was given to the planting layout to maximise sunshine and shelter. The plantation is north to south with rows 7 feet apart and at spaces of 4 feet; and allowed to grow to a height of 7 feet. This results in one side catching the morning sun and the other the evening sun. The spacing of the rows and a bare vineyard floor, means they afford each other shelter.

Wine Production
The still wines are made on site by Martin Millington. Bunches of grapes are almost

BIOGRAPHY David Millington

David Millington is a farmer's son who went into large-scale farm management after leaving agricultural college. He was the Estate Manager of the one of the CWS Estates, one of the largest farmers in the United Kingdom. After this he farmed on his own account and ran an agrochemical company in the West Midlands. David sold his agrochemical business in 1993 to concentrate on running the vineyard full time. His son Martin was trained at horticultural college and by Gillian Pearkes in wine production and joined the family business.

always de-stemmed before being pressed for two hours to extract the juice. The residue is used as manure for the vineyard, whilst the juice or must is clarified either by centrifugal separation or up to 24 hours settling. Sometimes it is chaptalised at this stage, whereby sugar is added if required to ensure that the eventual alcohol content is as high as desired. Prior to fermentation, the must is inoculated with a pure culture of wine yeast. The fermentation is maintained at an average temperature of not more than 15 °C. in order to capture freshness, aroma and delicacy of flavour. After fermentation the new wine is racked off its sediment into clean tanks (60 per cent stainless steel and 40 per cent fibreglass) and then left to mature in temperature-controlled conditions.

Young vines in bud

A large range of wines are produced; from the entry level Roman Villa (a cheap and cheerful medium wine made from varying grapes depending on the vintage) through to a quite serious Sparkling Rosé. The sparkling wines are finished at Three Choirs (see page 139). It is anticipated that from the 2008 vintage onwards, many of the still wines will be bottled with Stelvin screwcap closures.

Visiting
There are a number of special vineyard tours from Easter to October, from a simple vineyard tour to the "Special Experience". To book, please contact the vineyard at least 10 days in advance.

Whilst refreshments are available at the site at present, it is anticipated that a fully serviced restaurant will be opened in the spring of 2009. You can stay in the grounds of the vineyard in one of four self contained chalets or a 2 bedroom cottage and there is also a caravan site.

The Wroxeter sparking rosé

The Wines

Viticula Solaris 2007
Biscuity and smooth, this is a medium dry wine with plenty of body although it has crisp acidity to balance.

Shropshire Rosé 2006

Mainly Dornfelder with a little Rondo, made with double skin contact for six or seven days to obtain some darker colour, this has good colour and fruitiness with a little sweetness on the finish.

Rondo Red 2006
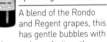
100% Rondo, deeply coloured, chunky with wild cherry tones on the palate.

Sparkling Rosé 2005
A blend of the Rondo and Regent grapes, this has gentle bubbles with nice raspberry fruit on the palate which is not too dry.

HOW TO FIND US
- Address: Wroxeter Roman Vineyard, Wroxeter, nr. Shrewsbury, Shropshire SY5 6PQ.
- From 9 am to 5 pm, Monday to Saturday and 12pm - 5.30 p.m. on Sundays.
- The vineyard is located between Shrewsbury and Ironbridge. From the Shrewsbury, take the B4380 towards Ironbridge. Take the Wroxeter Village turning and follow the road. Continue through the village turning left after the last house.

Tel: 01743 761888
Email wine@wroxetervineyard.co.uk
Web: www.wroxetervineyard.co.uk

BUZZARD VALLEY
Tamworth, Staffordshire

The Jones family has a sizeable vineyard and now a
modern winery where visitors can visit, taste wine and
enjoy the tea rooms, bar and restaurant and various
vineyard walks and tours.

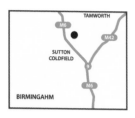

Ivan and Pat Jones came to the property in
1962 with a farming background and they
have developed a substantial wine
wholesaling business, as a part of Excelsior
Wholesale from which they not only sell
their own wines but a very impressive
range of wines from around the globe. The
wholesale operation also offers a wide
range of other products. They developed
their business in the 1970s and 80s as
market gardeners, as well as growing
flowers for drying and dyeing. Dried flowers
were replaced by silk flowers in the 1990s
and much of their land was free for
planting other products. Christmas trees
and woodland have been established and
more recently the vineyard, for which
planting commenced in 2001.

The vineyard
The vineyard, which consists of 8,000 vines
was planted in 2001. The varieties
cultivated include white Madeleine
Angevine, Phoenix, Reichensteiner and
Seyval Blanc. The red varieties are Pinot
Noir, Regent and the increasingly popular
Rondo. The vineyard is planted on a south-
facing slope and is planted on generally
clay soils.

Early season growth

Wine production
An extensive range of wines, all of which
are estate grown and bottled is produced
using modern winemaking facilities in an
equally modern winery.

VINEYARD FACTS

- Vineyard first planted in 2001.
- 8,000 vines planted.
- All wines produced from estate grown grapes.
- Modern winery fully equipped with stainless steel tanks, automatic bottling and wine processing and stabilisation equipment.

BIOGRAPHY   Ivan and Pat Jones

Ivan and Pat Jones have a background as dairy farmers. In the course of establishing their varied, "catering, arable farming and wine-growing and selling business" all the family has become involved to create what is very much a family enterprise. They established the property in 1962 but it is only in the last decade that they have become vignerons. Leon and Andre Jones have moved the vineyard project onto its most recent stage in overseeing the construction of the firm's new winery.

Stainless steel tanks abound and there is an automated bottling line with labelling equipment and all the necessary filtration equipment to provide fresh, clean and well-made wines. White, red, rosé and sparkling wines are all produced from estate grown grapes. Work began on construction of the winery in 2006 and was completed in 2007 along with the tea rooms and restaurant.

Varietal whites are produced from Madeleine Angevine, Phoenix, Reichensteiner and Seyval Blanc. Blended whites include a dry white style from Madeleine Angevine and Reichensteiner, a medium style from Reichensteiner and Phoenix, as well as a sweet white dessert style available in 50 cl bottles, coming from a mix of

Seyval Blanc, giving desirable acidity, and Phoenix. Reds are produced varietally from Regent, Rondo and Pinot Noir and there is an unusual sweet red dessert Rondo. Red, rosé and white sparkling wines are all produced as well.

Visiting

This is an important destination for wine enthusiasts and indeed for an enjoyable alternative day out. On site there is a modern tea room, restaurant and a bar which has a viewing platform where you can take in the activity in the winery. There is a well-equipped wine shop, created in the same style as the restaurant, where all the Buzzard Valley wines can be purchased, along with wines from other parts

of the world as well as other goodies and gift hampers.

As well as the restaurant and shop, visitors can explore the vineyards and a range of organised tours is offered which will normally end with a full tasting. For those interested in fishing there are also nine lakes which are well stocked with trout and many other species. Weddings, Christmas parties and other special events can all be catered for. Future plans include holiday lodges with a classic English vineyard and winery backdrop.

HOW TO FIND US

- Address: 37 Shirral Drive, Drayton Bassett, Tamworth B78 3EQ
- Take the A446 — Lichfield. Stay on the A446 for approx. 2 miles. At big island, take the A453 — Tamworth. At the end of the central reservation, turn right down Shirrall Drive. Buzzards Valley is the 2nd farm on the left.
- Open: Telephone for opening time details for the shop, tea rooms and restaurant.

Tel: 0121 308 1951

Email: buzzardvalley@btconnect.com

Web: www.buzzardvalley.co.uk

Sales of Christmas trees are also important

HALFPENNY GREEN
Halfpenny Green, Staffordshire

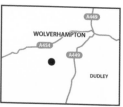

This is not only one of the larger of the Mercian vineyards but one of the larger in the country. A wide range of grape varieties is planted and an extensive range of wines can be purchased in a very attractive, airy vineyard shop.

The Halfpenny Green Vineyard was first planted in 1983. Martin Vickers planted the first vines and continues to oversee this part of the operation while his son Clive now makes the wines. Those early plantings are now of real age in English vineyard terms. They have continued to plant and expand their vineyard holding from what was originally a hobby and now have some 30 acres (12.15 ha) in all under vine. The whole operation is a commendable example of what can be done from less than profitable arable farming land.

The Vineyard
The vineyard has reached its current 30 acres (12.15 ha) after a series of planting programmes. 22 acres (8.9 ha) had been added to the original 0.5 acres (0.2 ha) by 1991. The site is good for growing vines with a south and south-west facing aspect and well-drained loamy sand soils avoiding a

real build up of vigour and vine growth during the summer. As such, the vineyard has, by English standards a relatively high plant density of around 1,300

VINEYARD FACTS

- 30 acres (12.15 ha) under vine. Approximately 39,000 vines planted.
- Vineyards use Double Guyot trellising.
- Trellising ensures good levels of photosynthesis and sugar in the grapes.
- Wines produced on site.
- Contract winemaking available for other vineyards.
- Modern winery with stainless steel tanks, bladder press and gravity fed bottling.

Visitors relaxing in the Tea Room

vines to the acre (3,200 vines/ha). In order to optimise the quality of their fruit the Vickers have their vines trained by the Double Guyot method, with vertical shoot positioning of the fruiting wood and good exposure to sunlight. An extensive range of grape varieties is planted. Among the whites, Huxelrebe, Reichensteiner, Seyval Blanc,

BIOGRAPHY   **Martin Vickers**

Martin Vickers established the vineyard in 1983, making better use of arable farmland than would be possible with conventional farming. He has now been joined by his son Clive in this endeavour. After bringing in their first harvest, they have been producing award winning wines since 1988. Their vineyard and winery has been consistently developed since then to its present position as one of the best facilities in the country. The Queen and Prince Charles have tasted their wines and they provided the wine for the G8 summit in Birmingham with President Clinton.

Madeleine Angevine, Chardonnay, Schönburger, Faber, Findling and Kernling. Red varieties consist of Triomphe d´Alsace, Rondo, Regent, Pinot Noir and Dornfelder.

Wine production

As you would expect with such a large operation, the Vickers have their own winemaking facility on site. It's fully equipped and state of the art. There are stainless steel tanks for fermentation with temperature control, modern bladder presses for perfect juice extraction and ageing and the focus is in this respect on fruit-driven styles. The wines are automatically bottled and processed on site, which helps the logistics for the winemaker considerably. Both reds and whites get pre-bottling maturation in stainless steel. As for the wines themselves, the range is comprehensive with three sparkling wines, a red, a rosé as well as no fewer than six whites. The original winery was constructed in 1994 although this was replaced with the current modern facility in 2005. With such resources and storage immediately to hand it is understandable that as well as making the family wines, Clive Vickers is also able to offer contract winemaking for local vineyard owners.

Visiting

There is now a very impressive direct sales facility with not just wines for tasting and sale but also a restaurant and tea room, in which both lunches and cream teas can be enjoyed. A craft centre offers an extensive range of bespoke goods including homemade jewellery, homecraft goods, aromatherapy, garden furniture, prints and artwork, glassware, woodcraft and soft furnishings. When stocks are available the range of wines is also available to purchase via mail-order over the internet. The wine shop is open seven days a week for wine sales between 9.30 am and 5.00 pm. In the shop wines can be purchased as gifts with appropriate boxes and packs and case discounts are available. The Vickers are also regular visitors to local farmers' markets and an updated schedule of where they will be is available on the website. Wine and vineyard tours are available, check with the vineyard for complete details. The tea room and restaurant are also worth a visit.

HOW TO FIND US

- Address: Tom Lane, Halfpenny Green, South Staffordshire, DY7 5EP, UK
- Halfpenny Green is situated close to Wolverhampton, Dudley and Stourbridge just off the B4176 near Halfpenny Green Airfield.
- Open: The Vineyard and Tea Rooms are open daily all year from 10:30am – 5:00pm.

Tel: 01384 221122
Fax: 01384 221101
Email: sales@halfpenny-green-vineyards.co.uk
Web: www.halfpenny-green-vineyards.co.uk

CHEVELSWARDE
South Kilworth, Leicestershire

This small organic vineyard, owned by John Daltry, is recognised by the Soil Association. A range of organically grown vegetables are available in their farm shop, as well as their wines.

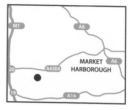

The origins of the small village of Chevelswarde date back to the Domesday book. John and Ruth Daltry purchased the property in 1973 and shortly thereafter decided to plant an acre (0.4 ha) of their land to vines. Their vineyard was the first in the UK to be recognised by the Soil Association and was of course England's first organic wine producer. The rest of the land is given over to vegetable growing on the Daltry family market garden and the whole property is farmed organically.

Wine production

The vineyard is small at just 1.3 acres (0.53 ha) and the vines are planted at moderate density to just four grape varieties, Phoenix, Solaris, Regent and Rondo. The soil, a sandy clay loam over gravel, has been treated organically for well over 30 years and two different trellising systems are employed. In addition to the more traditionally found Geneva Double Curtain (GDC), part of the vineyard is also now trained by the Scott-Henry system and all the vines are spur pruned. A grass cover crop is grown in the vine rows and compost added when required.

The Dry Red

Since 2003 the wines have all been made on site. This is a small property and the logistics involved in getting the four varieties, which ripen at different times, to an outside wine-making facility was as much of a challenge as vinifying them on site. The small winery is well-equipped with crusher and press, and variable capacity as well as glass-fibre tanks. Two wines are produced, a dry white and a red. Both get a short ageing period until the spring/summer following the vintage which helps to stabilise them.

Visiting

The property is open to the public but an appointment is requested before visiting. Visitors are welcomed between 9am and 6pm except Thursdays. Wines sales are possible at the shop and tours for small groups can also be arranged. Refreshments are not generally available except on the occasional open days. Visitors will be able to see how all the crops are grown, some open air and some under polytunnels, which does not include the vineyard which is cultivated traditionally.

EGLANTINE
Loughborough, Nottinghamshire

This small property near Leicester is the only commercial vineyard currently operating in Nottinghamshire. Joint owner and winemaker Tony Skuriat also makes wine for Renishaw Hall (see page 167) as well as his own range.

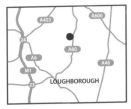

The Eglantine vineyard was first established in 1979 and was named after the wild rose of the English hedgerows. The first commercial crop was produced in 1984 and planting continued during the early 1980s. It confounds visitors that grape growing is possible as far north as this. The vines have been harvested under the Northern Lights and the finest wine produced here the North Star sweet white, is one of the country's best.

French award winners

Wine production
The vineyard is on a gentle south-facing slope planted on calcareous clay over limestone soils. These conditions will help to achieve not only fully ripened grapes but also good acidity and balance in the resulting wine. Vine density is sensibly kept to a reasonably low level with around 4,000 vines planted in total. The vines are all spur pruned and trained on a vertical shoot position trellis to aid exposure to sunlight during the summer months.

The wines are all vinified in the Skuriats' own well equipped small winery. There is a dry white, the sweet late-harvest North Star, a rosé, a red and a sparkling white. The North Star late-harvest white is also made from Madeleine Angevine. It has truly impressive depth and intensity with beguiling hints of citrus and dried fruits and excellent acidity and balance. It is possibly England's only ice-wine. The Traditional Method sparkler comes from a blend of varieties and vintages. It sees 18 months on its yeast lees before disgorging.

Visiting
The vineyard is open to the public most days between 10am and 6pm. There is a winery shop and tasting of the wines is also possible. Vineyard tours can also be arranged by appointment. As well as the small range of wines, mead is also made from home-produced honey and there is an additional sweet wine produced from cherries. As for most small English producers, cellar door sales are extremely important. The wines are also distributed by Best English Wines and Vintage Wines of Nottingham.

HOW TO FIND US

- Address: Costock, Loughborough, Leicestershire LE12 6UX Take the A60 north from Loughborough passing through the village of Rempstone and then Costock, which is by-passed. After around one mile take a left turn into Ash Lane (the turn is easy to miss) and the vineyard is around half a mile along Ash Lane on the lefthand side.
- Open: The tasting cellar is open 10am to 6pm. Telephone or email to make an appointment to view and tour the vineyards.

Tel: 01509 852386
Email: tony@skuriat.freeserve.co.uk

VINEYARD FACTS

- 3.2 acres (1.3 ha) in total under vine. South to south-east facing vineyard slope.
- Soil is a calcareous clay over limestone.
- Vineyards trained with a vertical shoot position trellis and spur pruned.
- Wines vinified in well equipped winery on site.

WELLAND VALLEY
Market Harborough, Leicestershire

This small Leicestershire vineyard is one of the better outposts of winegrowing in England's more northerly climes. It is open to the public for wine sales and certainly worth a visit.

VINEYARD FACTS

- 1.85 acres (0.75 ha) under vine.
- Vines planted on clay loam soils.
- Vineyards vertically trellised and Single and Double Guyot.
- Except for sparkling wines, vinification is on site.

WELLAND VALLEY
Farndon Dale

Welland Valley's story only began in 1991, when it was established by David and Jane Bates. They specialise in sparkling and given their vineyard's latitude, more surprisingly red wines, although a number of whites are also made.

Wine production

The vineyard currently has around 1,500 vines. The planting density is quite low but there will be reduced summer growing problems with too much foliage in the vine canopies. The soil though is ideal for vines and is low in fertility and there is replacement cane pruning during the winter months. The canopy can be easily opened up after véraison allowing good ventilation and exposure for the ripening bunches. A surprising number of grapes are planted given the size and scope of the operation here. The white varieties consist of Bacchus, Reichensteiner, Madeleine Angevine, Phoenix, Seyval Blanc, and Orion. Solaris has also been established in 2008. For the reds, Rondo, Regent, Dornfelder and Acolon are planted.

Unlike many other small vineyards the wines are vinified on site. The winery has stainlees steel tanks for settling, fermentation and storage and blending. There are also a couple of Burgundy barrels as well. The juice for the sparkling base wine is fermented on site and then sent to Three Choirs for lees ageing in bottle and disgorging. Of the wines, Farndon Dale is a crisp medium-dry Madeleine Angevine. There is a varietal off-dry Bacchus

as well as an aromatic Phoenix which is driest of the trio. Steeplechase is the bottle-fermented white sparkler vinified from Seyval Blanc and Reichensteiner and is a touch sweeter and fruitier than other styles. Two rosés are made, one the sparkling Tickled Pink and also Hunting Pink which is a dry still style. The small range is completed by the red Naseby, a blend of Rondo, Regent and Dornfelder.

Visiting

The vineyard is open for wine sales by appointment, there are no fixed times.

HOW TO FIND US

- Address: Marston Trussell, Market Harborough, Leicestershire LE16 9TX There is an accurate map on the website.

- Open: Telephone or email to make an appointment.

Tel: 01858 434591
Email: welland@tiscali.co.uk
Web: www.welland-vineyard.com

Sparkling Tickled Pink Rosé

RENISHAW HALL
Renishaw, Derbyshire

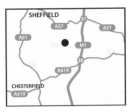

Renishaw Hall is the private seat of the Sitwell family and has been for over 400 years. It is a classic 17th century stately home with beautiful gardens in a 300 acre (121 ha) park that are open to the public.

The Renishaw vineyard itself was first planted in 1972, when at that time it had the distinction, or otherwise of being the most northerly in Europe at a latitude of 53 degrees, 18 minutes North. Grapes though are now being grown in locations as far north as Norway.

Wine production
The growing of grapes in such a climate and environment is not easy, although crop levels have improved here over the last half dozen years. It would seem almost certain that the current trend of global warming has contributed to this. The best years here are when there are two consecutively warm summers, first to ripen the fruit bearing wood and then the crop itself.

Seyval Blanc, Madeleine Angevine and some Phoenix are now planted, with a vineyard development programme that commenced in 1997 and was completed in 2002. Winemaking is now in the capable hands of Tony Skuriat at Eglantine (see page 165). Both still and sparkling white wines are now being produced.

Visiting
As well as the gardens, visitors can also visit the Sitwell Museum, the performing arts gallery and enjoy the Gallery café for lunches and teas.

Appointments must be made to visit the house. The vineyard itself is not open to the public and visitors should ask about wine sales at the ticket kiosk.

HOW TO FIND US

- Address: Renishaw Hall, Renishaw, Nr Sheffield, Derbyshire S31 9WB
- Renishaw Hall is in the heart of England, 140 miles north of London between Sheffield and Nottingham. It is only three miles from Junction 30 on the M1, and is well signposted from the Junction.
- Open: The gardens are open daily 10:30am — 4:30pm from the end of March to the end of September. The vineyards are not open to the public.

Tel: 01246 432210
Fax: 01246 430760
Email: info2@renishaw-hall.co.uk
Web: www.sitwell.co.uk

VINEYARD FACTS

- Vineyards first established in 1972. Vertical trellising on wires now improves canopy exposure.
- Seyval Blanc is the only original variety still planted. It is particularly suitable for sparkling base wine.
- Vinification is carried out at Eglantine Vineyards.
- 2,000 bottles produced a year.

LEVENTHORPE
Leeds, Yorkshire

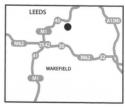

This is one of the most northerly of England's vineyards and unusually found within the boundaries of the city of Leeds. The key to being able to produce wine in such a location is a very unique local climate.

Winegrowing in Yorkshire though did not start in the 20th century. Monks, both the Cistercians and the Benedictines had been making wine successfully in the 12th century: a changing climate is not just a preserve of the current era. George Bowden and his wife Janet established Leventhorpe in 1985. George had identified and earlier purchased the site when he had noticed how its south facing slope had caught the sun and how well the soil drained, two of the key environmental ingredients here contributing to the vineyard's terroir. At the time Leventhorpe was unique as a vineyard at such a latitude, although others are also now being established with the gradual impact of global warming.

VINEYARD FACTS

- 5 acres (2 ha) under vine.
- Uniquely warm local mesoclimate, planted to early ripening grape varieties.
- Vineyard sited well drained sandy loam over sandstone soils.
- The oldest vines now 18 years.
- Vinification and ageing is all done on site.

The Vineyard

The first planting began in 1986 and there are now 5 acres (2 ha) in all of grape varieties that will ripen over a short summer growing season. Red Triomphe as well as the white grapes Seyval Blanc, Madeleine Angevine and Madeleine Sylvaner are planted and there are also a number of experimental varieties. Early ripening is the key here to achieving a consistent crop. Although the Seyval comes in a little later than the two Madeleine varieties, it provides good and consistent yields and can be used for dry whites and sparkling wine. The vineyard is located in a warm dry basin, which aids this process at such a latitude. A gentle south facing slope is also crucially important here as is the well drained and quickly warmed sandy loam over sandstone soil. Frost also tends to drift off the slope into the nearby River Aire. The local climate of the area is also warmer than the rest of Yorkshire with generally earlier summers, which helps in achieving good flavour ripeness in the grapes.

LEVENTHORPE
SEYVAL
YORKSHIRE REGIONAL WINE
11%vol   Estate grown in Yorkshire and   75cl
bottled by Leventhorpe Vineyard, Leeds, UK.
contains sulphites

BIOGRAPHY   George Bowden

Before becoming a vigneron, George Bowden taught chemistry, providing a good scientific background to understand the challenges of winegrowing in Yorkshire. He retired from teaching in 1999 and is now committed solely to his vineyard and winery. His advice is often sought from new world winegrowers who want to understand better the dynamics of cool climate viticulture and he also joins students at Plumpton College (see page 64) from time to time. Below: George Bowden shows HRH The Duke of Kent around Leventhorpe

Summer in the vineyard

Wine production

All the wines are made on site in a small well equipped modern winery with the facilities necessary to preserve aroma and flavour in the wines. The key to the whites being a long, slow fermentation which captures all those subtle and restrained aromas. Inevitably, given the latitude of the vineyard, the wines are marked by their quite piercing acidity and it is wise with the whites in particular to give them four or five years ageing to let them unfurl and open out. The small range includes as well as the Seyval Blanc and Madeleine Angevine, a dry Madeleine Sylvaner, a White rosé, a red from Triomphe and a Sparkling Brut produced from Seyval Blanc and aged in bottle on its lees.

Visiting

The wines are available from the vineyard shop as well as in local shops and restaurants. The vineyard is open to visitors most days including Sundays. It is advisable though to check first if you are travelling any distance. During the summer guided vineyard tours can be arranged for groups by appointment.

The Wines

LEVENTHORPE
MADELEINE ANGEVINE
YORKSHIRE REGIONAL WINE
11.5%vol Estate grown in Yorkshire and
bottled by Leventhorpe Vineyard, Leeds, UK. 75cl

Seyval Blanc

This is a tight and structured white, demanding of four or five years before approaching it. If you like dry Chenin Blanc from Vouvray or Montlouis, this is likely to be on your shopping list. The 2006 was very structured and restrained.

Madeleine Angevine

Still a backward style and needing a little patience, this offers a more floral and subtle aromatic style than the Seyval. Up to four years ageing is advisable though.

HOW TO FIND US

- Address: Woodlesford, Leeds LS26 8AF
- Take Junction 46 from the M1. Follow signs to Leeds. At next roundabout (Sainsbury's Retail Park) turn left, leading to Bullerthorpe Lane. Road crosses motorway and passes Gamblethorpe Farm on left. Take first turning right, signposted Newsam Green, then turn immediately left by the Lodge House onto Newsam Green Road. Winery on left hand side near bottom of road.
- Open: Most days. Telephone or email first if travelling any distance.

Tel: 0113 288 9088

Email: janet@leventhorpevineyard.freeserve.co.uk

EAST ANGLIA

East Anglia

Philip Williamson

Bedfordshire
1 Warden Abbey

Cambridgeshire
2 Chilford Hall

Essex
3 Bardfield Vineyard
4 Carter's Vineyards
5 New Hall Vineyard
6 Sandyford

Suffolk
7 Ickworth
8 Oak Hill Wines
9 Shawsgate
10 Wissett Wines
11 Wyken Hall

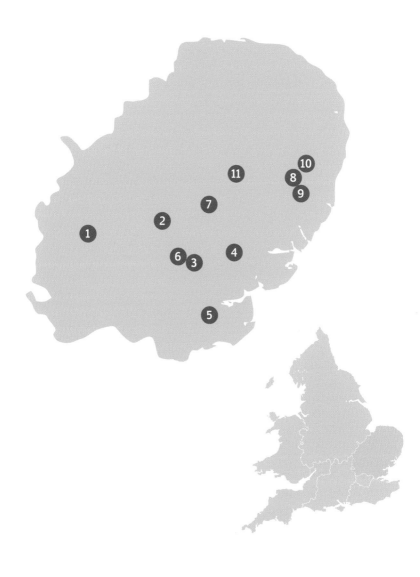

OAK HILL WINES
Fressingfield, Suffolk

Stretched across just a single acre of pleasant Suffolk countryside and below an oak tree estimated to be 800 years old is Willow House Vineyard, on a slope planted solely to the Bacchus variety.

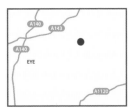

The vineyard was planted in 1987 by Martha Stevens in the grounds of 400 year old Willow House in the centre of Fressingfield, deep in the Suffolk countryside. Oak Hill is now owned by David and Carol Spenser. Carol, a style and fashion consultant, runs Style Directions, her fashion advice business from here. There are a further 7 acres (2.8 ha) available for planting.

Wine production
Given its small size, Willow House Vineyard can be adequately managed by just one person, Victor Barley. However, the grapes are picked with the help of a few friends — 20 people are needed to get the entire

The small and compact vineyard

VINEYARD FACTS

- Just a single acre (0.4 ha) of vineyard on clay and flint soils.
- Bacchus, the only variety used, is trained on a Geneva Double Curtain system.
- The site is south-facing and all the grapes are hand-picked.
- Differences in winemaking produce three distinctly different styles of Bacchus.

vineyard picked in a day — before sending them to Mark Barnes at Chilford Hall (see page 186) for the transformation into wine. The bottles are returned from the winery by the June following the vintage for hand-labelling. Not one but three Bacchus are made. Bacchus Dry is an unoaked, stainless steel vinified dry style while in Bacchus Medium more residual sugar makes for an off-dry version. A third, Bacchus Oaked,

sees some contact with French oak to give a broader example with a less pronounced varietal character.

Visiting
The vineyard is not open to visitors, except on the weekend of the Fressingfield garden festival in June but if you want the peace and pleasure of the Suffolk countryside it is possible to stay in the Granary, a large, free-standing farmhouse property. The historic market town of Harleston is also close by, just 4 miles away.

HOW TO FIND US

- Oak Hill Wines, Willow House Vineyard, Fressingfield, Eye, Suffolk IP21 5PE
- Fressingfield on the B1116 is just south of Harleston, which lies next to the A143.

Tel: 01379 586868
Fax: 01379 586858
Email: mail@oak-hill.co.uk
Web: www.oak-hill.co.uk

ICKWORTH
nr Bury St Edmunds, Suffolk

The striking 18th century rotunda that is the centrepiece of Ickworth House acts as a magnet drawing visitors to the park. Close by, within the walled garden, a vineyard has taken root providing the National Trust with its very own wines.

This large National Trust property extends for 1800 acres (729 ha). The house includes paintings by some of the great masters (including Velázquez and Titian), portraits by Gainsborough, and fine period fittings and furniture. The parkland includes a formal Italianate garden, wooded gardens and, since 1995, a vineyard within the walled garden. Frederick Augustus Hervey was the creator of Ickworth House and became both an Earl (the 4th Earl of Bristol) and a Bishop (Bishop of Derry). Known as the Earl Bishop this name has been used for Ickworth's red wine.

Wine production
The walled garden once included table grapes

VINEYARD FACTS

- First planted in 1995 and 1996, subsequently substantially replanted and expanded.
- 2.5 acres (1ha) of vineyard on clayey loam soils.
- Planted to Auxerrois, Bacchus, Rondo and a small amount of Pinot Noir.
- The vines are trained to the Scott Henry system with 2.5m between the rows.

amongst its crops but it was only thanks to the initiative of Charles and Jillian Macready in 1994 that modern wine production became a reality. The pair both planted and manage the vineyard but the wines have always been contract-made — recently, most of them by Chapel Down (see page 28). They are led by a sparkling Traditional Method rosé called Suffolk Pink, a blend of Auxerrois grapes with some Pinot Noir. Also produced are Walled Garden White, a dry varietal Bacchus, and a new still rosé, called Lady Geraldine's Blush. The red wine, made by Carter's Vineyard (see page 180) is Earl Bishop's Reserve, from 100 per cent Rondo grapes. With its deep ruby colour, somewhat Beaujolais-like texture and typical coarse Rondo flavours — an old-fashioned red fruits character with a slightly burnt, peppery aspect — this is a 'love it or loath it' style of red.

The vines on a south-facing slope within the walled garden

Alistair Carr and Charles Macready

Visiting
The vineyard may be visited at any time during a day out at Ickworth Park. Discovery days are on the second Sunday in the month between June and October. For a small charge there's a wine tasting and talk as well as the usual self-guided trail around the vineyard. The wine is sold in the shop and is also available in the restaurant by the glass or bottle.

HOW TO FIND US

- Ickworth House, Horringer, Bury St Edmunds, Suffolk IP29 5QE
- The park and house can be reached off the A143 just south-west of Bury St Edmund (use the M11, A11 and A14 if coming from London). The A14 also provides the link to Cambridge. Otherwise you can walk, cycle or bus from Bury St Edmunds – if you've come by train.
- Vineyard open from 11am-4pm.
- Ickworth House is open Mon, Tues, Fri, Sat & Sun from 1-5pm (mid March to end September); 1-4:30 during October. The gardens and shop have longer opening hours and the park is open all year from 8am-8pm. For more details on opening days/hours visit the National Trust website (use the alphabetical listing under Places to Visit).

Tel: 01359 251173 (vineyard); 01284 735270 (house, park, gardens)

Email: macready@ickworthvineyard.co.uk

Web: www.ickworthvineyard.co.uk

www.nationaltrust.org.uk

SHAWSGATE
Framlingham, Suffolk

Shawsgate is the leading Suffolk winery, equipped with a modern winemaking facility that produces not only the Shawsgate range of mostly white wines but also includes the output of several other wineries in the region.

Shawsgate dates from 1973 but much of its recent standing derives from its purchase by Ian Hutchinson in 1985. New vineyards and a new winery were part of the legacy when it came under new ownership in 2000. Shawsgate now forms part of the Jarrett Group based in Mendlesham, near Stowmarket, which includes Jarrett Seeds and Jarrett Teas.

VINEYARD FACTS

- 15 acres (6 ha) of vineyard running north-south on clay soils.
- Both Guyot and Geneva Double Curtain trellising systems are utilised.
- High windbreaks offer some protection on the relatively wind-exposed countryside.
- A leading proponent amongst those offering vine leasing schemes.

Wine production

The vineyard covers 15 acres (6 ha) and includes Bacchus, Müller-Thurgau, Reichensteiner, Rondo, Schönburger and Seyval Blanc. Shawsgate was one of the first to operate a vine leasing scheme whereby leasees rent a row or more of vines and can have the resulting crop vinified and bottled under their own label. They continue to promote this scheme and more details can be found via their website. Shawsgate's own wines are made by the well-respected Rob Capp. Led by a varietal Bacchus, they are amongst the best from East Anglia. The well-

equipped winery with plenty of stainless steel tank capacity together with a temperature regulated cellar have also made it possible for Shawsgate to serve as something of a regional winemaking hub, providing contract winemaking facilities for many other vineyards in the wider area.

Stainless Steel Tanks

Visiting

As well as self-guided tours of the vineyard, group vineyard and evening tours can be booked in the summer months. The vineyard shop is open every Friday (and some Saturdays) 10-4pm but every day of the week between April and October.

HOW TO FIND US

- Badingham Road, Framlingham, Suffolk IP13 9HZ
- From Ipswich take the A12 for 15 miles before following the B1116 to Framlingham. From here it is a further mile along the B1120 Badingham Road. From the west it can be reached via the A14. Continuing to Stowmarket. Join the A1120, east to Saxtead Green. B1119 takes you to Framlingham.

Tel: 01728 724060
Fax: 01728 723232
Email: wines@shawsgate.co.uk
Web: www.shawsgate.co.uk

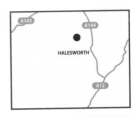

WISSETT WINES
nr Halesworth, Suffolk

This vineyard with tours, gardens and a chance to mingle with a herd of Alpaca lies inland from the delightful seaside village of Southwold. If the weather is too inclement on the coast then head inland.

Wine production

The first vines were planted here by the owner Jonathan Craft in 1987 after a visit to Alsace. Pinot Gris and Auxerrois grapes were brought back and still form an important part of the grape mix. The vineyard now extends to 8 acres (3.2 ha) and also includes Pinot Noir, Pinot Meunier and Madeleine Ange-vine. Vines in the original vineyard are trellised in the Geneva Double Curtain system while for the newer plantings the Scott Henry system is used.

After a break in production of several years, the Crafts are now making the most of the resurgence in English wine. The 2006 Wissett Dry white combines the two Alsace varieties to good effect with some peach blossom and good slightly pear-like fruit typical of the varieties. While there is not the extra concentration, depth or nuance of a fine Alsace example it is well-balanced and soundly structured and an attractive example of a dry English white in this vintage. Other wines include Wissett Pink, a rosé from Pinot Noir and Pinot Meunier, and Noah's First, a varietal Pinot Gris from late-harvested grapes made in a dry style. Traditional Method sparkling wine is also made, in both Brut and Brut Rosé versions.

Visiting

The winery includes a visitor centre in a restored 18th century barn and is open for vineyard tours and tastings. In addition there is both Bed & Breakfast accommodation and a farmhouse style self-catering option for those wishing to make the most of this attractive part of Suffolk.

VINEYARD FACTS

- 8 acres (3.2 ha) of vines on clay soils interspersed with flints.
- Two different trellising systems used: Geneva Double Curtain and Scott Henry.
- Windbreaks are especially important given the relative proximity to the coast.
- Later ripening Auxerrois grapes are planted in the warmest, most protected vineyard plot.

HOW TO FIND US

- Valley Farm Vineyards, Wissett, Suffolk IP19 0JJ
- From the A12 make for Halesworth. Here head north on the Norwich Road (A144), taking the first left after the third roundabout and following the brown Wissett Wines tourist sign.
- Open: from 10-6pm daily.

Tel: 01986 785535
Email: valleyfarmvineyards@tiscali.co.uk
Web: www.wissettwines.com
www.valleyfarmvineyards.com

WYKEN HALL
Stanton, Suffolk

Here is a vineyard destination that offers much more than just vines set amongst the splendour of the Suffolk countryside. Fine estate gardens, an ancient wood, a restaurant and shop as well as a regular Farmers' Market.

VINEYARD FACTS

- 7 acres (2.8 ha) planted to an assortment of early ripening varieties.
- The vineyard is south facing with mostly sandy loam soils.
- The grapes are transported to Framlingham to take advantage of Shawsgate's contract winemaking facilities.

Wyken Hall is an Elizabethan manor house owned by Kenneth Carlisle and has been in his family since the 1920s. In 1986 he married American journalist and activist Carla Cooper who set about transforming the estate. This included restoring a 400 year old barn, which now houses the Leaping Hare restaurant and shop, as well as planting the vineyard. Carla writes a regular piece about the estate and her experiences in the Spectator column of 'Country Life'. A selection of these have been reproduced as South Facing Slope which is available from the Wyken shop. The Carlisles continue to enhance the estate's ecosystem both for the long-term viability of the farm and in order to improve the quality of the produce.

Wine production
A Farmers' Market sells produce from both the estate and other local farmers. The 7 acre (2.8 ha) vineyard was planted in 1988 and the first vintage was in 1991. Production averages around 14,000 bottles per year but fluctuates significantly depending on the vintage. Rather than build their own winemaking facility the wines have been produced by Shawsgate (see page 176). A varietal Bacchus is the leading white wine. Also made are a sparkling wine, Wyken Moonshine and a rosé, Wyken Pink.

Visiting
As well as a restaurant, café and shop, for a small charge visitors can also enjoy the garden on summer afternoons.

HOW TO FIND US

- Wyken Hall, Stanton, Bury St-Edmunds, Suffolk IP31 2DW
- Close to the A143 about 9 miles (14.5km) north-east of Bury St-Edmunds. Leave the A143 at Ixworth or Stanton and follow the brown tourist signs.
- The restaurant, café and shop are open daily 10-6pm.

Tel: 01359 250262 (shop) 01359 250287 (restaurant) 01359 252372 (estate office)
Email: estate.Office@wykenvineyards.co.uk
Web: www.wykenvineyards.co.uk

Wyken's well manicured vineyard

BARDFIELD VINEYARD
Great Bardfield, Essex

Essex and wine are not an unusual association — at least in the context of drinking the stuff. Making it is however less common but Bardfield along with Carter's, New Hall and others are showing that successful cultivation is also possible in the county.

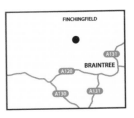

Anne of Cleves once owned the land here. Following the dissolution of her marriage to Henry VIII she received an honorary title and property which included Hever Castle and the Burgh of Bardfield. The latter included the Great Lodge, a 16th century house and barn. While the house has undergone subsequent rebuilds and extensions, the striking Grade I listed brick and tile barn built around 1540, survives. A single hectare of vineyard was added in 1990 which followed a series of gardening enhancements by Rosemary Alexander, who was resident at the Great Lodge during the eighties. Rosemary, author of several gardening titles, was the founder, and continues to be Principal, of the English Gardening School (at the Chelsea Physic Garden in London).

Wine production

Owner Alan Jordan's vineyard is planted to just two varieties, Bacchus and

VINEYARD FACTS

- 2.5 acres (1 ha) planted to Bacchus and Reichensteiner in 1990.
- The vines are trellised on a Double Guyot system in a south facing vineyard.
- The grapes are hand-picked before being dispatched for vinification and bottling.

Reichensteiner. The vines are planted on sandy loam soils typical in the area and the grapes are hand-picked prior to a cool stainless steel fermentation. The white wines are made by Rob Capp at Shawsgate (see page 176) in both medium-dry and dry styles and as well as varietal versions of both varieties. The most popular wine however is a vintage-dated

Extra Brut sparkling wine.

Visiting

The vineyard is open by appointment and tours and wine tastings can be arranged during the spring and summer months. Wines can also be purchased at the vineyard all year round.

HOW TO FIND US

- The Great Lodge, Great Bardfield, Braintree, Essex CM7 4QD
- Just to the north of Braintree, Great Lodge can be reached from the M11 by exiting for the A120 and then following the signs for Blake House Craft Centre before continuing for a further 4 miles almost as far as the village of Great Bardfield.
- Open: By appointment.

Tel: 01371 810776
Fax: 01371 811398
Email: info@thegreatlodge experience.com
Web: www.thegreatlodge experience.com

CARTER'S VINEYARDS
Boxted, Essex

A vineyard with a difference. Carter's offers a great opportunity for a stroll in the English countryside that includes wildflower meadows, ancient hedgerows, lakes and woodland nurturing local wildlife — including kingfishers if you're lucky.

The vineyard was planted here in 1990, a year after the farm had been purchased by Mary Mudd. She set the farm up in order to develop several different types of habitat for wildlife. Remarkably she successfully managed to establish the winery and farm independently without recourse to the national grid or the mains water supply, using renewable resources alone. The first crop was made at nearby Gifford Hall in 1993 and the first wines were sold on VE day in 1995 at a wine and food fair in Colchester — the same year winemaking commenced at Carter's after Mary had taken a winemaking course at Plumpton College.

The vineyard
The farm's poor soils with a light loam over sand and gravel on a gentle slope were considered well disposed for viticulture. Initially white varieties were chosen followed by red varieties from the mid-nineties. The vineyard has expanded to 7 acres (nearly 3 ha) of the 40 acre (16 ha) estate. While there are some plantings of leading vinifera varieties such as Chardonnay and Pinot Noir as well as the now widely seen Bacchus there are also

VINEYARD FACTS

- The winery is powered independently using only renewable energy.
- A reed bed waste filtration area is used to deal with waste and produce Comfrey for mulch to spread on the vineyards.
- Grapes from 7 acres (2.8 ha) are supplemented by bought-in supplies.
- The Scott Henry system of trellising is used to enhance ripening.

plantings of modern hybrid varieties Orion and Phoenix. However both have been classified in Germany as being vitis vinifera. Grapes such as these are capable of obtaining good sugar levels even in wetter or cooler years.

Vines planted to maximum acreage

BIOGRAPHY Ben Bunting

In an age when there is a resurgence in locally produced food and beverages it is perhaps gratifying to see that Carter's future is now secure as part of Bunting & Sons who continue to run the farm with Mary Mudd using only renewable resources. Bunting & Sons is a long established Colchester family business (1820) with a horticultural tradition, the sixth and seventh generation of the family now run the company's diverse holdings and projects. While Ben Bunting directs operations at Carter's, other properties include the Heritage and Conservation centre in Horkesley Park and the 15th century Anchor Inn pub in Nayland, on the banks of the river Stour, which is run by Carl Shillingford. Adjacent

to the Anchor Inn is the non-intensively farmed Heritage Farm and kitchen garden (both open to the public) that supplies it with fresh produce.

Carter's' addition to the growing range of sparkling wines

edge detract slightly but there is plenty of character and flavour as well as some potential for ageing.

Visiting
Following a self-guided tour through the vineyards, the wines can be tasted or purchased. Events are held in the vineyards during the summer months and functions can also be arranged. Also made and available for purchase are a range of fruit liqueurs. If you can't get to the winery, the wines are sold locally in outlets in Colchester.

The attractively labelled Boudicca

Crates of freshly picked grapes ready for pressing

Wine production
Around 25,000 bottles of wine are now produced every year from both estate grapes and some bought-in fruit. Wines are now also made under contract for other growers in the region. Carter's sparkling wines include bottle fermented Traditional Method Brut and Rosé. These are unusual in combining the hybrid grape Orion with Chardonnay. Both Bacchus and Orion are produced varietally as is Reichensteiner in a medium-dry style under the label St Helena. For red there is a varietal Pinot Noir which is sold as Boudicca. However the most celebrated wine made here to date is the King Coel red. Composed of Rondo, Dornfelder and Dunkelfelder there is good colour, especially in hot years like 2003 or 2006, and plenty of rhubarb, raspberry and plum fruit in a round and supple textured wine. Something of a burnt earth character and a slightly coarse herbal

HOW TO FIND US

- Green Lane, Boxted, Colchester, Essex CO4 5TS
- Carter's lies just to the north of Colchester and can be reached from the A134.
- Open: Every day 11-5pm from Easter Monday until the end of October.

Tel: 01206 271136
Fax: 01206 273625
Email: enquiries@ cartersvineyards.co.uk
Web: www.cartersvineyards.co.uk

NEW HALL
Purleigh, Essex

There is plenty for the visitor to the largest vineyard in East Anglia especially if you choose to visit in September when an annual English wine festival and open day are held.

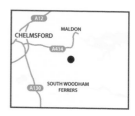

Wine was made locally in the Middle Ages with a vineyard planted at Purleigh in 1120. Subsequent 12th and 13th century records show its commercial importance, including an instance where the wine was taken to Bury St Edmunds in anticipation of the visit of King John. By contrast New Hall is a relatively recent manifestation, being established by the Greenwood family in 1969. However this still makes it one of the oldest vineyards in the modern era of English viticulture.

The vineyard
The vineyards, the largest planting in East Anglia, are widely spaced on a Guyot trellising system. Around 60-70 per cent of the grapes are sold off to others including the English Wines group (Chapel Down).

VINEYARD FACTS

- East Anglia's largest vineyard with 185 acres (75 ha).
- The location benefits from some of the warmest weather and lowest rainfall in the UK. Frost is rarely a problem.
- A wide variety of mostly Germanic varieties is planted.
- The vineyards are planted at relatively low densities on heavy clay soils.

New Hall's vineyard is the largest in East Anglia

NEW HALL Annual Wine Festival

An annual wine festival has been held here since 1975. On the first full weekend in September New Hall is open to all, providing entertainment, country dancing, local foods, wine tasting, guided tours and an arts and crafts show, all with an English country flavour. Guided tours of the vineyard and winery are also available at other times of the year. There is also ample opportunity to stock up on other local produce from other farms and shops in the surrounding area.

In the early years the wines were made elsewhere but the winery now is fully equipped with modern presses and rows of stainless steel tanks. Current production of around 400,000 bottles per year will double when recently planted vines come on stream in a couple of years.

Wine production

The wines are attractive, balanced and soundly made and sold as East Anglian regional wines. Although relatively undemanding, there is good consistency across the range from medium-dry whites to drier whites, rosé and red. Nearly all are produced varietally including the Signature white which was made from Siegerrebe in 2006. The Ruby Royalé red however is comprised of the unusual blend of Pinot Noir, Alcolon, Regent and Dornfelder. Just 15 per cent of the wine spends a short spell in French oak. As well as the other wines detailed here there are varietals made from Huxelrebe, Müller-Thurgau, Ortega, Pinot Blanc, Rülander (Pinot Gris) and Schönburger. A Traditional Method sparkling wine from Pinot Noir and Chardonnay is also made.

Visiting

Even if you don't make the wine festival in September (see above), for a glimpse at East Anglia's largest vineyard and the source of a consistent range of typical English wine production, this has to be worth a visit. It is also one of the most easily reached vineyards north of London.

HOW TO FIND US

- Chelmsford Road, Purleigh, Chelmsford, Essex CM3 6PN
- From the M25 take the A12 including the Chelmsford bypass until the A414. At the roundabout beyond Danbury continue on the B1010 to Purleigh where the winery is signposted.
- Open: Mon to Friday: 11am-5pm Saturday & Sunday: 11:30am-3:30pm

Tel: 01621 828343

Email: newhall@newhallwines.co.uk

Web: www.newhallwines.co.uk

The Wines

2006 Signature (dry white)

Floral and fruit scented white with an almost chalky edge. Soft, supple and sound – a wine that conjures up something of English hedgerows and countryside.

2007 Bacchus (medium-dry white)

A very herbaceous green-fruited Bacchus with nettle, crushed wild herb and grassy scents. Light and just slightly off-dry with reasonable lift and zing in the mouth. A 2005 Special Late Harvest version adds some ripe fruit flavours as well as more character and style.

2007 Pinot Noir (medium-dry rosé)

A pretty pale cherry pink, with hints of cherry, herbal and floral aromas. A soft, round and easy-drinking style with clean appley, cherry fruit that should be drunk lightly chilled.

2007 Ruby Royalé (red)

This youthful red combines spice, earth and lightly brambly berry fruit and wild cherry characters with a firmer herbaceous streak. Relatively light, soft, round and juicy, this forward red has only modest length and structure but is easy to drink and soundly made.

SANDYFORD
Great Sampford, Essex

This small 2 acre (0.8 ha) vineyard is in the heart of the East Anglian countryside. It forms part of a larger 400 acre (162 ha) farm that comprises wheat, barley and other crops, as well as some free-range turkeys.

Sue and Mike Lindsell run this small vineyard planted in 1999. The introduction of viticulture provided further diversification on their large family-run farm. The relatively mild and dry local climate encouraged them to plant some of the most successful German-derived vinifera and hybrid varieties. The first small crop was harvested in 2001. Because of the relative fertility of the soils the Scott Henry trellising system is employed. The aim is for better photosynthesis and improved wine quality.

Wine production
A diverse range of wines starts with the Clover Hill white, the first wine ever made here, a mix of Bacchus and Reichensteiner. There's also a floral and herbal-scented rosé called English Rosé, from Regent and Rondo grapes. It displays cranberry and cool red fruit

VINEYARD FACTS

- South-west facing slopes that are susceptible to late spring frosts.
- Italian alders have been planted to improve vineyard shelter.
- Scott Henry training is used. The canopy is split vertically with a part trained upwards and a part trained downwards, giving a curtain of foliage 2m high.

and, although capable of a couple of years' age, is best drunk fairly young. The Lindsells' Special Reserve red uses the same grapes as the rosé but in addition some Triomphe. It spends six months in oak before being released with plenty of bottle age. The 2003 is still deeply coloured (in part thanks to the Rondo) and supple with berry fruits and old fashioned plum and no lack of intensity and character, if finishing more robustly. Also made is Sandyford Brut, a traditional method fizz based on Bacchus and Reichensteiner.

Visiting
There are guided tours (May to September) for a minimum of 10 people. Appointments should be made for both tastings and tours.

Mike & Sue Lindsell

HOW TO FIND US

- Salix Farm, Great Sampford, Essex CB10 2QE
- Sandyford Vineyard is located to the north and east of Stansted airport – off the B1051 just south of Great Sampford. If coming up the M11 from London leave at junction 8 and travel up through Thaxted. If coming down the M11 from the north leave at junction 9 and travel through Saffron Walden.

Tel: 01799 586586
Email: info@sandyfordvineyard.co.uk
Web: www.sandyfordvineyard.co.uk

WARDEN ABBEY
Biggleswade, Bedfordshire

This small vineyard planted on the land of Warden Abbey and owned by Jane Whitbread, venerable viticultural history. The Cistercian abbey here was founded in 1135 and the monks established two vineyards.

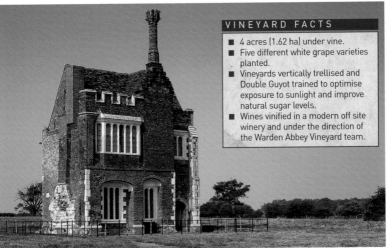

VINEYARD FACTS

- 4 acres (1.62 ha) under vine.
- Five different white grape varieties planted.
- Vineyards vertically trellised and Double Guyot trained to optimise exposure to sunlight and improve natural sugar levels.
- Wines vinified in a modern off site winery and under the direction of the Warden Abbey Vineyard team.

Infamously, the monks gained a reputation far removed from their celibate vows, women were said to have visited the abbey, and the monks were referred to as "common dronkerds". The vineyard eventually went into decline with Henry VIII's Dissolution of the Monasteries. It was not until 1986 that Jane Whitbread re-established the "lyttel" vineyard.

Wine production
A range of varieties is planted here. The vines are all vertically trained to Double Guyot, providing

The community at harvest

them with good sunlight exposure for the vine canopy and the site enjoys a nicely exposed sunny southerly aspect on well-drained soil.

The wines are vinified off site, although a careful control is taken over each stage of the process. There is the further benefit gained from the expertise of Master of Wine Derek Smedley who has advised here since the vineyards were first established. The wines produced are all whites. First a lightly floral Warden Vineyard white which is a blend of Regner, Reichensteiner and Bacchus. There is also a crisp varietal Bacchus. The Warden Abbey white blends Müller Thurgau with Regner and in 2006 a special white bottling was a blend of a range of grapes. The Special Reserve is Müller-Thurgau, Reichensteiner and Regner.

Visiting
The vineyard itself is a working farm and as such is not open to the public except on open days, contact Southill Park for details of these. All the wines can now be purchased online and via mail order. Warden Abbey itself is available for short breaks through the Landmark Trust.

HOW TO FIND US

- Address: Southill Park, Biggleswade, Beds, SG18 9LJ
- Visit the website for detailed directions for both Warden Abbey and Southill Park.
- Open: On special function and tasting days and the September Open Vineyard Weekend.

Tel: 01462 816226
Fax: 01462 812235
Email: sue@wardenwines.co.uk
Web: www.wardenwines.co.uk

CHILFORD HALL
Linton, Cambridgeshire

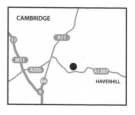

You might come to Chilford Hall to attend a conference or a dinner event. You might even be visiting the Curwen Studio renowned for its print making. However you must also take advantage of the complete winemaking entity by taking part in a tour.

The home of the Alper family since 1965, Chilford Hall incorporates 18 acres (7.3 ha) of vineyard and its own winemaking facilities. The Great Hall and House date from the first half of the 19th century while the winery is housed in a reconstructed barn that dates from the 17th century. Also forming a part of the centre's facilities, the Curwen studio, with an adjacent study centre was relocated here in 1989. At least something of what visitors can see is the legacy of Sam Alper. Marble pillars from the Long Bar at Waterloo can be seen in the wine cellar while granite pillars from the Embankment can't be missed on a stroll through the vineyard.

VINEYARD FACTS

- One of England's oldest established vineyards in the modern era.
- Vineyards are now planted to a typical blend of some of the most successful varieties for still white and red production in the UK.
- Vines are trellised high, in part to reduce the risk of spring frost.
- All grapes are hand-harvested.

The vineyard

The first vines were planted in 1972 with further planting in the mid-seventies, although much of it was re-planted in the nineties. Soils are variable but free-draining including sand and gravels, with varying amounts of clay and silt overlying chalk. White varieties including Müller-Thurgau, Ortega, Schönburger, Reichensteiner and Siegerrebe are supplemented by black grapes Regent, Rondo, Dornfelder and Pinot Noir. All the grapes are harvested by hand and fermented using active dried yeasts.

The Autumn harvest begins

BIOGRAPHY   Sam Alper

Sam Alper (1924 – 2002) bought Chilford Hall in 1965 and set about modernising the estate fired by his own particular blend of interests. He was the designer of Sprite caravans and the founder of the Little Chef chain, but a passion for wine, art (especially sculpture) and architectural relics more than compensate. Sam's art

collection and establishment of the Chilford Hall Press eventually resulted in the Curwen studio relocating to Chilford Hall, whilst Sam's passion for wine led not only to the development of the wine estate but promotional stunts that included driving samples of his wine to the George V hotel in Paris in his Vintage Rolls Royce Phantom II.

The Wines

2006 Chilford Hundred Schönburger

A scented white with pear, spice, floral and exotic aromas. There is both intensity and good structure for a wine from this variety. Plenty of fruit, well-balanced and suffused too with a cool English herbal expression.

2003 Chilford Hundred Sparkling Rosé

Even the colour is unusual with a salmon-cherry hue to this curious blend of Dornfelder and Müller-Thurgau. Floral, redcurrant and cherry aromas precede a ripe and fruity palate under-pinned with plenty of acidity. Has a Prosecco-like zest and freshness even with 5 years' age.

'Chilford Hundred' land

Wine production

The wines are all labelled Chilford Hundred (in reference to the Saxon measure of land divisions) and include whites bottled as Medium, Medium-Dry and Dry as well as a fine example of a varietal Schönburger and a sparkling rosé based on Dornfelder and Müller-Thurgau. The sparkling white wine is based entirely on Müller-Thurgau, a grape rarely used on its own in fizz in the UK. In Europe cheaper sparkling wines can sponge up excess quantities of the grape's production, especially as Sekt in Germany. The emphasis generally is on clean, fresh, aromatic styles with good intensity and as such they are among the best examples of East Anglian wines.

Visiting

Vineyard tours take in the whole winemaking process from vineyard practice through pressing and fermentation to bottling. Visitors can then purchase the estate's wines at the Vineleaf café and shop. If you're visiting Cambridge there are further opportunities to buy the wines at local outlets. In part due to Sam Alper's unstinting promotional efforts small quantities are also exported to the Netherlands, Norway, France and the USA.

HOW TO FIND US

- Chilford Hall, Balsham Road, Linton, Cambridge CB21 4LE
- Chilford Hall Vineyard, located on the B1052 between Balsham and Linton, is clearly signposted after exiting the M11 then A11 when coming from London or the west.
- Open Friday, Saturday and Sunday 10-5pm between 1st March and 1st December.
- Wines can be bought from the shop or via the office number below.

Tel: 01223 895600

Fax: 01223 895605

Email: info@chilfordhall.co.uk

Web: www.chilfordhall.co.uk

WALES

Wales

Neville Blech

Anglesey
1 Llanbadrig
2 Ty Croes Vineyard

Powys
3 Penarth Vineyard

Monmouthshire
4 Ancre Hill
5 Parva Farm
6 Sugar Loaf
7 Wernddu Wine

Vale of Glamorgan
8 Bryn Ceiliog
9 Glyndwr
10 Llanerch Vineyard

Carmarthenshire
11 Jabajak Vineyard

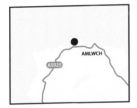

LLANBADRIG
Cemaes, Anglesey

Anglesey has a very long winemaking tradition dating back to Roman times. When the foundations for a Holyhead supermarket were being dug, roots were found which proved to be part of a vast area of vines belonging to the Romans.

Grape growing in polytunnels

Tom Barlow and his family started the vineyard in 1990 as a single row on a hillside to the east of the village of Cemaes. The vines did not grow and were replaced the following year by more suitable varieties. They now have approximately 6,000 vines growing on 2 acres (0.8ha) and continue to experiment with newer varieties, having some 20 or so different types on trial. They are not all producing yet, but the aim is to produce more than 20,000 bottles annually.

VINEYARD FACTS

- Llanbadrig is the most northerly vineyard in Wales.
- Sandy loam soil with good drainage, containing gravel and large stones.
- Vines planted in an east to west valley.
- Vines trained with Single Guyot method.

The Vineyard

The direction of the valley allows the prevailing south-west wind to ride high over it and a warm microclimate occurs with virtually no frosts and hardly any summer rainfall. Productive vines are: Madeleine Angevine, Triomphe d'Alsace, Seyval Blanc, Rondo and Phoenix. In polytunnels there are Merlot, Cabernet Sauvignon, Pinot Gris and Chardonnay.

Wine Production

Annual sunshine at Cemaes is one of the longest in the UK, with average mean temperatures providing ample time for ripening. However, even with that, production is subject to the vagaries of the weather and quantities can vary from 10,000 bottles down to 500 in a poor year, such as 2007.

The wines: Sant Padrig (medium dry Seyval Blanc), Pendragon (medium Triomphe d'Alsace rosé); Sant Seiriol (dry blend of Seyval Blanc and Phoenix); Mon (a sparkling wine made with Seyval Blanc and Phoenix); Santes Dwynwen (off-dry Madeleine Angevine) and Draig Coch (Cabernet Sauvignon and Merlot). All the wines are made on site and there is storage capacity for 10,000 litres of wine in stainless steel tanks for maturing.

Visiting

The vineyard shop is open 12 noon to 6pm from Wednesday to Sunday. Tea, coffee and light refreshments are available. Tours of the vineyard and winery can also be arranged on Thursdays, Fridays and Saturdays.

HOW TO FIND US

- Llanbadrig Vineyard, Gwinllan Padrig, Cae Owen, Cemaes Bay, Anglesey LL67 6RP
- Follow the A55 to junction 3, take the signs for Wylfa Power station, and turn right at the traffic lights, onto the A 5025 north coast road to Cemaes Bay. Turn right at village sign, passing the Gadley Hotel. The vineyard is a mile further on, on the right hand side as you drop into the Llanbadrig valley.

Tel: 01407 710416
Email: sales@llanbadrigvineyard.net
Web: www.llanbadrigvineyard.net

TY CROES VINEYARD
Dwyran, Llanfair P.G., Anglesey

One of only two vineyards in Anglesey, this can be considered Britain's most westerly vineyard. Vineyard tours, wine tasting and light refreshments are available.

Ty Croes vineyard was established in 2003 with 800 Phoenix vines, planted by owners Harry and Julia Dean and their family and friends. The next year they added a red varietal (Rondo), together with a little Seyval Blanc and some more Phoenix. For the following two years, Harry nurtured the vines, allowing them to mature and establish themselves and in 2005 a small harvest resulted in approximately 100 bottles of quality white wine. To make it possible to blend more grape varieties and enhance the flavour and range of their wines, in 2007 the Deans planted more Rondo, another red varietal (Regent) and some white Solaris.

VINEYARD FACTS

- The vineyard now covers 3.5 acres (1.41 ha) of land, on a north/south alignment.
- A light sandy loam soil on a shale base.
- Rows are 2.4m. apart running north-south on a gentle slope.
- Grapes grown: Phoenix, Rondo, Seyval Blanc, Regent and Solaris.

Wine Production

There was a plentiful harvest in the 2006 vintage and a dry and off-dry Phoenix were produced as well as some Rondo red. The grapes were sent to the Wroxeter Vineyard facility to be vinified by Martin Millington (see page 158). The dry Phoenix is very full in the mouth with crisp acidity although it is not very complex. Owing to the poor harvest in 2007, no white wine was made and only a few bottles of the red. Very little of the 2006 wines are still available for sale but the Deans are hopeful for the future.

Young vines at Ty Croes

Visiting

Ty Croes is part of a mixed farm, which includes holiday cottages, located nearby. Wines may be purchased at the on-site shop. There are no set visiting times, so it is best to telephone to ascertain if the shop is currently manned. Visitors are welcome to a tour of the vineyard.

HOW TO FIND US

- Harry and Julia Dean, Ty Croes, Dwyran, Anglesey, LL61 6RP.
- From the Welsh mainland (A55), turn left over the Menai bridge and take the A4080 to Newborough. Ty Croes is located after about 6 miles just behind Dwyran church (do not confuse this with Dwyran chapel) on the road between Dwyran and Newborough.

Tel: 01248 440358
Email: info@tycroesvineyard.co.uk
Web: www.tycroesvineyard.co.uk

JABAJAK VINEYARD
Whitland, Carmarthenshire

A new vineyard estate attached to an upmarket restaurant with rooms in the heart of West Wales whose first harvest will be in the autumn of 2009.

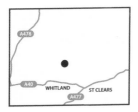

Julian and Amanda Stuart-Robson spent years renovating and transforming this 150 year-old Welsh farmhouse into a stunning restaurant with rooms. In 2006, they established the vineyard that surrounds the property with the help of consultants from Three Choirs (see page 139) where they are due to produce their first vintage in 2009. Jabajak is also a licensed Red Kite feeding station, where the public can watch these rare birds flying overhead and swooping down to feed.

Wine production
Wine production and vineyard consultancy is under the auspices of Mike Garfield of Three Choirs (see page 139). The intention is to produce a

Red Kites over Jabajak

VINEYARD FACTS
- 2,000 vines planted on 2.5 acres (1 ha) of red limestone soil deep under rocky slate.
- Vines trained by Geneva Double Curtain method.
- Grapes grown: Phoenix, Reichensteiner, Seyval Blanc, Huxelrebe and Pinot Noir.

sparkling wine from their 500 Seyval Blanc vines and their 100 Pinot Noir vines. There will be a single varietal wine made from their 600 Huxelrebe vines whilst a blend from their 500 Phoenix and 300 Reichensteiner vines completes the range. The first vintage will be in 2009. There is also a practice row of Rondo red grapes which the Stuart-Robsons are using for experimentation to cut their viticultural teeth.

Visiting
Whereas the vineyard is still in its embryonic state, you can visit the complex which consists of an upmarket restaurant, luxury accommodation and a wine shop which is currently selling wines from around

The recently planted vineyard

the world. Jabajak is open all year round and specialises in hosting corporate and business conferences and is licensed to conduct weddings.

HOW TO FIND US
- Jabajak Vineyard Restaurant with Rooms, Banc y Llain, Llanboidy, Whitland, Carmarthenshire SA34 0ED
- Go on to the A48 at the western end of the M4. After Carmarthen, take the A40 west towards Haverfordwest. At the Whitland roundabout turn right, following the signs to Pemberton Chocolate Farm and Llanboidy. Continue for approximately 2.5 miles and you will see Jabajak on your right.

Tel: 01994 448 786
Email: info@jabajak.co.uk
Web: www.jabajak.co.uk

ANCRE HILL
Monmouth, Gwent

A highly ambitious new estate in the Wye Valley whose first harvest will be in October 2008 with wines available from the cellar door in 2009.

Retired businessman and passionate winemaker Richard Morris and his wife Joy planted the first phase of the vineyard in April 2006, with a further plantation in April 2007. Previously, this was grazing land used as a paddock attached to the house. The Morrises always felt that this could make ideal land for viticulture, which was confirmed by the œnologists at Three Choirs (see page 139), so they decided to go ahead. The surveys were very positive — ideal limestone soils on south-facing slopes nestled in a protected valley and the first plantation went ahead in April 2006. Two trips to New Zealand and one to Australia to study vineyards and winemaking techniques had also been fitted in alongside similar exploratory excursions to France and Spain.

The Vineyard
The vineyard comprises two sites surrounding the owners' home at Ancre Hill on the outskirts of Monmouth. The Folly View site of 6 acres (2.42ha) is principally planted with Chardonnay (1,550 vines) and Seyval Blanc (2,200 vines), but also has some Pinot Noir (300 vines) and Triomphe (550 vines). The newer Town site of 3 acres (1.2ha) is totally dedicated to Early Pinot Noir (2,300 vines). Both sites are south-facing on limestone, loam and clay soils with excellent drainage and the long hours

VINEYARD FACTS

- 9 acres (3.64ha) of superbly sited vineyard easily accessible just outside Monmouth.
- 7,000 vines planted on south-facing slopes protected by the Brecon Beacons.
- Over 4,000 vines dedicated to the production of sparkling wines with plantings of the classical varietals of Chardonnay and Pinot Noir.
- Vines trained on Geneva Double Curtain trellising system designed for cooler climates.

of sunshine and comparatively low rainfall all combine to make it an ideal location for vines. The vineyard is blessed with its own unique microclimate and mesoclimate.

Wine Production
The estate will be specialising in quality sparkling wines, produced in the true champenoise style, but will also be producing still Seyval Blanc and Pinot Noir. They are dedicated to producing wines of only the highest quality, assisted by first class viticulture practices in the vineyard. When fully operational, they expect to be producing around 30,000 bottles a year. The first bottlings of still Seyval Blanc will be available in the summer of 2009 and the sparkling wines in 2010. They also hope to be able to produce a rosé and a red with the

Triomphe blended in for this purpose. The wines are being produced at the Three Choirs facility for the time being (see page 139), but the Morrises hope to open their own secondary fer-mentation operation for their sparkling wine by the turn of the decade and a full-blown winery is on the drawing board, if additional land can be secured adjacent to the current site.

Visiting

The vineyard is open from April 1st to September 30th, Wednesday to Sunday, 10.30am to 4.30pm. Closed Monday and Tuesday.

BIOGRAPHY   Richard & Joy Morris

Richard & Joy Morris are West Waleans from Cardigan who settled in the Monmouth area in 1982. They have 4 grown-up children with strong links to wine and vineyards, and planting and pruning still is a lively family affair. David, their son is in his final year at Plumpton College studying viticulture and œnology and makes sure his father knows exactly what he is doing wrong! Richard

and Joy's ambition is to create a boutique vineyard producing world class sparkling wines and also hope to produce a mean Pinot Noir red. Richard has been back to University having completed a year-long viticulture course at Plumpton and is an avid disciple of Richard Smart. He believes canopy management in the vineyard is the key to achieving his ambition of producing a world-class sparkling wine.

The Folly View site planted with Chardonnay vines

Vineyard tours are available twice daily at11.30am and 3pm. Tasting will be available from 2009 when their first wines have been produced. Locally produced wines made by their contract winery – Three Choirs at Newent are for sale — sparkling, white and rosé, together with a range of wine related merchandise. From 2009 their own wines made from grapes grown at Ancre Hill Vineyard will be available. Accommodation is available — a newly refurbished 3 bedroom cottage over-looking the vineyard, within 10 minutes walking distance of the historic border town of Monmouth.

The ripening process

HOW TO FIND US

- Richard and Joy Morris, Ancre Hill Vineyard, Rockfield Road, Monmouth, NP25 5HS
- Follow the B4233 out of Monmouth in the direction of Rockfield and Skenfrith. Cross, over three mini roundabouts until you reach the de-regulation sign for the 30mph speed limit and immediately after this you will see the vineyard entrance on the right hand side.

Tel: 01600 714152, 07885 984918

Fax: 01600 713784

Email: info@ancrehillestates.co.uk

Web: www.ancrehillestates.co.uk

SUGAR LOAF
Abergavenny, Monmouthshire

Nestling at the foot of the Sugar Loaf Mountains, between Abergavenny and Monmouth, the Sugar Loaf vineyards are set in an area of outstanding natural beauty, with panoramic views over the Usk Valley.

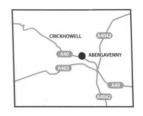

Three acres were planted in 1992 with two more in 1994, so the first crops are now getting reasonably mature.

The vineyard was closed to the public in 2001 after the outbreak of foot and mouth disease at a nearby farm before Louise Ryan and Simon Bloor bought the property and reopened the vineyard in 2003.

The Vineyard
There are currently four types of white grape grown (Siegerrebe, Reichensteiner, Seyval Blanc and Madeleine Angevine), and, unusually for Wales, three types of red grape (Triomphe d'Alsace, Regent and Rondo). Red grapes are usually more sensitive to climate, but the shelter offered by the Sugar Loaf mountain and the extra warmth generated by the proximity to the river Usk, seem to put the vineyard in an ideal location. The wines are made at the Three Choirs facility at Newent in Gloucestershire. (see page 139.) They can produce around 18,000 bottles in a good year, but as little as 7,000 when the weather is not at its best.

Wine Production
Three white wines, a rosé, a light red and a sparkling white wine are produced, which have achieved Quality status from the European Wine Standards Board. Little wine was made in the 2007 vintage due to the poor weather and many wines are currently sold out or are low in stock. At the time of writing (July 2008) the 2008 crop looks promising. The range consists of a Dry White Madeleine Angevine, a Medium Dry White, The "Sugarloaf Blush" Rosé (off-dry) and the "Deri

VINEYARD FACTS
■ The total area under vine is 5 acres (2 ha).
■ Approximately 5,000 vines.
■ Sandy soil over loam.
■ Vines trained with Geneva Double Curtain and Double Guyot.

Coch" Red Blend. Deri Coch means "Red Oaks," Coch being the Welsh for Red, quite an apt name as the Deri Hill turns red above the vineyard during harvest time. They also produce the "Hiraeth" Quality Welsh Sparkling Wine, made from Seyval Blanc grapes in the traditional method when they can, but none has been made since 2003. 2008 looks hopeful, but you will have to wait until at least the end of 2010 before it will be released. The wines can be found in a number of local hotels and restaurants — even as far away as Swansea.

BIOGRAPHY | Louise Ryan and Simon Bloor

Louise Ryan and Simon Bloor reopened the Sugar Loaf vineyard after a two year closure due to the foot and mouth crisis. They were running a poultry sanitising business together and were looking for larger premises when they were invited to view Sugar Loaf vineyard. Louise got the wine- growing bug, re- opening the vineyard on April 19th 2003. At the time she was the youngest wine grower in the country at the tender age of 25. The couple continue to run their poultry-house cleaning business, alongside the vineyard and now have two holiday cottages and their home on site.

Views through the vines to the Sugar Loaf mountain

Visiting

The Sugar Loaf experience includes tours and there is also a café on site where you can enjoy magnificent views of the Blorange mountain whilst enjoying your food and drink. The tasting facilities include a "buy and try" selection of tasters. You can take a relaxed, self-guided stroll around the vineyard, without any need to book, so turn up any time within their opening hours. Guided tours with wine tasting are available by appointment for groups of between 6-25 people. There is a gift shop where they stock locally made honey and preserves and some Welsh cheese. There are also vines for sale, as well as two one bedroom single storey cottages available as self-catering accommodation. Opening Hours: Easter – October 31st: Tuesday to Saturday 10:30 – 5 p.m., Sunday 12 – 5 p.m. (Open Mondays on Bank holidays and during school holidays). November 1st – December 23rd: Wednesday to Saturday, 12– 4 p.m.

HOW TO FIND US

- Address: Dummar Farm, Pentre Lane, Abergavenny, Monmouthshire, NP7 7LA
- From Abergavenney take the A40 towards Brecon. Pass Nevill Hall Hospital on your left. Approximately 200m take the first turning right into lane. Take the first turning left into another lane. Take the first left again, then immediately right into the Sugarloaf Vineyards and Cottages.

Tel. / Fax: 01873 853066.
Email louise@sugarloaf vineyards.co.uk.
Web: www.sugarloaf vineyards.co.uk

The Wines

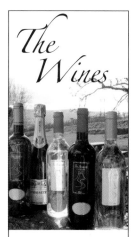

Madeleine Angevine 2006

This is fairly aromatic, but with a dry finish – a little spicy on the back palate with medium length on the finish. This wine was not made in 2007.

Sugarloaf Blush Rosé 2005

Made with 75 per cent Seyval and 25 per cent Triomphe d'Alsace, it displays a little red berry fruit on the nose and quite fruity on the palate with good structure and acidity.

Deri Coch dry red blend 2006

A blend of Rondo (50 per cent), Triomphe d'Alsace (35 per cent) and Regent (15 per cent), it has deep colour and good brambly fruit with softness and roundness on the palate.

Hiraeth Quality Welsh sparkling wine 2003

100 per cent Seyval Blanc, this has a good biscuity taste, rich bubbles and a good balance between the fruit and the acidity. Not much stock of this left and none made since.

Abergavenny Medium Dry White Blend 2006

A blend of Siegerebbe, Madeleine Angevine and Reichenseiner, this is a fragrant and fruity medium dry white wine with floral aromas, notes of tropical fruits and a good, clean finish on the palate.

PARVA FARM
Tintern, Chepstow, Monmouthshire

Believed to be on the site of a Roman winery, Parva Farm vineyard is located on a working farm with sheep, cattle and ponies on a hill behind the Wye Valley Hotel at the northern end of Tintern village.

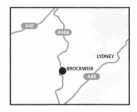

The modern vineyard was established in 1979, but by the time that Judith and Colin Dudley bought Parva Farm and Vineyard in 1996 it was in a run-down state. As they both had had horticultural and retail experience they decided to resuscitate the vineyard and produce wine to supplement the income from the sheep and cattle. What was a sideline is now the most important aspect of the farm's production.

Wine Production
The now mature vines produce high quality grapes which are used to make seven different wines — the main grape varieties being Bacchus, Seyval Blanc, Müller-Thurgau, Pinot Noir and Regent. There are

VINEYARD FACTS

- 2.4 acres (1 ha) under vine on a south facing slope above the River Wye at Tintern.
- 4,500 vines planted with Double Guyot training.
- Light sandy acid soil over limestone rock.
- 17 varieties of grapes are grown.

lesser plantings of Pinot Blanc, Pinot Gris, Auxerrois, Kerner, Scheurebe, Reichensteiner, Ortega, Huxelrebe, Eherenfelser, Regner, Grüner Sylvaner and Gewürztraminer. Apart from the 100 per cent Bacchus, they also produce a red and a rosé, three other still whites, a sparkling white and a sparkling rosé which are all vinified at Three Choirs. (see page 139). Welsh mead is also made.

Visiting
Tasting is available in the shop where the wines may be purchased as well as their plants and flowers and a selection of Welsh cheeses and other local produce.

A selection of Parva farm wines

The Wines

Parva Farm Vineyard Tintern
Parva Bacchus 2006

Their best selling wine – this is a clean, crisp and aromatic wine. Ideal summer drinking wine with salads, smoked fish and charcuterie.

HOW TO FIND US

- Address: Parva Farm, Tintern, Chepstow, NP16 6SQ
- The farm shop is open from 11:30 am to 6:00 pm daily except Wednesdays.
- Take the A466 Chepstow to Monmouth Road to Tintern. The drive to the vineyard is located to the right of the Wye Valley Hotel's car park up a steep sheep track. Visitors are free to stroll among the vines on the south-facing slopes enjoy the magnificent views of the Wye Valley at the same time.

Tel: 01291 689 636.
Email:
parvafarm@hotmail.com

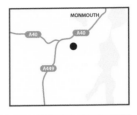

WERNDDU WINE
Pen-Y-Clawdd, Monmouthshire

Wernddu Wine is a family-run, organically-farmed vineyard, owned and run by Frank and Leigh Strawford between Monmouth and Raglan in the South Wales countryside.

After retiring, the Strawfords moved to Wernddu farm in April 1999 and seeking a new challenge, decided to produce their own wine. From the first planting in 2002, they carry out the whole wine-making process themselves, growing, fermenting and bottling — and all with organic farming methods.

Wine Production
The vineyard was established in March 2002 with 200 Reichensteiner vines. The growth of the vines in the first year convinced the Strawfords that the site was favourable. In March 2003 they planted a further 600 vines; 300 white Phoenix and 300 Pinot Noir. The following year, 1100 new vines were planted including some test

Grapes being poured into the stainless steel hooper

VINEYARD FACTS
- Gentle, south-facing, sloping, sheltered one and a quarter acre (0.5 ha) vineyard on clay loam.
- Grapes grown organically and matured organically in stainless steel tanks.
- Double Guyot and spur vine training on 2000 vines.

plantings of Ortega, Faber, Bacchus, Sauvignon Blanc and Chardonnay. The vineyard was registered with the Soil Association in September 2004, which is still the only one in Wales. As from the 2007 vintage, their wines are fully certified organic. The vineyard is high (around 200 metres above sea level) and it is a struggle for the grapes to fully ripen, especially since only organic farming methods are used.

Only one wine was produced in 2006 — a blend of Bacchus and Seyval. The 2007 will not be released until 2009. This 2006 Dry White is still fairly astringent on the attack, but there is reasonable fruit on the finish. It's also quite full-bodied and reminiscent of a sur lie Muscadet. It still

needs more time to develop, but should produce an excellent accompaniment to seafood in due course.

Perry and Cider are also produced.

Visiting
There is a tasting shop, but currently the vineyard is open by appointment only.

HOW TO FIND US
- Address: Wernddu Farm, Pen-Y-Clawdd, Monmouth NP25 4BW, Gwent
- Leave A449 at Raglan. Take minor road north-west out of town, passing under A40, and head in direction of Monmouth. After about 2 miles, turn right at Coed y Fedw, and up steep hill to Pen-y-Clawdd. Go past the church, and take right fork in road. Then after about 50 yards, turn left. Farm is about half a mile up this road on the right hand side.

Tel: 01600 740 104
Email: info@wernddu-wine.co.uk
Web: www.wernddu-wine.co.uk

BRYN CEILIOG
Leckwith, Vale of Glamorgan

A vineyard and cider apple orchard that forms part of a larger farming operation comprising three farms, Beggan, Cock Hill and Mill Farms which extend, with woodlands, to some 300 acres (120ha) in the Vale of Glamorgan.

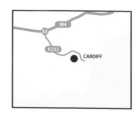

Ian Symonds is a farmer, rearing pedigree Welsh Black cattle organically. In 1996 he and his wife, Fernanda, or Maria Fernanda Candelaria Yanes Gonzales, to give her full name, originally from Tenerife in the Canary Islands, purchased 130 acres of land next to the family farm, Beggan, and after seeing Fernanda's family's vineyard at La Laguna on Tenerife, decided to plant vines in 1998. With advice from Peter Andrews, the former owner of Llanerch Vineyard nearby (see page 204) there are now 2000 of them across their 4

VINEYARD FACTS

- The land is well drained, faces south-west, with vine roots going down 40 feet (12m.) into limestone.
- Vine training is by the Geneva Double Curtain method.
- The grapes are Phoenix, Reichensteiner, Bacchus, Kernling, Findling, Rondo, Dornfelder and Regent.

acre (1.6ha) vineyard. The vineyard is on Cock Hill, which is the name of the wine and Bryn Ceiliog is its Welsh translation.

The Vineyard

Vineyard management has not come easily, battling with the marauding birds and trying to scare them off with all sorts of methods — scarecrows, streamers, flags on poles, aluminium strips and CDs on string — to name but a few methods of preventing them from eating the crop. Other problems such as mildew and coping with the hostile elements has not deterred Ian, nor has the considerable investment needed — he reckons that it takes six years for a vineyard to become commercially viable.

Wine Production

The south sloping vineyard

Ian Symonds is originally from a farming background in Caernarfon in North Wales, but has spent most of his life living in the Vale of Glamorgan in South Wales. He graduated with a degree in economics from the University of Wales but after university, changed direction and became a quantity surveyor, eventually becoming a senior partner in a major international consultancy. He sold the business to a French utilities company in 1993 and set up on his own.. Because of his affinity to the birds and the wildlife in the vineyards, Ian has been described in various articles as a "larger version of Bill Oddie" or a "Doctor Doolittle", although his preference would be to be called "a younger version Clint Eastwood"!

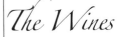

The Wines

Aromatic on the nose, with Granny Smith apple crispness and a fruity dryness on the palate hinting overtones of elderflower and it has body to take creamy dishes.

Mr Scarecrow helps with the harvest

The grapes are sorted and then transported to Martin Fowke of Three Choirs vineyard at Newent in Gloucestershire (see page 139) for vinification. Ian's white wine is the Cock Hill White Blend, a blend of Orion, Phoenix, Reichensteiner and Kernling. The 2005 had a little süss reserve added which had the effect of making it into a medium rather than a dry wine but also lowered the alcohol content to 10.5%. The 2006 is dryer, aromatic on the nose, with Granny Smith apple crispness and a fruity dryness on the palate with overtones of elderflower. It also has enough body to take creamy dishes. The 2007 is blended only of Orion and Phoenix because of the poor vintage, these were the only grapes that ripened sufficiently. The red is a blend of Rondo, Dornfelder and Regent with the 2006 being of much better structure than the 2004 or 2005. Again, no red was made in 2007 and in 2008 no wine will be produced at all owing to the heavy rain at flowering time.

Visiting
The vineyard is located on the family farm, Beggan, at Leckwith. Visits by small groups only can be arranged by contacting Ian Symonds. No direct sales are made from the vineyard but the wines can be bought at The Village Stores, Dinas Powys, in the Vale of Glamorgan and can be found in various local restaurants.

Flowers carpet the vineyard

GLYNDWR
Llanblethian, Vale of Glamorgan

An impeccably kept vineyard behind the owner's house in the Vale of Glamorgan.

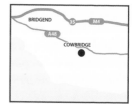

The Glyndwr vineyard was planted in 1982 and is the oldest established vineyard in Wales. The wines have been served in the House of Lords, the Welsh Assembly and at European State banquets. Richard Norris and his wife, Susan, both share a passion for gardening, and have opened their garden to the National Garden Scheme. In addition to the 6,000 vines, they grow quite a large selection of old English apple trees, experiment with a variety of unusual plants and tend their herbaceous borders and ponds. The wines, which includes three styles of white, a rosé, a red and a sparkling rosé as well as a vintage sparkling white, are distributed throughout Wales to various hotels, restaurants, and delicatessens.

The Vineyard

Glyndwr vineyard was planted with 3 acres (1.21ha) of vines in 1982, by the Norris family of Llanblethian. Today, the vineyard covers some 6 acres (2.42ha) with 6000 vines and produces over 12,000 bottles making it one of Wales's largest vineyards. Grapes grown are Reichensteiner, Siegerrebe, Madeleine Angevine, Seyval Blanc, Rondo, Regent, Triomphe d'Alsace and Leon Millot. The Siegerrebbe and Madeleine Angevine make good aromatic whites, whilst Richard is particularly fond of the red Rondo variety, because it is very high in natural sugars thus making wines with a certain amount of body. The vineyard is also environmentally friendly; chickens, ducks and wild pheasants roam about, hedges are left to grow wild to encourage birdlife and the vines are treated with organic material.

Some of the wildlife on the estate

BIOGRAPHY   Richard Norris

Richard was born in 1948 in a small rural village in Kent. His father kept a fruit orchard and bees and loved gardening. Perhaps the seeds of fruit-growing began sprouting all those years ago! He was educated at Tonbridge School and then went on to read Ancient Roman and Greek History at Aberystwyth. His first job was teaching English in Finland, and afterwards he worked in a shoe factory near Paris. Finally, he took over the family business in Cardiff. He was the sixth generation to head Edward England, which is one of Cardiff's oldest companies, importing, exporting and growing potatoes. He managed the company for 33 years, before taking over the running of Glyndwr vineyard.

Richard is passionate about his wines and growing and tending the vines in all types of weather. He often wonders how his love of Greek and Roman history fits into his current work, but perhaps it is just a long continuation of a great and ancient way of life!

Hibernation in the Vale of Glamorgan

The Wines

Brut 2003

100 per cent Seyval Blanc, ripe and biscuity with gentle bubbles and good persistence on the palate. Seyval is frequently used in sparkling wine production in England and Wales for its minerality.

Rosé 2005

60 per cent Seyval Blanc – the balance is approximately one third Leon Millot and two thirds Triomphe d'Alsace. This has a pinkish hue – quite fruity and not too dry but nevertheless quite crisp.

Dry Aromatic 2006

This is a blend of Siegerrebe and Madeleine Angevine in roughly equal proportions. Not very perfumed on the nose, but quite aromatic and grapey on the palate.

Red 2006

A blend of Rondo, Triomphe d'Alsace, Leon Millot and Regent – it is a good food wine, dry and digestible on the palate with good weight and length, perhaps lacking a little generosity of fruit.

Wine Production

A number of wines are produced from the vines that grow on the estate, which are all vinified at the Three Choirs facility (see page 139) at Newent in Gloucestershire in dedicated stainless steel vats and American oak barrels for the estate. These are: Glyndwr Medium White (a blend of Madeleine Angevine and Seyval Blanc), Glyndwr Medium-Dry White (a blend of Reichensteiner and Seyval Blanc), Glyndwr Dry Aromatic White (a blend of Siegerebbe and Madeleine Angevine), Glyndwr Rosé (a blend of Triomphe d'Alsace, Leon Millot and Seyval Blanc), Glyndwr Red (oaked in new American oak barrels, a blend of Rondo, Regent, Leon Millot and Triomphe d' Alsace) and Glyndwr Vintage Sparkling (100 per cent Seyval Blanc).

Visiting

The vineyard is not open to the public as such and all visits are arranged by appointment only. Tasting and buying facilities are available on the premises and meals/snacks from local Welsh/organic produce can easily be arranged. They also keep a pretty Bed and Breakfast and arrange tours with food in the vineyard. There is a large wine cellar underneath the farmhouse from where the wine can be collected. Visitors are also welcome to stroll around the beautiful gardens, which were recently opened for the National Garden Scheme.

HOW TO FIND US

- Glyndwr Vineyard, Llanblethian, Cowbridge CF71 7JF
- From the A48 at Cowbridge, take the ramp onto A4222/Primrose Hill. Continue to follow A4222 for about a mile. Turn left at St Athan Rd and then turn right at Broadway. Continue on to Bridge Road and after a short while turn right at Piccadilly. After 100 yards or so, you will see the Glyndwr House sign on your left.

Tel: 01446 774564
Email: glyndwrvineyard @hotmail.com
Web: www.glyndwrvineyard.co.uk

LLANERCH VINEYARD
Hensol, Vale of Glamorgan

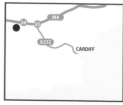

Llanerch is one of the largest and oldest vineyard in Wales, situated in the Vale of Glamorgan, just 15 minutes from Cardiff, among meadows and grazing pastures, woodlands and gardens and two tranquil lakes.

Vines were first planted at Llanerch in 1986 by Peter and Diana Andrews, on a south-facing slope about 50 metres above sea level and there were subsequent plantings each year up to 1991 when a total of nearly 7 acres (2.8ha) of vines were growing. Llanerch is currently the largest commercial vineyard in Wales producing between 24,000 and 30,000 bottles of estate-grown wines. It also attracts tens of thousands of visitors a year to enjoy the natural beauty of the site. The wines are marketed under the Cariad label, which means "love" in Welsh. In 2007, the Andrews sold out to their business partners, Scott Williams and Carole Growcott who have continued to develop the vineyard and have added a number of additional attractions for the visitor.

The Vineyard

The grapes grown are Kernling, Leon Millot, Bacchus, Huxelrebe, Reichensteiner, Triomphe d'Alsace and Seyval Blanc. There is a small experimental area containing two new German hybrids and three Melon de Bourgogne vines (from which Muscadet is made in the Loire-Atlantique area of France). All vines have been planted through thick black polythene mulch, which has three main advantages over planting

VINEYARD FACTS
■ Vines planted on 6 acres of heavy loam about 160 feet above sea level.
■ Planting is arranged North/South on a gentle south facing slope.
■ Vines trained by lyre system for the Kernel and Huxelrebe and by Double Curtain Guyot for the rest.
■ Not a lot of frost is experienced although the vineyard is prone to damage by the prevailing westerly winds.

directly in the soil — firstly, to provide a weed-free area around the vine during important early years, secondly, to attract warmth and thirdly, to help retain moisture in the soil. With the prevailing winds coming from the west, wind breaks of grey alders have been planted at around 30m. intervals and maintained as a hedge 5m. high by annual pruning. Whilst air circulation is essential in cool climate viticulture, as it minimises fungal diseases, strong winds have a cooling effect on the plants and delay growth and ripening of the fruit.

Cariad
Gwin da o Gymru

Welsh Regional Wine
75cl℮   11%

Wine Production

The following wines are produced from the vines grown on the estate: Cariad Dry White

Vines under a Welsh sky

The Wines

Cariad Celtic Dry White 2006

A crisp blend of Kernling and Bacchus, this has tones of Granny Smith apple, quince and gooseberry. It is quite dry yet aromatic with good persistence on the palate.

Cariad Rosé 2006

100% Triomphe d' Alsace, this has quite a deep colour with a good depth of flavour of strawberry and other red berry fruits. Dry on the attack, but finishes with a little sweetness to emphasise the fruit.

Cariad Medium Dry White 2006

This is a blend of Kernling, Huxelrube and Bacchus. There is fair aromacy on the nose and a touch of grapefruitiness on the palate without being overbearing. Finishes very long.

Cariad Blush Vintage Quality Sparkling Wine 2005

Made with Seyval Blanc and Reichensteiner grapes with a touch of Triomphe d'Alsace to give it the colour. It has a lively mousse and is pretty dry, perhaps lacking a bit of the fruitiness one would expect from it.

(SeyvalBlanc/Reichensteiner), Celtic Dry (Kernling/Bacchus),Rosé (Triomphe d'Alsace), Cariad Medium Dry (Kernling/Huxelrebe/Bacchus) Blush Vintage Sparkling (Seyval Blanc/Reichensteiner/Triomphe) and Bacchus. The wines are made by Martin Fowke at Three Choirs (see page 139) in Newent, Gloucestershire.

Visiting

Visiting is one of the delights of this estate and great efforts have recently gone into providing a great "day out" for the visitor, whether it be family, corporate or the foodie-orientated. There is an estate shop where you can buy their wines and locally produced foods as well as wine and food oriented accessories. The shop is open from Tuesdays to Sundays, 10.00am-4pm. Groups by arrangement.

The estate specialises in providing facilities for corporate conferences and additionally has recently opened an in-house restaurant in partnership with Hywel Jones, the talented, Michelin-starred chef of Lucknam Park in Wiltshire. Of course, Hywel is there only on limited occasions, but standards are ably maintained by his protégé, Michael Edwards and his team. The quality of the cuisine is excellent and the bonus is that there is an extremely affordable lunch menu.

On top of this, there is a cookery school headed up by Welsh TV chef, Angela Gray and a wine school is also planned. There are also wine tastings and self-guided tours of the vineyard and the nearby woodlands, which form part of the estate. If you feel too tired to travel home after all this, the estate provides bed and breakfast accommodation on a nightly basis at relatively modest prices.

HOW TO FIND US

- Hensol, Pendoylan, Vale of Glamorgan, CF72 8GG,
- From the M4 motorway, exit at junction 34 and follow the signs to the vineyard.

Tel: 01443 225877
Email: enquiries@llanerch-vineyard.co.uk
Web: www.llanerch-vineyard.co.uk

PENARTH VINEYARD
Newtown, Powys

In a unique location above the River Severn just outside Newtown lies the Penarth Estate Vineyard growing international classical grape varieties as well as some of the more traditional varieties grown in England and Wales.

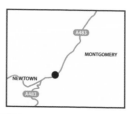

Bernard and Tanya Herbert planted their first vines in 1999, and the acreage was increased 2 years later, so that all 8 acres (3.2 ha) of the vineyard are now bearing fruit from some 8,000 vines. In the beginning crops were limited, as the vines were young. But the small yield helped the Herberts to maintain quality — in 2003 the entire harvest was gathered in two days — just before a spell of heavy rain began.

The Vineyard
Penarth vineyard is located in the Montgomeryshire region of Powys in mid Wales. Set on the Severn, the vineyard is in a unique microclimate which makes it possible to cultivate grape varieties which are usually considered unsuitable for the Welsh climate. The reason for this is that the Gulf Stream has a direct influence on the valley where the vineyard lies — so

VINEYARD FACTS

- Unique microclimate allowing grapes to be grown successfully outdoors.
- 8 acres (3.2 ha) of vines bearing fruit from some 8,000 vines.
- Vines trained by Geneva Double Curtain.
- Vineyard situated on an old river bed of loamy shale.
- Grapes grown: Pinot Noir, Pinot Meunier, Chardonnay, Merlot.
- A small section of the vineyard devoted to experimental varieties.

much so, that even a few hundred yards away, there could be a temperature difference of as much as 5 degrees C. Given that the Severn Vale around Newtown is sheltered, with westerly winds warming as they descend from Plynlimon, the site has many advantages. The grapes are grown outdoors, facing the elements, resulting in a depth of character and richness of flavour.

Wine Production
The vineyard has no winery, and wines are being produced by Three Choirs at Newent, (see page 139) and a brace of sparkling wines are currently being sold. The sparkling wines are produced in the traditional method — two years in stainless steel tanks on lees and a 12 month bottle maturation.

Vines sloping south towards the River Severn

BIOGRAPHY Bernard Herbert

Bernard Herbert's passion for food and wine has led him to become a successful operator of a number of wine bars and restaurants in London, but he is now disposing of some of them to concentrate more fully on the vineyard and the Egyptian Arabian horse-breeding businesses which he and his wife, Tanya have set up in Wales. The wines can be found at Tiles in Buckingham Palace Road, Victoria, Covent Garden Kitchen and Piazza Café, Covent Garden and Metro in Clapham, all of which he continues to own, as well as numerous local shops, delicatessens, restaurants and hotels in Wales. Bernard believes that the UK wine producers should take their courage in both hands and concentrate more on international varietals rather than German hybrids. He cites New Zealand as an example where not so many years ago, grapes such as Müller-Thurgau dominated their viticultural scene but have now been discarded for more suitable vines. He has set his own example by planting 1,000 Merlot vines from which he hopes to reap his first harvest in 2008.

Vines trained by Geneva Double Curtain system

Two interesting still wines are also produced — a Chardonnay/Pinot blend and a 50/50 Pinot Meunier and Pinot Noir blend. 1,000 Merlot vines were planted in 2006 and it is hoped that they will yield their first wine in 2008. No wine was made in 2007 owing to the bad harvest.

Visiting

A self-selected picnic from the Tasting Room Farm Shop and a self-guided tour is available. Plans are in place to open a picnic site and a fully operational restaurant on the estate in 2009 as the estate is becoming popular as a tour destination. These tours include parties of children from local schools who come to witness the production of the only outdoor grapes in Powys.

Contact the vineyard to arrange a group for a guided tour or tasting evening; the cost includes tastings of all of their wines and some locally produced foods which are available for purchase in larger quantities in the Farm Shop Tasting Room.

HOW TO FIND US

- Address: Penarth Vineyard, Pool Road, Newtown, Powys, SY16 3AN
- The Farm Shop is open daily from Easter to Christmas, Noon-4 p.m.
- The vineyard is situated on the A483, two miles outside Newtown on the main road to Welshpool.

Tel: 01686 610383

Email: info@penarthvineyard.co.uk

Web: www.penarthvineyard.co.uk

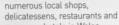

The Wines

The Penarth Estate sparkling pink (Pinot Noir & Pinot Meunier)

There is a little sweetness on the back palate, but the wine has some real complexity, gentle bubbles and raspberry fruit.

Blanc de Blanc (Chardonnay)

A blend of 2003 and 2004 wine with a soft and gentle mousse. It is tender on the palate without some of that rasping acidity you can get with German hybrid wines.

Pinots 2006

A 50/50 blend of Pinot Noir and Pinot Meunier, pale in colour but a little darker than the sparkling wine. There is some astringency with a tendency to feel that the grapes were picked under-ripe, but the wine has a very long finish with some complexity

Pinot/Chardonnay 2006

A still wine in the style of still wines produced in Champagne — crisp, refreshing acidity in the mouth and fair complexity on the finish.

THE WINEMAKERS

WILLIAM BIDDULPH

William Maitland Biddulph is one of the newer names emerging in English winemaking. New Zealand trained, he has recently taken over as the winemaker at Wickham Vineyards (see page 100). With a winery capacity that is to be expanded over the next two or three years this is likely become an important contract winemaking source for southern vineyards. William also has a number of key vineyard clients through his own consultancy.

OWEN ELIAS

Owen could be fairly described as the colossus of the UK wine industry, the winemaking behemoth that bestrides the vineyards of southern England. His output at Chapel Down (see page 28) alone would be enough to earn him this reputation but he also makes fine wines such as Hush Heath's sparkling rosé. More than that he salvages the reputation of many small wineries through making wines that are more than drinkable where others would have failed.

MARTIN FOWKE

Martin is another key winemaking figure in the industry. With the considerable capacity in the modern state of the art Three Choirs (see page 139) winery facility, he oversees the winemaking for most small vineyards in the

Marches, Wales and beyond. He has been a leading figure in the English wine industry for over 20 years and like a number of his peers, often overcomes considerable limitations in the quality of fruit he is provided with by his vineyard clients.

VINCENT GOWER

Vincent Gower is the winemaker at Stanlake Park (see page 86), originally Valley Vineyards where contract winemaking remains of great importance

as well as making the excellent Stanlake wines. Vineyard owner Peter Dart has invested heavily in the modern, very well equipped winery which has a capacity now of over 200 tons. Vincent not only makes still red, white and rosés for an extensive clientele but is also an important source for sparkling winemaking, both ageing and disgorging wines for vineyard clients.

SAM LINDO

Sam Lindo is very much the hands-on winemaker now at Cornwall's most important winery facility at Camel Valley (see page 122). While

contract winemaking is less a priority here than of old, the Lindos have been instrumental in creating some excellent wines for clients as well as themselves in the past. Nearby Polgoon was among their most recent successes with its rosé. While Sam heads up the team, this is still very much a family operation with great input from his father Bob.

PETER MORGAN

The lack of skilled viticultural and winemaking personnel is still a real concern in the UK industry. Peter Morgan and his colleagues at Plumpton college (see page 64) have extensive knowledge of English growing conditions and the type of grapes winemakers are faced with. Their teaching is a big part of the solution, as is already evident in the wines produced by graduates of the college who have more than found their feet. Over the next 4-5 years a further crop of students will have the opportunity to put their wines before consumers.

MIKE ROBERTS

Business acumen allied to a passion for winemaking make a scintillating combination for a highly professional sparkling wine operation. Ridgeview (see page 66) might be one of the big boys in terms of sparkling wine production, but Mike Roberts and his wife Chris have also interwoven their business with a sound family structure. There seems little doubt that son Sam, with the support of the family team, can take Ridgeview to a still greater level of recognition.

MARCUS SHARP

If Denbies (see page 44) stand out for one thing, it is the consistency of style and the accessibility of the wines. Marcus Sharp has been with Denbies for a decade with his first vintage as head winemaker in 2003, the subsequent period coinciding with the winery's best wines to date. Marcus has also overseen the increase in the sparkling wine range where Denbies, from their best slopes have the potential to challenge leaders such as Nyetimber and Ridgeview.

STEPHEN SKELTON

Over the past four decades no one who has been more immersed in the English wine scene than Stephen Skelton. He currently works as a consultant to vineyards and wineries in the UK, including the establishment of new sparkling wine operations. His long personal experience of grape growing and winemaking includes having established Tenterden Vineyards in 1977 where he continued to make the wines until 1999.

CHERIE SPRIGGS

Several people besides the owner, Eric Hereema have made a serious commitment to further developing the Nyetimber name (see page 60). Canadian-born Cherie Spriggs brings her talent and experience to add to the financial bedrock. She is also working with her husband Brad Greatrix, also a fully qualified oenologist, further reinforcing the team ethos that will be critical to Nyetimber's ambitious programme for success.

DERMOT SUGRUE

This individual has a lot riding on his shoulders. At Wiston Estate (see page 72) he has undertaken the establishment of a major new project from scratch. That includes vineyard management, building a winery, establishing a label and delivering high quality wines, both for Wiston and others. With a single-minded and exhaustive approach to quality, he will be watched closely by others in the industry. The degree of his success with grapes from chalk soils, as opposed to greensand or any other, could influence future plantings for sparkling wine production.

JULIET WHITE

Juliet is Devon's most important winemaker producing not only her own Yearlstone (see page 132) range but also wines from a number of other local vineyards. Notable among her clientele is Geoff Bowen at Pebblebed Vineyards. Her ability with each vintage to handle so much fruit in a relatively confined space is commendable, particularly in a vintage like 2006.

JOHN WORONTSCHAK

One of the leading consultant winemakers in the UK — a claim as valid now as almost two decades ago. Born and raised in England, John brought new a zeal and an Australian approach to winemaking in the UK from the late 80s, following his studies and experiences 'down under'. At Thames Valley vineyards (now Stanlake Park, see page 86) he applied new tools and brought a surer control to winemaking to give fresher, more fruit-driven wines that also revealed greater depth and expression.

Grape glossary

Those of you who have more than a passing interest in wine must be familiar with many of the world's greatest grape varietals, knowledge of which has been gleaned from books, TV presentations on wine and the internet. Some of these are grown in Britain, where it has been possible to adapt them to the vagaries of the British climate, but until recently at least, most English and Welsh producers have been dependent on crossings of grape varieties specially bred to ripen in a marginal climate. Initially, these were German or French varieties (such as Seyval Blanc) which were thought to be the most likely to be able to cope with our climate, but over the years, other clones and crossings have been discovered, albeit mostly in Germany, and sometimes from EU-shunned hybrids. Varieties such as Bacchus, Ortega, Phoenix, Regent and Rondo have been particularly adapted to give, whilst there is no particular terroir or regional style, something that is quintessentially English in character.

Yet there is much more to the story of grapes suited to UK conditions, even though, for the moment at least, this is largely centred on the best sites in the warmest southern regions. It is based instead on classic varieties, specifically the triumvirate of Chardonnay, Pinot Noir and Pinot Meunier that either alone or in some combination (often all three together) make up all Champagne. Thanks to several bold and enterprising growers and the subsequent unexpected success and acclaim for English sparkling wines based on the same grapes since the mid-nineties, there has been a transformation of the English vineyard over the past five years which continues unabated.

WHITE GRAPES

Auxerrois
Good quality white variety capable of producing refined floral and fruit scents. Better known in Alsace and Luxembourg, it was one of the original recommended varieties for planting in England. Plantings are small if widely distributed. While it is sometimes used to produce lightly oaked whites, it can also be used as a blended component of some sparkling wines due to its relatively late-ripening characteristics. Lower acidity levels can make it more suitable than other late-ripeners. At Davenport Vineyards it is combined with Pinot Noir.

Bacchus

Bacchus
Popular early ripening — Silvaner x Riesling crossed with Müller-Thurgau — that does well on chalk or limestone rich soils. The grape gives wines that are fruity and have a distinct, grapey, Muscat scent and are crucially less vigorous in their growth than Müller-Thurgau. In England Bacchus wines tend to be aromatic and dry with a hint of Sauvignon Blanc grassiness in cooler years. Its low acidity makes it one of the most widely planted varietals in the UK, successful almost everywhere from Kent in the east to the damper climes of Wales and the Marches. The only downside is that it has poor mildew resistance and as a result can yield very poorly. Almost everyone other than those dedicated to producing sparkling wines makes an example, with the big guns such as Chapel Down, Denbies and Three Choirs challenged by a host of smaller producers.

Chardonnay

Chardonnay
The leading variety in an explosion of new planting in southern England. Every major wine producing country has some and in England there exists great potential as a sparkling wine base. As a component of the classic Champagne blend of Chardonnay, Pinot Meunier and Pinot Noir it has contributed to the greatest success story of the English and Welsh vineyards, particularly in the south-east of England. Nyetimber and Ridgeview are two of the most celebrated producers where it has performed

admirably on greensand soils. Its affinity with chalk soils (the same strata as that in Champagne) has yet to be fully tested but the limited small-scale results to date are very exciting. Historically it was deemed to struggle to ripen fully in the UK and some growers resorted to using polytunnels. Yet the combination of the right soils, new clones, warmer summers and a particularly favourable mesoclimate more than does the trick. Although it is rarely produced as a still wine, Denbies is a leading producer making one, albeit in an oaky style.

Faber (Faberrebe)
A cross between Weissburgunder and Müller-Thurgau created to achieve frost resistance. Only rarely encoutered, it is a variety that produces fruity wines with crisp acidity and is used mainly for blending. Although it is easy to grow, it is not helped by naturally vigorous growth during the summer.

Findling
A mutated version of the Müller-Thurgau grape originally found in Switzerland. It is early ripening and a reliable cropper but the few plantings seen in the UK usually provide grapes for blending. With some grubbing it up it doesn't appear to have much of a future.

Huxelrebe
German-bred crossing of Chasselas with Courtillier Musqué extensively planted in England for single varietal wines with a slightly Muscat flavour (medium or dry depending on the year) that provides fruity wines with both good sugar and acidity levels. Late season disease is a problem, with fruit sometimes picked under-ripe. Also used for botrytis-enriched sweet wines.

Kerner
Kerner is a potentially good quality and productive German crossing of Trollinger (Schiava in Italy's Alto Adige) with Riesling. Its green skins turn gold when very ripe and it has good aroma with nuances of Muscat and tropical fruits. It also ages well and is a popular planting in the UK, due to the fact that it buds late and is therefore rarely susceptible to spring frosts. The disadvantages, however, mean there are better alternatives as it is a very leafy vine which grows sideways and is often difficult to control. Its high acidity and the fact that it ripens relatively late also make it a challenge to grow in many UK locations.

Kernling
This is a bud mutation of the Kerner grape, with a pink to greyish red skin colour, first identified in Germany in 1974. It is similar to Kerner but slightly riper, with a fruity acidity which is just a touch less sharp than the acidity of Kerner. It is late-flowering with reliable fruit set and produces higher sugar levels than Kerner if harvested at the same time. The growth of side shoots is less prevalent than that of the Kerner which makes it easier to manage. Late-ripening and high natural acidity remain an issue in less propitious vintages.

Madeleine Angevine
Known in the UK as "Mad Angy", this varietal is descended from the French Madeleine Angevine and has only female flowers. It is entirely different from the original French variety due to subsequent breeding and shows more Germanic characteristics. An early-cropping grape, it is rarely blended due to good aroma and crisp acidity. It is widely planted in the UK and generally easy to grow thanks to moderate natural vigour and its suitability for both cane and spur pruning. On the downside it can show poor disease resistance in cooler and or wetter years and can easily lose its refreshing acidity in warmer years. The bulk of Sharpham Vineyards is planted to the grape.

Madeleine Sylvaner
Little seen, very early ripening grape with consequent susceptibility to attack by birds and wasps. Normally the wine is aromatic and light, and is usually blended with other intensely flavoured varietals to produce dry wine.

Müller-Thurgau (Rivaner)
Although it once formed the major part of white wine production in England and still yields generously for basic plonk in Germany, this German crossing has few admirers. It lacks the structure and class of one of its parents (Riesling) but still makes attractive wine in good hands, particularly as a blending agent. Much of it has now been grubbed up and replaced by better quality varietals.

Optima
Relatively recent crossing (1970) of (Silvaner x Riesling) and Müller-Thurgau producing an intense, spicy wine. It is very early ripening with potentially high natural sugars.

Orion

A cross between Optima and the hybrid Villard Blanc that was bred for disease resistance. Orion produces aromatic, fruity and easy to drink wine with a pleasant soft acidity. The wines age quickly and should therefore be bottled and consumed early. It is often blended with stronger varietals, including Schönburger which ripens at the same time.

Ortega

One of the modern crossings (Müller-Thurgau and Siegerrebe) that is now widely used, both as a flavoursome blending component but also increasingly as a dry white varietal. In fact some of the best dry whites are based on it — Kenton Vineyards in Devon is an excellent example. Ortega ripens early, is not sensitive to frost and is quite weighty with a good natural sugar content. It can also be used for sweet wines in the right conditions with some cellaring potential.

Phoenix

A recent crossing from Germany (1984) between Bacchus and the hybrid Villard Blanc. Like others of its ilk, it was bred for disease resistance. There are plantings in vineyards in the south-west and Wales but it is also found in the other regions. High yielding, it has a pronounced Muscat bouquet, with crisp acidity and fullness in the mouth and a flavour similar to Bacchus. Astley Vineyards in Worcestershire produce a notable example.

Pinot blanc

Pinot Blanc

Widely planted grape making dry, rather intense white wines in many parts of the world. The variety is most associated with Alsace and Italy's Alto Adige and Friuli (as Pinot Bianco). It is not widely planted in England, but where it is, it produces a crisp, dry wine. It is also used by some in England as a component of sparkling wine, just as it is in Italy's best sparkling wine region, Franciacorta.

Pinot gris

Pinot Gris

Excellent white grape most associated with Alsace, where it produces distinctively flavoured whites of intense spice, pear and quince flavours, and north-east Italy. In

England there are only occasional plantings and little has been produced that is much more than a slightly washed-out imitation. Despite this there is considerable potential for use in sparkling wines.

Regner

Regner is a German crossing of a white Italian table grape, Luglienca Bianca and Gamay. In the cooler English climate its early ripening is a bonus with good yields and high sugars as well as higher acidity than in Germany, resulting in crisp dry white wines.

Reichensteiner

Reliable, early ripening variety bred from Müller-Thurgau that is widely planted in England. In a good vintage with sufficient acidity and ripeness it can make a good dry wine on its own (such as the 2004 varietal version from Dunkery Vineyard) but is often blended with other wines. It is also used as a base for more everyday sparkling styles and has some potential as a late-harvest wine.

Sauvignon blanc

Sauvignon Blanc

Internationally renowned varietal very rarely seen in the UK and then, usually grown under polytunnels or glass. In more temperate regions, it can exhibit anything from grassy, herbaceous or gooseberry flavours to ripe capsicum or even tropical fruits such as melon and fig. In the UK it tends to be more nettley and less pronounced than in New Zealand or even the Loire valley. Controlling alcohol and preserving flavour can also be a challenge when growing it under cover.

Scheurebe

Little seen and of very marginal importance in the UK, this late-ripening crossing from Silvaner and Riesling is unlikely to ever achieve anything like the respectability (for late-harvested and sweet styles) gained in its native Germany.

Schönburger

Crossing of good standard, used both varietally and for blending in English wines. It is one of the UK's best varietals with distinct Gewürztraminer and Muscat tones. However, the acidity can fall very quickly and the wines can lack structure. The grapes change colour as they ripen, turning light pink then a pinkish tawny colour when fully ripe. It can work as a late-harvested, slightly off-dry style if the balance is right.

Seyval blanc

Seyval Blanc (Sevre Villard 5/276)

Seyval Blanc has suffered somewhat unfairly at the hands of the EU who have ruled in favour of Vitis vinifera grape varieties or vinifera-derived crossings. Although currently permitted for planting, as a hybrid it does not qualify for Quality Wine status (which allows the grape variety and vintage to be shown on the label). It buds and ripens very late but is famous for its resistance to both disease and the cold, providing an alternative in marginal climates to the likes of Chardonnay and Sauvignon Blanc. Dry, crisp versions have vaguely citrus aromas and flavours as well as a certain minerality, sometimes compared to Sauvignon Blanc from the Loire valley. Its relatively neutral flavour profile also lends itself to oak and malolactic fermentation but it is now used almost exclusively in producing a unique English (and Welsh) style of sparkling wine. Breaky Bottom and Camel Valley make particularly fine examples. It remains widely planted in England and Wales but is now conceding ground to the new clones of Chardonnay and Pinot Noir, especially in the warmest parts of southern England.

Siegerrebe

Siegerrebe

This is a very early variety which can achieve high ripeness levels in summer heatwaves, when it is at its best. It is low in production and beloved of wasps and if it gets past the wasp attacks can go on to produce excellent dry and dessert wines. In poor years it can be flabby. Those from Three Choirs are among the best made.

Solaris

A Merzling x (Saperavi Severny x Muscat Ottonel) crossing that is mostly grown in a few vineyards in the north and west of England. It is a hardy, very early ripening variety giving very high sugar levels but very low acidity, yet can yield a flavoursome white wine.

Würzer

Würzer

A German crossing of Gewürztraminer and Müller-Thurgau now in decline due to the better performance of Bacchus and other crossings. It is early ripening but without great disease resistance and tends to be blended to improve aroma and spiciness. Würzer is successfully grown at Wickham Vineyards in Hampshire.

RED GRAPES

Acolon

Very recently approved (2002) crossing of Dornfelder and Blauer Limberger (Blaufränkisch) developed in Württemberg, Germany. It is early ripening and has good yield, producing red juice with high colour intensity and a moderate tannin content. It has a fruity bouquet, good structure and is capable of a long finish. It is grown at New Hall in Essex where it is included in the Ruby Royalé red. It has also been planted by Biddenden in Kent and most recently by Bothy Vineyard in Oxfordshire.

Cabernet Sauvignon

Cabernet Sauvignon

Internationally renowned grape varietal generally grown under glass or in polytunnels in the UK by a small number of producers in an attempt to obtain full ripeness in both fruit and tannin, something which doesn't usually occur naturally in our climate. The most credible example made so far is the Beenleigh Red (that includes 30 per cent Merlot) made by Mark Sharman of Sharpham Vineyards.

Dornfelder

Dornfelder

Bred in 1955 as a crossing between Heroldrebe (Portugieser x Limburger) and Helfensteiner (Pinot Noir Précoce x Black Hamburger), Dornfelder is now considered one of the better red wine grapes for cool climates but needs to be cane-pruned. The wine is notable for its colour and good acidity and the vines generally do well in the UK, having been introduced in the 1980s. The fruit yields light to medium-bodied but dark coloured and rich wines, which would also benefit from oak ageing.

Dunkelfelder
A relatively sparsely planted cultivar used for red wines, Dunkelfelder is a very early ripening German variety. A teinturier (red fleshed grape) it produces intense red juice. Although it lacks for flavour and acidity, it is particularly useful for blending and adding colour to wines.

Gamay
There are only miniscule plantings in the UK of the renowned Beaujolais grape variety. The fruit is usually added to a blend (often also including Pinot Noir) to make still or sparkling wines. The important Kent winery, Biddenden, uses it in its sparkling rosé and even made a varietal version in the very hot 2003 vintage.

Leon Millot
Another minor red wine grape variety in the UK and a hybrid originally grown in the eastern United States. A teinturier (red fleshed grape) it is mainly used as a blending wine to give more body and colour to paler reds. Legislation in favour of Vitis vinifera varieties meant the chop in northern France, where it was once popular. In England it also seems set to disappear soon.

Merlot

Merlot
Like Cabernet Sauvignon planted beyond its limits in the UK, requiring polytunnels, glass or an extraordinarily hot and long summer to stand any chance of getting fully ripe. Bookers in Sussex makes a tiny amount varietally.

Pinot Meunier
Important component in most Champagne blends if rarely used for anything else. Early ripening and as a wine, early developing, it complements both Chardonnay and Pinot Noir. Although it is being increasingly planted in England and Wales as one of the three traditional varieties for producing first class sparkling wines, opinion is divided over its true worth. It has yet to make its debut as a still wine in the UK.

Pinot Noir

Pinot Noir
This sometimes demanding variety is capable of producing some of the greatest wines in the world under the right conditions of climate, soil and toil. Its true strength in the UK lies as one of the traditional components of a good sparkling wine and it has seemingly been planted almost with abandon over the last 4-5 years and there's more to come as it establishes itself as one of the country's premium varieties. It needs moderately high average temperatures during flowering (minimum 15°C) for quick fruit set and a dry location but with the right viticultural expertise, it can out-perform many of the Germanic crossings (both red and white) that the English wine industry has laboured so long and hard with. Very decent pale-coloured, light still Pinot Noirs have also been produced over the years — some marketed as Pinot Noir rosé.

Pinot Noir Précoce (Frühburgunder)
Some of the existing plantings of Pinot Noir are in fact Pinot Noir Précoce, an earlier ripening variant that has been classified as a separate variety. The name Frühburgunder, though used by some to describe the variety in the UK, is officially restricted to Germany.

Regent
Regent is a crossing bred for red wine production that includes a hybrid progenitor but is approved as Vitis vinifera. Introduced, and grown since 1993, by Derek Pritchard at Dunkery Vineyard, Regent is now very common in Wales and the west and south-west of England, and on the increase in other UK wine growing areas. Amongst the most important new varieties, its high resistance to fungal attack also make it particularly suited to organic viticulture. Some of the wines produced to date show real promise with intense colour, good acidity, high sugar levels and good yields.

Rondo

Rondo
Like Regent, another crossing with hybrids lurking in its ancestry yet now approved as Vitis vinifera. It has responded well to UK conditions and

plantings have been increasing since it was first planted on an experimental basis in 1983. Rondo produces wines with very good colour, fruit and acidity although it can be susceptible to powdery mildew and berry drop can occur when ripe (making it more difficult to pick). It is considered to blend well with other varieties such as Dornfelder and Pinot Noir. At Wickham Vineyard in Hampshire they blend it with Pinot in the Special Reserve red. Although some make it in an easy drinking style it has greater potential and refinement in flavour if made in a full-bodied oak-aged style.

Triomphe

A hybrid variety bred in Alsace that produces a red wine with a disagreeable foxy taste. Some growers still refer to it as Triomphe d'Alsace as it was known until the EU rejected the name in order to protect the Alsace appellation contrôlée region. In fact it is little known outside Britain and is now in decline here, although quality has improved in recent years and some vineyards produce acceptable, if not earth-shattering reds. Its main use is for blending with other, often lighter coloured, reds to give wines with more depth of colour. It is judiciously combined with Dornfelder and Pinot Noir in the Camel Valley Red blend.

Glossary of terms

Assemblage This is the final blend of a wine prior to its bottling.

Autolysis Enzymatic process in sparkling wine whereby dead yeast cells add increased flavour to wine. The longer the period, the richer and more complex the characteristic becomes. Sparkling wines with less than 18 months on their yeast sediment will have little or no autolysis character.

Barriques The most well-known barrel type of 225 litre capacity. The Burgundian Pièce is fractionally larger with thicker staves than the classic Bordeaux barrique.

Biodynamic Method of organic farming that seeks to promote the natural balance of the land. This includes both soil and plants. Natural treatments are used to protect the vineyard and applications carried out in line with lunar and planetary activity.

Botrytis Botrytis or Botrytis Cinerea is a fungal infection of the vine that is particularly harmful to red grapes. In certain unique conditions though it provides for the development of 'Noble Rot' in areas such as Sauternes in Bordeaux. In late warm harvests with early morning humidity followed by dry sunny days the grapes will dehydrate concentrating their sugar and flavour. Wines produced from such grapes have a uniquely intense, peachy character. The odd English example has been produced.

Botrytised Wine produced from grapes affected by 'Noble Rot'.

Calcium carbonate Used to de-acidify must and wine (also see De-acidification).

Cane pruning Pruning method with fruiting buds on canes replaced each season.

Canopy The vegetative growth of the vine including its shoots and leaves.

Canopy management Vineyard management techniques designed to improve yield and quality as well as minimising risk of vine disease. Utilises a number of trellising/training systems to better expose the vines' foliage and fruit to sunlight, resulting in improved photosynthesis and grape ripening.

Chalk Form of limestone composed solely of the mineral calcite and formed under relatively deep marine conditions. Used here to refer to the more erosion resistant uplifted downland deposits seen in southern England as well as the plateau of Salisbury Plain.

Champagne method See Traditional Method.

Chaptalisation The addition of sugar to grape must to increase its alcoholic strength. Winemakers may also use concentrated grape must (see Sweet Reserve).

Chlorosis Vine malady affecting photosynthesis. Usually found in chalk soil and rectified with an appropriate choice of rootstock.

Clonal Selection See Clones.

Clones Vines reproduced by taking cuttings of original plants. Vines reproduced by clonal selection provide for uniformity of yield and flavour but wines produced from whole vineyards of the same clone can lack complexity.

Cold maceration Period prior to fermentation where crushed red grapes are kept in solution with the juice at a cool temperature to extract both colour and primary fruit flavours.

Cold soaking See Cold maceration.

Cold stabilisation Process of removing unsightly although completely harmless precipitated tartaric acid by chilling the wine below freezing. Precipitated acid may look like shards of glass.

Cordons Permanent vine wood with fruiting buds on spurs.

Cork taint See TCA.

Coulure Incomplete fruit set after flowering caused by cool or wet conditions. Some fruit loss can be positive to quality.

Crossing The result of a cross between two different grape varieties of the same vine species, usually Vitis vinifera. Some modern crossings used in England (such as Orion and Phoenix) are the product of a Vinifera variety with another that includes a hybrid in its parentage but have been approved as Vinifera — all important for Quality Wine status.

Débourbage Period where white grape juice or wine is left in order for solid matter to settle. Lighter aromatic and fruity whites will require all solids settling.

De-acidification The use of any

number of techniques to reduce high levels of acidity in wines. The acidity may be reduced through dilution or by the addition of calcium carbonate, resulting in precipitation as calcium tartrates. In England high acidity levels are exacerbated by poor summers yet deacidification is rarely necessary for wines from well-managed vineyards in the best sites.

De-stemmed Most red grapes will be crushed and de-stemmed prior to fermentation. Some whites may be whole bunch pressed and reds may include whole bunches added to the fermentation vat, particularly with Pinot Noir.

Demi-Muid A 600 litre oak barrel used in some parts of France.

Disgorging Removing the yeast deposit from the neck of the bottle by freezing it and removing with a disgorging machine.

Dosage Traditional Method sparkling wine will be topped up after disgorging with a mix of wine and sugar (liqueur d'expédition) and this dosage determines the style and sweetness of the final wine.

Downy mildew (Peronospera) Fungal disease that is a big problem in England and Wales in summers characterised by warm, humid conditions. The disease impacts adversely on photosynthesis and sugar levels. Some crossings show good resistance to it.

Extraction Process where tannins, colour and other matter is extracted during Maceration.

Filtration The removal of solid particles by means of a filter prior to bottling. While it saves the time required for a natural

settling it may also rob a wine of flavour and character.

Fining Process used to clarify grape juice or wine by removing the smallest (soluble) microscopic particles which attach themselves to the fining agents added. Great care should be used to avoid stripping the must or wine of flavour.

Foxy The term used to describe a distinctive but unpleasant flavour common to many hybrids that have been produced from one of the wild American vine species (also see Hybrid).

Geneva Double Curtain (GDC) Important training system employed by many UK vineyards. Vines are high trained on two wires and the fruiting wood and canopy foliage directed downwards. It helps in reducing vine density and vigour and boosts yields, sometimes at the expense of quality.

Giropallet/Gyropalettes Automated machines for riddling Traditional Method sparkling wines.

Guyot Old and very well established French vine training system. One (Single) or two (Double) fruiting canes are trained along wires with the new season's shoots trained above on a second wire. Now widely used in England and Wales.

Hybrid Vine variety produced by crossing two different vine species. Although it should not be confused with a Crossing which is produced from two varieties of the same species some modern crossings include hybrid ancestry. Hybrids usually refer to Vinifera varieties that have been crossed with those of the more hardy and disease resistant wild American (such as Riparia or Rupestris) or Asian species

(Amurensis). Such hybrids are generally held in low regard but a few such as Seyval Blanc can yield good quality wine without any trace of a so-called 'foxy' quality. Also see Crossing, Foxy, Vinifera.

Lees The sediment left after fermentation, including the dead yeast cells. White wine will often be racked off the gross lees but some sediment will remain which is known as the fine lees. This is important in providing additional flavour and texture as well as acting as an anti-oxidant during early barrel maturation.

Liqueur d'expédition See Dosage.

Liqueur de Tirage The addition of sugar and yeast to provoke the second fermentation in Traditional Method sparkling wines.

Maceration The period during which flavour, colour, tannins and other components are leeched from the grape skins before, during and after fermentation. Temperature plays an important role with primary fruit aromas and colour extracted at cooler temperatures whereas more tannin is released with heat. The cap of grape skins formed during fermentation needs to be kept in solution with the fermenting must and various methods are used which also aid extraction. Pre-fermentation maceration (see Cold Maceration) is regularly practised in England.

Malolactic fermentation Chemical process whereby malic acid is transferred into softer lactic acid. All red wine is put through malolactic but for whites it depends on the variety and style. For aromatic varieties the process is generally avoided.

Marc / Pomace Used here to

refer to the mass of skins, stems, seeds and pulp after free-run juice has been run off. With red wines, it is the solid matter that remains after fermentation. Marc is also a French brandy made from the pomace.

Mesoclimate The localised climate found generally within a vineyard or small specific area and responsible for particular characteristics found in the resulting wines. Often incorrectly referred to as a microclimate. The latter is in fact the very specific climate of the vine canopy.

Millerandage Irregular fruit development after flowering caused by cool weather. Yield is reduced because some berries are smaller. Quality though is likely to improve.

Must Can refer to either unfermented grape juice or the mix of grape juice, skins, pulp and seeds prior to or at the onset of fermentation. Also see Marc.

Noble Rot See Botrytis.

Organic An increasing number of winegrowers around the world are now producing wines without recourse to chemical treatments in the vineyard and with a minimum of chemical additives during vinification. Also see Biodynamic.

Oxidation Exposure of must or wine to air. Controlled oxidation is important in the maturation of barrel-aged wine before bottling. Reduction is the opposite of oxidation.

Phenolics Compounds found in grapes and extracted during vinification. These include tannins, flavour compounds and anthocyanins (responsible for the colour in red wines). See also Extraction and Maceration.

Phylloxera Vine aphid which was the great scourge of the world's vineyards in the 19th century. It can be resisted by planting vinifera varieties on resistant American species rootstocks.

Powdery mildew (Oidium) The 'other' mildew, now less of a problem in England and Wales than Downy Mildew. It similarly attacks the green parts of the vine and thrives in warm conditions. Can reduce yields and fruit quality but is inhibited by sunlight and good canopy management.

Propagated Meaning reproduced. In viticultural terms this most commonly refers to vegetative propagation using cuttings taken from other vines.

Quality Wine scheme Official wine status accorded to UK grown wines subject to passing analytical and tasting tests. Approved wines may add a 'psr' designation (produced in specific regions). This is similar to the French AC (Appellation Contrôlée) system but is currently labelling is restricted to either English Vineyards or Welsh Vineyards. Quality Wine status is restricted to approved Vinifera varieties. Without it, the vintage and grape variety may not be shown on the label.

Racked Winery procedure where must or wine is pumped or transferred under gravity from one container to another. This is both to remove the wine from solids but also to provide adequate aeration during maturation.

Reduced This is the opposite of oxidised. Excessive reduction can result in the development of foul smelling sulphides during cask ageing and so wines need to be exposed to controlled aeration during this phase.

Reductive Refers to wines that are in a reduced state.

Residual sugar There is always a small portion of unfermentable sugar in wine even those that are technically classified as dry. It is commonplace in some whites particularly straightforward fruit-driven styles to purposely leave a hint of residual sugar. Late harvested wines are deliberately left on the vine to accumulate sufficient sugar to ensure considerable sweetness after vinification. Also see Botrytis.

Riddling Process of moving the lees deposit after secondary fermentation in sparkling wine to the neck of the bottle for disgorging.

Rootstock The plant formed from the root system of the vine to which the scion (fruiting part) is grafted. Most Vinifera vines (the European species to which most quality grape varieties belong) are grafted on to rootstocks of American vine species (or hybrids of them) due to its resistance to phylloxera.

Saignée Running off some free run juice prior to fermentation in order to increase the ratio of skins and solids in the must and therefore flavour and tannin. Regularly practised in the production of top quality Pinot Noir.

Scott Henry Vine training system popular in some British vineyards. There are two layers of fruiting wood with the canopy trained both upwards and downwards. Growers will seek to increase their crop while maintaining quality.

Screw cap See Stelvin/Stelvin Cap.

Smart Dyson A cordon-trained variant of the Scott Henry training system that similarly produces a vertically divided canopy. Both systems are also suitable for mechanical harvesting.

SO2 See Sulphur Dioxide.

Spur pruning Pruning method where small spurs carry the fruiting wood, which is trained from fixed cordons.

Stelvin/Stelvin Cap Screw cap enclosure used instead of cork to avoid any possible contamination of the wine by TCA, oxidation or other potential spoilage from external sources.

Sulphur Dioxide All purpose wine antiseptic. It is both an anti-oxidant and anti-bactericide.

Sur Lattes Period during which sparkling wines are stored on their sides and on the lees prior to riddling and disgorging.

Sweet Reserve (Süssreserve) The addition of unfermented grape juice used to add sweetness to wines as a means of improving the balance between sweetness and acidity. It is less satisfactory than when balance is achieved naturally.

Sylvoz Training system where the vines are trellised on a high single wire and trained downwards from spurs.

TCA Chemical compound, its full name is 2,4,6-trichloroanisole, responsible for most of the off flavours in wine caused by contaminated corks. Eliminated by the use of screwcaps.

Tartaric acid The main acid in wine. Some may precipitate at low temperatures (see Cold Stabilisation). High levels of acidity can be reduced by De-acidification.

Terroir French concept which considers the unique physical environment of a site or vineyard. Also refers to the character in a wine that is derived from its origins rather than the grape variety.

Traditional Method The classic method of Champagne production as it is referred to in other regions for sparkling wines made in this way. A second fermentation takes place in bottle and the wine is left to age on the resulting yeast lees. All of the finest sparkling wines are made in this way including those from England and Wales.

Unfiltered See Filtration.

Vertical shoot positioning (VSP) Training method where the fruit wood of the vine is trained upwards on wires to optimise exposure to sunlight. Used in conjunction with a Guyot trellising system (including the Pendelbogen variant on Double Guyot).

Vinifera Vitis vinifera is the European species of vine to which nearly all the grape varieties used in global wine production belong. However there is some use of hybrids or modern crossings (that may include a hybrid somewhere in their parentage) in more marginal climates for viticulture such as England and Canada.

Volatile acidity The volatile acids in wine are those that are unstable and chief among these is acetic acid. Excessive exposure of a wine with high volatile acidity to air will encourage a bacterial reaction that causes off volatile aromas (similar to nail varnish) and will eventually convert wine to vinegar.

Yield The size of crop yielded from a vineyard. Yield is fundamental to wine quality. In general the smaller the yield the greater the wine quality. Older vines are naturally less productive. Yield per acre (or hectare) in England and Wales is often low but usually as a result of low planting densities or inclement growing conditions rather than a lack of fertility.

OTHER VINEYARDS IN ENGLAND & WALES

South East

Kent

Chalksole Estate, Green Lane, Alkham, Kent CT15 7EE

Groombridge Place, Groombridge, Tunbridge Wells, Kent TN3 9QG

The Mount, Shoreham, Kent TN14 7SD

Mystole Members Vineyard, Mystole, Canterbury, Kent CT4 7DB

Squeyrres, Squeyrres Court, Westerham, Kent TN16 1SJ

Terlingham Vineyard, Hawkinge, Folkestone, Kent CT18 7AE

Surrey

Godstone Vineyards, Quarry Road, Godstone, Surrey RH9 8DQ

Goose Green Vineyard, Wallington, Surrey SM6 8PN

Greyfriars Vineyard, The Hogs Back, Puttenham, Surrey GU3 1AG

Thorncroft Vineyard, Thorncroft Drive, Leatherhead, Surrey KT22 8JD

East Sussex

Barnsgate Manor, Herons Ghyll, nr Uckfield, East Sussex TN22 4DB

Battle Wine Estate, Leeford Vineyards, Whatlington, Battle, East Sussex TN33 0ND

Bluebell Vineyard Estates, Furners Green, East Sussex TN22 3RU

Charles Palmer Vineyards, Winchelsea, East Sussex TN36 4AG

Herons Ghyll Estate, Chillies Lane, Crowborough, East SussexTN6 3TB

Hidden Spring, Vines Cross Road, Horam, Heathfield, East Sussex TN21 0HG

Hobdens, Wellbrook Hall, Mayfield, East Sussex TN20 6HH

Mount Harry Vineyard, Ditchling Road, Offham, East Sussex BN7 3QW

West Sussex

Highdown Vineyard, Ferring, Worthing, West Sussex BN12 6PG

Rother Valley Vineyard, Elsted, Midhurst, West Sussex GU29 0JS

Upperton Vineyard, nr Petworth, West Sussex GU28 0RD

Warnham Vale, Warnham, West Sussex RH12 3SQ

Central South

Berkshire

Binfield Vineyard, Forest Road, Wokingham, Berkshire RG40 5SE

Buckinghamshire

Daws Hill Vineyard, Church Street, Radnage, Bucks HP14 4DY

Hale Valley Vineyard, Wendover, Bucks HP22 6NQ

Manor Fields Vineyard, Weedon, Aylesbury, Bucks HP22 4NR

Dorset

Charlton Barrow Vineyard, Charlton Barrow, Charlton Marshall, Dorset DT11 9DD

Doles Ash Farm Vineyard, Piddletrenthide, Dorset DT2

Parhams Vineyard, Melbury Abbas, Dorset SP7 0DE

Portesham Vineyard, Waddon, Weymouth, Dorset DT3 4ER

Wodetone Vineyard, Wootton Fitzpaine, Bridport, Dorset DT6 6DF

Hampshire

Birchenwood Vineyard, Brook, Hants SO42 7ZN

Bishops Waltham Vineyard, Tangier Lane, Bishops Waltham, Hants SO32 1BU

Cottonworth Vineyard, Andover, Hants SP11 7JX

Court Lane Vineyard, Ropley, Nr Alresford, Hants SO24 0DE

Exton Park Estate, Exton, Hants SO32 3NW

Hattingley Valley Vineyard, Medstead, Hants GU34 5NU

Laverstoke Park, Overton, Hants RG25 3DR

Hertfordshire

Frithsden Vineyard, Frithsden, Herts HP1 3DD

Hazel End Vineyard, Hazel End Farm, Bishop's Stortford, Herts CM23 1HG

Isle of Wight

Adgestone Vineyard, Upper Road, Adgestone, IOW PO36 0ES

Rossiters Vineyard, Wellow, IOW PO41 0TE

Oxfordshire

Chiltern Valley Vineyard, Hambledon, Oxon RG9 6JW

Fawley Vineyard, Fawley Green, Oxon RG9 6JA

Grange Farm Vineyard, Swerford, Oxon OX7 4AX

Linch Hill Vineyard, Linch Hill, Stanton Harcourt, Abingdon, Oxon OX29 5BB

Wiltshire

Bow-in-the-Cloud Vineyard, Noahs Ark, Garsdon, Wilts SN16 9NS

Fonthill Glebe Wines, The Winery, Teffont Evias,Wilts SP3 5RG

Southcott Vineyard, Southcott, Pewsey, Wilts SN9 5JF

South West
Cornwall
Barras Moore Vineyard, Perrananworthal, Truro, Cornwall TR3 7PE

Lambourne Vineyard, Truro, Cornwall TR2 5NL

Pemboa Vineyard, Rosehill, Penzance, Cornwall, TR20 8TE

Polmassick, St Austell, Cornwall PL26 6HA

Devon
Blackdown Hills Vineyard & Winery, Oaklands Farm, Monkton, Devon, EX14 9QH

Lily Farm Vineyard, Budleigh Salterton, Devon EX9 7AH

Manstree Vineyard, Shillingford St George, Devon EX2 9QR

Summermoor Vineyard, Swimbridge, Devon EX32 0QH

Willhayne Vineyard, Colyton, Devon EX24 6DT

Gloucestershire
Cowley Estate Vineyard, South Cerney, Glos GL7 6HS

Kilcott Valley Vineyard, Wotton-under-edge, Glos GL12 7RL

St Anne's Vineyard, Wain House, Oxenhall, Nr Newent, Glos GL18 1RW

Somerset
Head of the Vale Vineyard, Stoke Trister, Wincanton, Somt BA9 9PH

Lopen Vineyard, The Bartons, Yeabridge Somt TA13 5LW

Quantock Hills Vineyard, Rhode, Bridgwater, Somt TA5 2AD

Staplecombe Vineyard, Burlands Farm, Staplegrove, Somt TA2 6SN

Wraxhall Vineyard, Wraxhall, Somt BA4 6RQ

Midlands and North
Herefordshire
Coddington Vineyard, Nr. Ledbury, Hereford HR8 1JJ

Four Foxes Vineyard, Longworth Lane, Bartestree, Hereford HR1 4BX

Sparchall Vineyard, Tarrington, Hereford HR1 4EY

Sunnybank National Vine Collection, Eywas Harold, Hereford HR2 0EE

Treago Vineyard, Treago Castle, St. Weonards, Hereford HR2 8QB

Lancashire
Mount Pleasant Vineyard, Bolton Le Sands, Carnforth, Lancs LA5 8AD

Plot 19 Vineyard, Flixton, Lancs M41 5RU

Northamptonshire
Harlestone Vineyard, Lower Harlestone, Northants NN7 4EW

Kemps Vineyard, Hargrave, Northants NN8 6BW

Vernon Lodge Vineyard, Tiffield, Towcester, Northants NN12 8AB

Shropshire
Commonwood Vineyard, Weavers Loft, Wem, Salop SY4 5SJ

Hargrove Vineyard, Church Stretton, Salop SY6 7DP

Morville Hall, The Gatehouse, Bridgenorth, Salop WV16 5NB

Morville St. Gregory, Valentine Cottage, Aston Munslow, Salop SY7 9OW

Tern Valley Vineyard, Hall Farm, Tern Hill, Market Drayton, Salop TF9 3PU

Yorkshire
Holmfirth Vineyard, Woodhouse Lane, Holmbridge, Yorks HD9 2QR

Ryedale Vineyards, Westow, Yorks YO10 7LS

Summer House Vineyard, Skellow, Yorks DN6 8JU

Womacks Vineyard, Harrogate, Yorks HG1 3HU

Yorkshire Heart Vineyard, Nun Monkton, Yorks YO26 8EJ

East Anglia
Cambridgeshire
Elysian Fields, Bedwell Hey Farm, Ely Road, Little Thetford, Cambs CB6 3HJ

Essex
Mersea Island Vineyard, Rewsalls Lane, East Mersea, Essex CO5 8SX

Pages Farm, Debden Green, Essex CB11 3LX

Norfolk
Tas Valley Vineyard, Hall Farm, Overwood Lane, Forncett St Peter, Norwich NR16 1LW

Thelnetham Lodge Vineyard, Lodge Farm, Thelnetham, Diss, Norfolk IP22 1JL

Suffolk
Brook Farm Vineyard, Lavenham Road, Brent Eleigh, Sudbury, Suffolk CO10 9PB

Coggeshall Vineyard, Fletchers Lane, Middleton, Suffolk IP17 3NZ

Giffords Hall, Hartest, Bury St Edmunds, Suffolk IP29 4EX

Melton Lodge Vineyard, Melton Lodge, Melton, Suffolk IP12 1LU

Staverton Vineyard, The Rookery, Eyke, Suffolk IP12 2RR

Willow Grange Street Farm, Crowfield, Ipswich, Suffolk IP6 9SY

Wales
Cardiff
Gelynis Fruit Farm and Vineyard, Morganstown, Cardiff, CF15 8LB

Credigion
Ffynnon Las Vineyard, Aberaeron Ceredigion, SA46 0ED

Gwynedd
Pant Du Vineyard, Penygroes, Gwynedd LL54 6PY

Monmouthshire
Monnow Valley Vineyards, Monmouth, Monmouthshire NP25 5DL

Pembrokeshire
Cwm Deri Vineyard, Martletwy, Pembrokeshire, SA67 8AP

Wrexham
Worthenbury Vineyard, Worthenbury, Wrexham LL13 0AW

INDEX

ACKNOWLEDGEMENTS

The Publishers would like to thank the following for their assistance and contribution to the preparation of this book.

Julia Trustram Eve, English Wine Producers

Peter Dart, Stanlake Park Wine Estate

Linda Wade, Linda Wade Design Ltd.
DTP Management

Tony Barrett Photographic Services
Pre press production

Cartography and Illustration

Maps
Jamie Crocker Artista Design

Illustration
Stuart Lafford (pages xvi-xvii) at Linden Artists Ltd

Clive Spong (pages xx-xxi) at Linden Artists Ltd

Photography Permissions

The publishers would also like to thank the following people, companies and picture libraries for permission to reproduce their photographs in this book.

CEFAS vi; Tony Barrett vi; British Library x; CFAS xii; Getty Images xiii; 22-23 Richard Balfour-Lynn; Leeds Castle 38; National Maritime Museum 39 top; Lisa Fulcher 40; N Edmonston 41; RHS Garden Wisley 49; Painshill Park 50-51; Tony Barrett 60-63; Royal College of Physicians of London 67 top; Simon J Tuck, Colin Smith middle.75; Tony Barrett 76-77; Alan Bostock, Stanlake Park Wine Estate 86-89; Beaulieu Enterprises Limited 90; Jim Champion 91 top; New Forest Tourism 96; Peter Facey middle, New Forest Tourism bottom, 97; Colin Smith 99; M Simons DCC 103; James Dawson 106; Sherborne Castle Estate 107; The Choice Forum 111 top; Richard Robbins 114-115; Von Essen Hotels 138; Mike Hardingham 142-143; Richard Greenwood 156; Betty Longbottom 158; Organic Growers Alliance 164; Ben Bunting 170-171; The National Trust 174-175; The Landmark Trust 185; Mrs. Sam Alper 187 top; The Photo Library of Wales Ltd. 188-189; Martin Jones 192; Steve Robards (Mid Sussex Times) 206 top left; Tony Barrett 207 centre; Alan Bostock/Stanlake Park 210-214; Geograph.org.uk